THE BOOKS
IN
FRED HAMPTON'S
APARTMENT

Books of Richard Stern

RICHARD STERN

The Books
in
Fred Hampton's
Apartment

HAMISH HAMILTON
LONDON

First published in Great Britain 1974
by Hamish Hamilton Ltd
90 Great Russell Street London WC1
Copyright © 1973, 1953, © 1956, 1957,
1959, 1962, 1963, 1964, 1965, 1966, 1967,
1968, 1969, 1970, 1971, by Richard Stern

SBN 241 02451 X

Printed in Great Britain by
Compton Printing Ltd., Aylesbury

CONTENTS

A NOTE ON THE TITLE

The original title of the miscellany was *One Person and Another*. The present title—that of the piece on page 70—was suggested by Hal Scharlatt, the editor.

The title of my last book (*1968*) had been suggested by its editor, Aaron Asher. I'd been hooked by it. Bloodily. Reviewing-snipers claimed that the story writer was hiding behind the newspapers. (Pinned, he cried, "Never. No." Unheard.) So I rejected Scharlatt's suggestion. I didn't want to hang my book on poor Hampton's story.

But the title grew on me. I tested it on a few reliable people. They felt as I did, uncertain, but they too liked its specificity and slight unexpectedness. It does reach a number of the book's organizing notions: the ways men, events, and books get formed and reported; the connections between active men and the often surprising things they know; and books themselves, energizing or lethal, beautiful or false. Then too there's much in the book about Chicago; and Hampton's story is important in this city. City power took its ugliest turn with him: from pain and wild rhetoric to bad death and mendacious concealment. (One of the hero-villains of the story, a smart, vain, dutiful, careless, assiduous, mean state's attorney, a pure Chicago strutter, clown, and bumpkin, has just won a primary election and thus once again dimmed city lights.) So Fred Hampton and his books do stand for much that follows, and thanks are due Hal Scharlatt for fishing out the title.

R.S.

Chicago
March 28, 1972

. . . the world is based on gettin' a little bit of the pie . . . but as soon as you're not gettin' it, the first thing you say is, "Why aren't I in that?" . . . Chicago is the only area of a big city that I've ever been . . . where I know everybody . . . A lotta bullshit goes on there, but you have to pass on it . . . you can't get away with anything here . . . If you know somebody, you can give him an even break, and if you don't know him, you screw him . . . Everybody's human. You have to change the human being to change the world. The world is beautiful in itself, terrainwise and etcetera . . . As long as there's man, then that's it.

> Gene Willis,
> from *Division Street: America,*
> edited by Studs Terkel

Il y avait en moi un personnage qui savait plus ou moins bien regarder, mais c'était un personnage intermittent, ne reprenant vie que quand se manifestait quelque essence générale, commune à plusiers choses, qui faisait sa nourriture et sa joie . . . Comme un géometre qui, depouillant les choses de leurs qualités sensibles, ne voie que leur substratum linéaire, ce que racontaient les gens m'échappait, car ce qui m'intéressait, c'était non ce qu'ils voulaient dire, mais la manière dont ils le disaient, en tant qu'elle était révélatrice de leur caractère ou de leurs ridicules; ou plutôt c'était un objet qui avait toujours été plus particulièrement le but de ma recherche parce qu'il me donnait un plaisir spécifique, le point qui était commun a un être et à un autre.

> Marcel Proust,
> *Le Temps Retrouvé*

IN DEFENSE OF THE MISCELLANY

miscellanea (Latin), a mix of different sorts of broken meats

Why defense?

Because the habits of most modern readers, editors, book-sellers, catalogue makers, librarians, reviewers, and award committees screen out the pleasures of the miscellany. If gourmets can relish snacks and marathon runners strolls in the park, why can't novel-and-history readers enjoy miscellanies?

Can a miscellany be *a real book?*

1. "No. Miscellanies are grab bags, wastebaskets, old files, office sweepings, throat clearings, leftovers, hash, rubble, transient hotels. Nonbooks. Antibooks."

2. "Not so fast. How about the Bible, *Mahabharata,* Greek and Confucian anthologies, *Arabian Nights,* Burton's *Anatomy,* Montaigne? We're not talking about hash but bouillabaisse, the Plaza, not a fleabag."

Novels and epics are also assemblages of divers scenes, characters, notions. Their assemblages are fusions, their progress from seed to bloom is clearer; but miscellanies have their own sorts of coherence. (There are, of course, miscellanies and miscellanies: between a "gathering of fugitives" and a *Leaves of Grass* there are conceptual and executive miles.)

Going over pieces, published and unpublished, a miscellanist sees recurrences, developments, potential symmetries. His job is to organize the pieces, make links, add and amputate until coherence and a single perspective dominate the variety; and to do this while preserving whatever original flavor doesn't stale.

A miscellany should be read better in its given sequence than in a series of dips here and there, now and then.

There is an omitted story in every miscellany: that of its

observer-reporter(s) and its assembler(s). In some miscellanies much of this story gets told, and the result is a form of autobiography.

This miscellany contains but isn't autobiography. The hope is that its "I"—not one of the earth's major figures—is visible enough to be a reference point, even a leverage point, for the small universe of the book.

The Miscellanist's Creed goes: "What I've seen, thought, and written about somehow counts." There is sufficient narcissism in it to warrant early apology for presumption, but again the hope here is that this miscellany is more outward than inward bound. The aim is less that of Gene Willis (Epigraph 1) than of Proust (Epigraph 2), a human geometry which relates one person to another.

CLOUDS

I

So many poems about clouds.
Still. Tonight, driving around
the mountains, within a great blue
gap, there was a pack of tiny
golden clouds; some were almost
letters: a T, an almost-*epsilon*,
an O (as if some smoke-ring puffer
had, just once, really made it).

My ancestors were message-hunters,
and though their alphabet is dark
to me, and I believe in next
to nothing they believed in, I
can use an unexpected message.
(There's been no mail out here at all.)
For seconds then, I pressed
that cirric alphabet like
a scholar with a new papyrus bit.

II

Now, against a ravishing
Tiepolo cloud, an almost straight
white line grows and grows.
A jet. Visible only in
its own debris. A straight white
line, as if the Scribbler
in Clouds decided to surprise
His readers with a human form.

But that's just it.
Like lines you make in manuscript
to signify italics, that jet
had sent its message: "Geometry
is here. Look sharp. Yours truly."

PART I

1. Riding in Their Cars

All I want is that municipal ownership be postponed till I get my bill repealin' the civil service law before the next legislature. It would be all a mess if every man who wanted a job would have to run up against a civil service examination. For instance, if a man wanted a job as motorman on a surface car, it's ten to one that they would ask him: "Who wrote the Latin grammar, and, if so, why did he write it? How many years were you at college? Is there any part of the Greek language you don't know? State all you don't know and why you don't know it. Give a list of all the sciences with full particulars about each one and how it came to be discovered. Write out word for word the last ten decisions of the United States Supreme Court and show if they conflict with the last ten decisions of the police courts of New York City."

Before the would-be motorman left the civil service room, the chances are he would be a raving lunatic. Anyhow I wouldn't want to ride on his car . . .

George Washington Plunkitt,
boss of the Fifteenth Assembly District,
New York City,
from *Plunkitt of Tammany Hall,*
recorded by William L. Riordan

The piece on Kennedy and Nixon in Washington is the only one in this book which appeared in another. I include it because it introduces the sniffing, pontificating outsider "I" in his naivest version. The "I" may be a little naive even for this first dip in Lake Politics, but then he comes up with a few fish which tougher types would have thrown back in the lake. To read about Nixon's 1959 view of Tolstoy in 1972, for instance, is to feel a special tremor at the stupendous root of public banality. The piece also introduces the art-politics strain which dominates the first half of the book.

THE PURSUIT OF WASHINGTON: KENNEDY AND NIXON IN THE SUMMER OF 1959

1

Flying to Washington for the first time must be a little like passing the bar exam: seventeen dollars and fifty minutes from Idlewild and you feel you've launched a career. The Empire's man summoned to Downing Street from the Gulf of Oman would know the feeling. The air approach is over the pink estates of Maryland, curled with green lawn, an augury of grandeur, and perhaps a warning to freshmen Congressmen not to forget their place. There is a city, though, not the blank spaces which a hundred years ago met visitors and which caused Dickens to wonder if "the houses had gone out of town with their masters" for the summer.

The driver of the airport limousine points out the Fourteenth Street Bridge, the Navy Department, one of the Agriculture buildings, the National Archives. I spot what I need no introduction to, the Washington obelisk and nearly risk telling the driver it was once stolen by the Know-Nothings; unsure of detail, I bank on something more familiar and trip myself up: "No suh, that there's the Jefferson. The Lincoln's down a piece." I doff my confidence. At First and Maryland a statue of Garfield keeps before the legislators in back of it a reminder of the wrath of the insulted and injured.

My appointment is with Senator [John] Kennedy in the Old Senate Office Building at two o'clock. It's only twelve. I ask a guard where the Vice President's office is: we have been corresponding about an appointment. The VP is off for Moscow in six hours; porters wheel out boxes of "the Boss' speeches." A blonde receptionist has a tough time parrying my inquiries while sustaining the indispensable tone that Washington officialdom takes with unknown quantities: pleasantness. This boiling city opens its pores so hospitably that only at the failure of a mission does one realize that the receptivity, gentleness, and amiability are Southern forms of refusal.

I go across the hall to a door marked "Mr. Kennedy—Walk In" and tell a perfectly beautiful red-haired girl of my appointment. There are pictures of yawls and the Senator all around, a red carpet, plants, a marble fireplace, a few books—*I Married the Veep,* the *Congressional Directory*—and magazines—*The New Leader* under *Sports Illustrated* and that under *U.S. News and World Report;* the last is a current number. Phones ring every twenty seconds. "There's a run on autographed pictures for Congressmen's children," the beauty tells a girl at the second desk. Two young Germans come into the office, one explaining Washington to the other. At two-twenty, a thin, young fellow with glasses and a gait so casual it looks as if he's being dangled comes up to me and introduces himself as Fred Holborn, one of the Senator's legislative assistants. He asks if I can come back at four, when they'll have some of "the rubble" cleared out of the way. Embarrassed for the Germans but bolstered by the implicit view of my own status, I nod confidently and make my way—with a couple of Senators and tourists—to the Capitol via the Toonerville trolley in the basement. I've stopped in another Senator's office for a pass to the Senate Gallery and in a third—for I am trying to get the feel of things—for a letter to the Senate librarian. Two girls are leaving the second office, one saying to the other, "I suppose he'll just be finishing up when I get to the floor." The other says, "You can read it in the *Record*." "I read it yesterday," says the first, and I mark down this fragment of devotion in my Woolworth notebook.

Over in the Capitol, a couple of guards misdirect me to the Library, but a third aims me past the Printing Office to the petite, lovely, deep-chaired rooms where, with my letter, I am almost affectionately welcomed by what seems a curiously large staff. There is not a great collection of books, and a librarian is pleasantly surprised that they have the Senator's first one, *Why England Slept*. It turns out to be a dull but careful account of England's failure to prepare for Hitler, and I find none of the Cliveden stigmata which I have been told the Senator displayed along with his father.* Such stories about the Senator turn out to be one of Washington's parlor games: I hear about immense, sequestered public relations staffs, wondrous attentions paid to potent vote swingers; jets of anti-Romanism discovered like oil in abandoned lots.

Back in the Senate Office Building at four, I go with Holborn into the Senator's office. The Senator isn't there: he is speaking on the floor in behalf of the anti-loyalty-oath addendum to the education bill. While he champions my profession, I sit with Holborn under a hundred-pound bluefish—"though he's not really much of a fisherman, I think his wife caught this one"—and more pictures of the occupant. I learn that the Senator isn't musical but that his wife is; that he is a great novel reader, now

* *The Wartime Journals of Charles Lindbergh* (New York: Harcourt Brace Jovanovich, 1970). To Joseph Kennedy, Lindbergh, and the members of the Astor set at Cliveden, it looked not only as if "the English are in no shape for war" but that an attack on Germany would "result in the destruction of European Civilization."

on those of Mary Renault (inside accounts of mythical Greeks); that he doesn't read foreign periodicals or books but that his wife does; that he reads the standard magazines but not such as *Encounter*.*

It's time to go over to the floor. We make our way the outside route through a fog of heat behind a teetering, white-suited old man who is identified by Holborn as Senator Harry Byrd. Outside the Senate chamber Holborn leaves me with the page boys— loud, menacingly polite Southern college boys up for an official lark—and I fill out a card which is taken in to the Senator. I wait in the public reception room, which looks like the inside of a baroque toaster, flaming rosettes barely interrupted by swooning murals and catatonic portraits of the Senate greats: Calhoun, Webster, La Follette, Taft, Clay. Two or three Senators are there pacifying or amusing constituents.

Not Senator Kennedy but a bald man with the monogram M.F. on his pocket handkerchief and a bundle of papers strangled in his fist comes out to me and regretfully reports that there are going to be a couple of riders on the bill, and that the Senator will be on the floor for at least two or three hours. How about after that, I ask, prepared to change my return reservation. Unfortunately, there are people to see then, some of them on tap for weeks. "Will he stop for a bite to eat?" M.F. says that the Senator will be lucky to stagger home at ten for nourishment. I am beginning to feel rubble-like. M.F. offers me the Senator's college roommate, "who knows him like a book," but proud, I refuse the substitute. He offers profuse regrets; these I accept and depart to call my St. Bernard, Mr. Holborn, who says that I ought to stick around. "Nothing much doing tomorrow," he says. I debate, decide suddenly that I've had it, and charge the visit to soaking up atmosphere.

A Senator with whom I trollied over earlier nods smilingly at me, and I have the feeling that he wishes to borrow something.

---

* Kennedy commented on articles and quoted poems from *Encounter* during his presidency. (Did he know "he" was paying some of its bills?)

It restores my self-possession. I walk down the Capitol steps as if from my inauguration. When the cab driver asks me respectfully if the widow of his Army buddy who had a heart attack yesterday ought to try to get some money from the VA, I advise him to have her try. "Nothing to lose but a stamp," I throw in for nothing, and feel that I have brought some quasi-official comfort to a bereaved civilian.

2

My Washington expedition had begun with an editor's invitation to do a piece of reportage. I came up with something that had been fishing in me for years, the character of men in power, the nature of their intellect and of the culture which nourishes it. I suppose envy as much as curiosity stokes such interest. How many of us without public power wonder if we could wield it, or wonder why we don't? The wonder is usually fruitless * and is often succeeded by contempt for the politician and his practice. I had been reading essays of Professor Shils which traced such intellectual contempt for politics to the romantic identification of all politics with ideological politics, the politics of fanaticism. What Shils calls the politics of civility, the politics of adjustment —small gains, large compromise and larger tolerance—struck me as an arena fit for the very best citizens of the modern state as it was for those of the *polis*.

What was the new American politician like behind the seven veils of his press agentry? My notion was to find out by indirection, to try to talk with one or two important men not about affairs of state but about their intellectual and imaginative experience, the books they'd been moved and instructed by. I wanted to take down those incidental observations which used to appear in collections of table talk.

I decided that the Vice President [Nixon] was the most inter-

* For many intellectuals, the wonder was replaced in 1961 by the labor, the delight, and sometimes the "arrogance" and madness of power. The balance sheet of their contribution to weal and woe hasn't been drawn.

esting possibility: an antipathetic stereotype I'd formed had been curiously altered when I saw a picture of him in a garden carrying books among which was the *Collected Stories of Faulkner*. Even if it were a posed picture, the posing involved an appeal which boded well for my enterprise. I wrote, therefore, stated my interest, and asked for an hour or two of his time. Three weeks went by without an answer. I decided to switch to Senator Kennedy, who was not only a leading contender for the Democratic nomination but who had put himself on record with two books, one of which I had then read. Then, a month after my letter, I received a call from a colleague who was on leave in Washington working with the Vice President. My letter had been turned over to him and he had agreed to act as a liaison. It seems that Nixon's staff would be quite interested in such a piece, my colleague said. The Vice President tended to ally himself, at least temperamentally, with intellectuals. He was introspective, somewhat shy, a student. Better than some of his friends, he sensed the resentment he'd aroused since the Hiss case, and felt that the time for *rapprochement* with intellectuals was at hand. I was to sit tight and an appointment would be carved out for me, probably after the VP's return from the Soviet Union. The VP was very busy preparing for this trip: he and his wife rose early every day to study Russian, and he was reading everything he could put his hands on that would gear him for it.

A week later Kennedy wrote that he'd be happy to talk to me in Washington, or if that were not convenient for me, to answer in writing any "leading questions" I put to him. I answered that if he were free I would come to Washington on July 17. On July 21 I received a kind note to the effect that he was going to be in Massachusetts on July 17. I wrote Mr. Nixon again suggesting possible appointment times in September, wished him luck on his Russian trip, and in the spirit of the enterprise recommended a couple of books for his jet trip, Herzen's *Memoirs* and Wilson's *To the Finland Station*. I received a letter from him thanking me for recommending the Wilson book and suggesting that I arrange an appointment with Herbert Klein, his press secretary, after his return from abroad. Meanwhile I called Senator Kennedy's office. A secretary seemed to ignite at my name, apologized for the July 17 failure, and asked me when I could come to Washington. All this lay in back of the Washington trip.

On my return from Washington that night, I wrote Holborn of my disappointment and asked him if it might be possible to see the Senator in Hyannisport some weekend. There the filigree nature of my enterprise would not be so conspicuous, and since I would be in Rhode Island for three weeks the trip over to the Cape would save me time and money. I swore not to rob the Senator of more leisure time than I would have consumed in Washington. Again I received a gracious answer, but after I'd left Rhode Island. The Senator apologized for the futility of the first journey, described the delight he would have had in seeing me in Hyannis, and regretted that he had not been there during my Rhode Island stay. Perhaps I would be coming to Washington again.

Before going to Rhode Island, though, I had watched something in New York which fused oddly with my Washington views. I had spent a morning up in the old Gold Medal Studios in the Bronx ogling Anna Magnani and Marlon Brando, who were making a Tennessee Williams movie there. What intrigued me at this first sight of film-making was the exhausting pauses between the numerous takes, and the actors' reactions to them. Magnani, mop-haired, powerfully subdued, the lava of a marvelous volcano, sat back in chairs, rubbed her stomach—*Ho fame, ho fame* —or slapped her forehead after forgetting a cue—"Right here I had it, right here"—while Brando arched around, encouraged a couple of youthful beards to tear the shirts off each others's backs, and proclaimed an imminent bowel cleansing. In different ways the actors seemed to be at wit's end; for me the source of their trouble lay in the difficulty of sustaining the passion which, every ten minutes, they had to project into the camera as an uninterrupted continuity. Off the set they were staying close to the emotional life of the characters whom they had to haul back under the lights at the disposition of the technicians.

It struck me that movie actors and legislators had to have large powers of insulation and tenacity to sustain the contours of character or history making which to outsiders seemed unflawed by interruption. Although outsiders desire the illusion of continuity—mental parallel to that odd persistence of an image on the retina after the source of the image has disappeared—the burden of creating it rests on the actors and public men. They are responsible for concealing the crudities of process. The tax on personality was commensurate with the glittering rewards.

For a couple of weeks after this I went about my ways working on a novel about double agents,* people who of all others were most constricted, between whose inclinations and expressions the greatest difference existed. Then, toward the end of August, I called Herbert Klein and asked for an appointment with Mr. Nixon. He was cordial and discouraging: all the writers were lining up outside his office and he didn't know when he would be able to fit them in. Nonetheless, I should be sure to come to see him when I came to Washington. I tried Mr. Holborn, who was as ever hopeful. We arranged an appointment for September 3, "when the labor consultations were sure to be over and there'd be very little doing." I assured him that I would be in my chair at the proper time, and that I'd bring along a healthier supply of flexibility to ride out any legislative squalls that might blow up.

3

The second trip to Washington was a lark. I had the feeling that I had been returned by a constituency. I walked unhesitatingly through the right doors, identified the monuments with ease, and entered the Senate Office Building as assured as a sleepwalker. In the Senator's office I was told to rush to the floor, where he was supervising the parturition of the Landrum-Griffin

---

* *In Any Case.* (New York: McGraw-Hill, 1962).

labor bill. I waited under the flaring rosettes of the public reception room while a Texas page boy, calling my name, brought out
the Senator. Then ten yards from me, a young man in a fine blue
suit started to whirl. While I caught the flash of brilliant blue
eyes and a face which surprised me—after all the photographs—
by the depth of its indentations at cheek and eye socket, the
powerful grip of politics pressed my hand and an adenoidal, boyish voice * rattled off "How-are-you-good-to-see-you-fine-of-
you-to-come." Into this I could only mutter that I was sorry to
drag him out of the scrimmage. "It's hectic," he said. "I wish I
could give you more time. It'll be going on for five or six hours."
(I thought this an exaggeration; it proved to be an understate-
ment.) When then could we talk? "I just don't know," he said,
but why didn't I go to his office. They'd take care of me, it was
good to have seen me, and he whirled to another, unintroduced
person as I stumbled out, the peripheral casualty of a tornado.
I telephoned Holborn, who told me to try back at the office in
a couple of hours. "They ought to vote pretty soon." I told him
that this was not the Senator's estimate, but he repeated it. I said
I'd try, and then made an appointment with Mr. Nixon's blonde
receptionist to see Mr. Klein. As I left, she was saying over the
phone, "Next time you call from London, you better do it person
to person."

I decided I'd take a look at the National Gallery, but first I
called my colleague and was invited to meet him in the West
Lobby of the White House, from which we would go to dinner.
I had never seen the White House. The thought of meeting someone there for dinner seemed a spectacular introduction.

Taxis in Washington operate by zone,† which reduces by half
the tension of transport. Fifty cents seems to cover the area of
government and the arts. The National Gallery presents its fantastic wares air-cooled, and though a bad peepshow would have
earned my grateful attention here in the city's ninety degrees,

* Which, like so much, changed.
† 1959.

stupefaction was the meanest initial response this art innocent could pay that monument of collectivitis. I narrowed my stunned sights, looked at the five Vermeers, then at Bernini's bust of Louis XIV, whose swelling ease of nose and cheek told of that absolute assurance which survives no longer in political nostrils. Across from the Vermeers was a portrait of an almost-Kennedy by Dürer, the blue-eyed, jutting face suggesting, as the guide sheet had it, "that mixture of idealism and fanaticism so common among the leaders of the Reformation." On my way back to the original, I luckily passed Jan Van Eyck's *Annunciation* and Washington slipped out of mind. Gabriel's remarkable smile was telling the Virgin, "Oh, you're going to be so surprised!" This and the figured robe, lily, and the book were so clearly *there,* as if condensed from a single, remarkable breath.

Mr. Nixon's receptionist said "Hi, Mr. Stern." She took me down the hall, where a pleasant-looking man who looked and talked like the actor Eddie Albert said it was very nice to see me. He remembered that I wanted to do a "philosophic" piece on the VP, said that that sounded fine, lots of the writers asked deep questions, and cited some recent ones about our relations with Russia. The schedule, though, was packed. He showed me Mr. Nixon's list for the day, a series of ten or twelve television appearances with Congressmen to be filmed in the congressional studio. Then he advised me to stick close to the Vice President when he came out to dedicate the new University of Chicago Law School. I could "observe him in action." We talked half an hour, and I went across to Senator Kennedy's office full of the milk of Mr. Klein's kindness, hardly aware that I had been weighed on the only scale that could count for him now, my usefulness to the Vice President. Washington had no scale sensitive enough to weigh that.

Senator Kennedy's office was the inside of a washing machine, the Senator whirling with the rest. Holborn dangled some papers at his nose, telling him to make sure that "the analysis made the *Record.*" Another assistant, Mr. Reardon, called him inside, then shouted for "somebody from Joint Atomic." M.F. now was talking to someone on the phone; the secretary (not the redhead) was trying to get a page to take some papers over to the House. Then the Senator was gone, a flower with bees foaming instructions from all sides at him. "How long is Morse going to be?" another secretary called to Reardon. "It'll take him an hour for each point, and I assume he'll have three to five points. Keep after Saltonstall." A girl named Rafferty came up to me, said sweetly that she had nearly "had me" as an instructor at college. I wished her continued success, and left for the floor. Senator Morse was at Subsection Three or Four of Point Two or Three. I listened for a while to the impassioned sense and nonsense, then saw Holborn sitting in the aides' section, climbed over the seats, and asked how things looked. "Fine," he said. Morse would be finished in an hour, then the Senator, then Goldwater, then the vote. Why didn't I go to dinner and come back to the office after that? Fine. Morse was finishing and Senators were filing into the chamber. Kennedy got the floor. He talked briefly about a bill to establish a national park on Cape Cod, yielded to Saltonstall, and then read his report on the Landrum-Griffin labor bill. Not the bill he wanted, he said two or three times, but the best that was available. He yielded to Senator Carroll of Colorado, who said that his mind and vote had been changed by Kennedy's masterful presentation. He said that he and most of his colleagues didn't understand a thing about labor legislation, and that he thanked the Senator for explaining it. Then he asked whether the Denver case had been dealt with. Kennedy thanked him for asking that, so that the response could make "legislative history," and said that it had not been dealt with. Senator Carroll had not finished: he repeated his view of his colleagues' ignorance, his praise of Kennedy's ability to change his— Carroll's—mind, and his regret that the Denver case had not been faced up to. Then Senator Russell praised the hard work, skill, knowledge, and intelligence of the subcommittee and its chairman, the young Senator from Massachusetts.

I left and taxied to the northwest gate of the White House. I asked the guard if it were indeed the NW gate. "Mr. Stern?" he asked. "Come right in." Washington tumbled into my lap. I was admitted and walked up the drive past the shade elms and oaks which disguise the extent of the painted sandstone. In the West Lobby a soft-spoken, tough-looking guard greeted me by name.

My colleague took me for a tour of the formal rooms, the President's Office, the Cabinet Room. The great world shrank. He spoke of the Eisenhower's kindness and the President's skill in making his way through a complex briefing. We passed the putting green and then were taken by official limousine to the Cosmos Club for dinner. We talked about Washington, about the hard work done there and the pressure of doing such work on a spotlit highwire. Back in my friend's office in the Executive Office Building, I put in my last call to Holborn. If I hurried over to the floor, he said, I might just catch the Senator. They were about to vote. I left my friend and taxied to the Capitol under the stars.

As I sent in my card by the tired page boys, it struck me that I was like the fruit peddler who interrupts the lovers in the old Olson and Johnson review *Hellzapoppin'* with "Anyone wanta buya banan'?" I rather hoped for the answer that the Senator sent out, namely that he was very sorry but that he had to beg off; after the vote he had some paperwork to attend to in his office.

I decided that I'd write him the "leading questions" he'd invited me to send him. Although I shall not be able to tell from the answer I expect * how much or little of the Senator there is in them, this will do for me. I will at least be able to gauge the climate of his opinions. Perhaps that is all that really matters in Washington. I mean it strikes me that legislation and politics are too difficult for men to handle as, say, a good mechanic handles a car or a good writer a book. A man of power is the center of a system: if he is a sun, instead of, say, a cloud

*but never got.

or breeze, he dominates his system. As far as his national personality goes, that is an illusion; a kind of allegory, standing for this, stemming from that, aiming here, avoiding there. The graceful manner of the city is the allegorical setting. At the end of the second long Washington day I felt my original need to translate the allegory slaked instead by its charm.

Slightly tipsy with my own allegorical person—the man about to return from Washington—I walked down the darkened Capitol steps without feeling the need of climbing them again.

4

There is an afterward to my two-day bike race: I actually caught up with something more than my own shadow.

A month after the second return from Washington, the Vice President showed up in Chicago for the "informal question-and-answer session with the faculty" about which I'd been told. Five or six hundred people filled half an auditorium, more students and faculty relatives than card-holding instructors. The VP started off with a few barbed graces about such nonpolitical, off-the-record sessions, made himself the butt of a story about a cool New Hampshire reception, and then opened himself to questions "on any subject." Relaxed, intelligent, pleasant, his face was more of a piece than in those pictures which show its odd fat deposits deforming its little-boy features.

The first question was my now rusted key to his interior: "What were some of the books which had moved and instructed him during his formative years, and what were some he managed to look at now?" The VP said he assumed that "formative" meant high school and college years. He'd had the usual training of a liberal arts major. He'd never taken a political science course—Whittier had none—and advised en route politicians against them. There'd been an "inspirational teacher" who'd told him to expose himself to everything Tolstoy had written, so he exposed himself to *War and Peace, Anna Karenina, Possession, Etcetera.* He did not assess the third and fourth works but said that he preferred the first to "the greatest love story in the world." How he had been affected by it all he didn't know. Of the English philosophers he'd been exposed to, he liked Locke and, uh, Hobbes. He had a minor in French and read Voltaire, Rousseau, Etcetera, and this accounted, he supposed, for his radical tendencies. Laughter. Finally, in law school he'd taken a two-hour course in international jurisprudence and this had interested him very much. Now he had little time to read anything but the secret reports which Chairman Khrushchev also claimed to read, but he relaxed more with history than with detective novels or with light novels. Toynbee, Etcetera relaxed him, and in fiction historical novels. He apologized to the audience for taking such a long time with his answer.

With the next question about disarmament—and all the other questions were about such crucial topics—something remarkable happened to Nixon. His hands seized the podium, and then, as he answered, they were off, soaring, twirling, weaving, hammering, a graphic version of the policies of what he once referred to—without the definite article—as "You Ess" (U.S.). The answers were those he'd given a thousand times and would give a thousand more until the policies changed, but it was as if he had never answered them before. At times, the strain of not being able to meet the questions on more natural terms told in a storm of clichés, a swoop of arms, the bloat of false dreams. "The cold and calculating Communist who fought his way up through that web of intrigue"—the hands spinning a terrible, tangled web—"defying the UN in Korea"—fist batting the air— "peace-loving nations"—this coming out as "peaceful-loving" as the tired interior squirmed—"freedom will prevail," "striking the first blow" (which we'll never do, unless we have incontrovertible evidence, but—hastily—we could never have that)— and so it went. Out of these rocks a stalk of well-groomed bitterness occasionally thrust itself: "I have no power to negotiate— in fact, no power." It was the Greek archaic statue straining against its Egyptian stiffness. But more. Here was this expert, not unpleasant, young—younger than his age—rather funny, even slightly offbeat fellow on a train he couldn't get off. Worse, he was part of the train, a wheel driven by Washington gas. In something else he said one felt he knew the interior was being depleted. The commonest coin of his remarks was "When I was in X," "When I saw Y," "I had a six-hour talk with Z," "I've been there," "I've seen this." It was more than a build-up which no Rockefeller or Kennedy could match. It was a loud version of a soft cry, once illustrated by a womanish flop of his hand after a finger skimmed sweat off his forehead: "I'm really alive. Washington hasn't buried me." It was an appeal demand by this hard-soft, oppressed-oppressive, witty-bedulled, mechanical man-boy that he be seen as a man capable of reaction as well as action, an untrammeled Mensch, a real person, no allegory, a man.

He had recently seen such a man, a man who was free in his power, and the complexity of his feeling about Khrushchev seemed deeper than consciousness, so that the name was talismanic for him and contradictions often circled about it: Khrushchev is completely materialistic—and nervously, "as my experts tell me"—like this table (bang on podium), and "talking about his sincerity is like talking about this table's sincerity—this is the expert now," followed a minute later by identifying the "good things of life" with "consumer goods." It was the engine's exhaust discharge. And the earthy talk ("Try to spread the excess wheat around and you have the Canadians on your back") and cultural arabesques ("I visited Leningrad, it's a quite beautiful city—Italian architecture") were the mechanical gestures of farewell to whatever personality had been used up in the lunge ahead.

The audience applauded, and the Vice President modulated his boy's triumph smile into wise assurance as the photographers aimed commemorative weapons.

Could it have been this way with Gladstone, John Adams, Bismarck? Or is it only in the great world which lives on images

—"that terrible public relations word," as the Vice President said with a real grimace *—that its politicians manufacture out of antiquated dreams and performance tips that someone could feel as I did for the young man gathered in by his limousine, a splurge of fellow feeling followed by a jolt of fright at the distance a man could travel from himself? †

* And before the debates with Kennedy.

† 1972: this formulation won't do. A man becomes himself. With untroubled—he claims he's never had a headache—descent into anesthesis, Richard Nixon has become himself.

June, 1973: Now the swamps of Watergate reveal the Nixonian skeletons. Like Ivan the Terrible's return from the monastery with his Kautilya-Machiavelli network of spies (the *oprishniki*), Nixon's return from the 1960 defeat has brought moral disaster to his country.

GEORGE McGOVERN

July 13, 1972

Two miles high in Colorado, the un-antennaed television set doesn't transmit pictures, but the noise is clear: the Democrats have just nominated George McGovern.

In the fall of 1969, I spent about twelve hours with him going up and down Chicago, ending at midnight in the apartment of a delightful political lawyer—William Clark—who'd assembled half a billion dollars of Chicago money to look him over. (The prize Croesus for me was an adipose pyramid named Arthur Wirtz who within minutes of meeting me told me his assets—thirty-eight apartment houses "free and clear," the Black Hawk restaurant, the Chicago Black Hawks, the Chicago Whatever . . . —hoisted his passing wife's arm to display the ruby as big as the Ritz she "got me to buy her," told me how he and Jim Norris had signed an agreement to keep their widows from getting hold of their sports interests, and finally where I should moor my yacht. "They let you fire the cannon after six.") One remembers what goes against the grain of a personality, the expectations of it you've had. Between McGovern speeches, we were in a penthouse of the gorgeous Lake Point Tower apartments. McGovern relished the gawdy beauty of the place. (If memory isn't kidding me, I think the host took a panoramic picture of Chicago every half hour.) We talked about skyscrapers. I said Bettelheim thought the height of housing developments was ruinous, kids playing downstairs couldn't relate to the scale, the gigantism reinforced their sense of being overwhelmed, their lives' root problem. McGovern was "up" on Bettelheim and wanted that clear. I was surprised and pleased at the insistence. I hadn't read the Merryman interview in *Life,* hadn't realized intellectual force had spilled over long-disciplined watchfulness into a form of aggression. It made him more of a

37

person. In the car which shuttled us up and down Chicago, he'd said little while two counselors—one my friend Richard Wade—pelted him with sensible advice. (A question was which anti-war rally should he address. McGovern's practical contribution was, "You can't be heard there. It's outdoors and they always yell a lot.") Mostly he was alert, unironic, pleasant. What I remember of his face—trying to discard a thousand recent pictures—is that it's slightly too emphatic at eyes, eyebrows, jaw, lips and forehead to be what you might quickly take it for, a handsome face. Nice-looking, yes, with the veiled and set-back eyes the door to something more.

I objected to only one thing he'd said. When we came from the airport where we'd met, I sat in the front seat, and he called from the back, "Are you writing something now, Dick?" A very small thing, but Wade's briefing had been too recent, the question was intrusive, cornball, and I was uneasy at the first name. The rest of the impressions were first-rate. McGovern had the ease in ten different sorts of places that comes from a hundred discoveries of superiority. There was also, I think, a deep modesty which bespeaks an even greater intelligence that knows it isn't of the first order. Plus a deep lode of feeling, and convictions with them. Yet there was little memorable said. Politics is repetition. I do remember that we were discussing the recently-discovered North Vietnamese massacre at Hué. Were we sure of the published fact, I asked? McGovern said to his aide that it should be checked, but said, yes, he thought it true and then something about the worst part of war being the increased brutalization of everybody.

We said goodnight at two A.M. in front of the Blackstone. He seemed fresh. I wrote him about the pleasure of meeting a public man who was so close to the private man—"private faces in public places are much nicer than public faces in private places" —and got back a Dear Dick letter that was a heavy-phrased version of his decency.

I'm past the stage of the Kennedy-Nixon piece, and proximity to the world's caesars isn't much of a thrill. (I don't know what I'd feel in a room with a political monster.) Even the staggering, the anti-human power of office isn't one of the world's marvels for me. A Tolstoy-Dostoevski reader like McGovern would appreciate that, I think, in a more interesting way than his opponent, the "exposed" reader of Tolstoy. (Without his discounting the enchantment of the sensations and activity of power which private dredgers like me can only try and imagine.)

Naturally I'll vote for him. With joy. Not only because of his personal qualities, but because of the Jeffersonian program. That he might end dynasty life—rockefellerism—in this country is something terrific.

In 1960 an editor asked me to do a piece about Charles Percy, then president of Bell and Howell and a comer in Republican politics. I drove up to the home plant, talked with Percy for an hour, and then wrote a piece which I sent him to check over.

It was a mild little account. Its strongest judgment was that the Bell and Howell plant looked like a bunch of electronic Mars bars trying to look like a garden and that its president was the prince in a fairy tale who'd just learned politics and now wanted to be the protagonist of a realistic novel. A bit fancy, but it was the way I saw it.

Percy was upset about it. He told me his wife had wept (they were new to politics then) and said she'd have to keep the children home from school if it were published. This reaction mystified me. I compared it to that fear of images which certain people we used to call "primitive" have: the subject of such exposure feels he's being buried, not described. Of course, there is a whiff of aggression in the most benevolent analysis. (I once asked Sartre what Genet's response had been to his seven hundred memorial pages on him. "He claims not to have read it, but I think everything he does is an attempt to refute it.") My Percy piece wasn't published, so its only effect was on me. The experience was distasteful, and I took it as a hint to go back to my vocation, making up stories more or less from scratch.

Until the mid-1960s I kept my politics for the living room and for letters to the editor. By this time, the betelevisioned American womb had brought Political Expertise into every home. Sitting in one's armchair, one was closer to the center of things than many a nineteenth-century Congressman had been in Washington. Today's Congressmen were getting lots of their own hot news from the same kitchen. (At times the televised event was the news.)

The brief pieces printed here are those of an armchair sitter. Their temperature rises as the discrepancy between res and verba heated up more and more of the world.

THE FLOTSAM OF WAR AND PEACE:
DECEMBER 2, 1967

Deaths, anniversaries, protests, politics. A cold day, windy, full
of autumn color, a football day fringed with iced squalls. America's most bellicose priest* and most luxurious traveler—the
Twentieth Century Limited—made their farewells. In Chicago
Eugene McCarthy made his first campaign speech, an invocation
of noble losers: Adlai Stevenson, Hannibal, Captain Dreyfus. In
late afternoon, on the site of the squash rackets room under what
had been the west stands of the country's first college football
stadium, Stagg Field, the widow of Enrico Fermi, the sculptor
Henry Moore, and the president of the University of Chicago
yanked at the sheet which draped the enormous red bronze which
commemorated the twenty-fifth anniversary of Fermi's nuclear
baptism: "The reaction is self-sustaining. The curve is expo-
nential."

A Fellini scene, the grand peppermint awning, the wind-
snapped flags, the Farragut High School Band squirting Sousa
marches, the inquisitive steel cranes suspending their excavation
of the field for the university's new library, the SDS banners en-
joining the university to "Get Out of IDA" (the Institute of
Defense Analysis) and advising the guests within earshot of
their loudspeaker to remember what this atomic nostalgia meant.
LBJ, with the new wisdom which keeps him off his country's
streets, sent his greetings by closed-circuit television. The great
face, incised by a kind of baffled ferocity, looked unearthly, an
Orwellian apparition.

The survivors of the nuclear band were mostly old and
famous. Some were retired, some ran great corporations, all
figured in scientific establishments here and abroad. There were

* Cardinal Spellman of New York.

41

Nobelists—Libby, Segre, Calvin, Seaborg, the last as dark, vertical, and infolded as a Warner Brothers inquisitor. The old nemesis, General Groves, was there in the distinguished jowls, mustache, and mufti of an English banker. Hatchets were buried deep in the wash of recollection and historic triumph.

The small, gray-haired sculptor, as inconsequential- and irreducible-looking as a rock, sat in front with Mrs. Fermi. He was finely attentive to the brief talks, and only when the dark sheet revealed his work did he seem to drift.

The work dominated everything. Red, eyeless head, ruptured tomato, bloody molar, nuclear cloud, whatever, it shone in the strange stormy light of the afternoon. On an early sketch of it, Moore had written: "The great . . . problem (for me) is to combine sculptured form with human energy." The Italian Henry, the nuclear navigator, might have reversed this: "the energy of things, organized by human forms."

One sought parallels between the two. Both worked with earth stuff, both knew its recalcitrance and possibilities, both were extraordinarily inventive and independent of the apparatus of large-scale enterprise. From the day's scientific recollections one saw that the Fermi Project (as Walter Zinn said) "was finished with unprecedented speed, though it lacked the computers, elaborate organization, and scientific managerial techniques now considered indispensable for such undertakings."

The recollection was bucolic. In those days, the artful inventors needed but six thousand dollars' worth of graphite, and that unprecedented sum they got via Einstein's famous letter to Roosevelt. The relationship between science and government was almost like that of gods and men in the myths.

Then the serpent showed up. The land was reached, the Indians were destroyed, and the explorers felt the chains on their feet. Chicago Pile One became Hiroshima, and the administrators gave way to the urbane theoreticians who like General Pfuhl in *War and Peace* "so love their theory that they lose sight of the object of the theory—its application to practice . . . immutably conceited men, ready to face martyrdom for their own ideas."

That night, at the Conrad Hilton, the weary, reflective Senator from Minnesota spoke his contempt for the latest package of maggoty theory. Yet his speech sounded ethereal in its purity: "A single legal crime, a single dishonorable act will bring about the loss of one's honor, the dishonor of a whole people." This from the noble Péguy, but if this were the case, on such a day as this, it was clear the game was over already. No one present had failed to earn a share of dishonor.

Reading such words, a participant in the atomic ceremonies wondered why the pursuit of power had to sound so much further removed from ordinary standards of human decency than the simpler pursuits of the Moores and Fermis, whose work after all endures in usefulness and beauty by coming to grips with the recalcitrance and impurity of natural things.

YARMOLINSKY, EISENHOWER,
AND THE CANNIBAL

On Armistice Day [1966] the former special assistant of the Defense Department, Professor Adam Yarmolinsky of Harvard, spoke in the handsome, bowl-shaped courtroom of the University of Chicago Law School about the relationship of arms and foreign policy. For those of us whose knowledge of Yarmolinsky was limited to the notion that he represented the most temperate —and thus eventually ejected—element of Defense Department policy, the hour and a half had its surprises.

He was introduced by a fellow defense strategist, Professor Wohlstetter, who described his first sight of Yarmolinsky in Secretary McNamara's office at the beginning of the Kennedy administration. McNamara was instructing a group of white-faced generals about the new sorts of questions for which he needed answers. In the back of the room Yarmolinsky snored away, an obbligato of self-confidence amidst the brass collapse.

Yarmolinsky, a small, bristling man with a haycock of gray-specked black hair, read a thoughtful paper which went more or less as follows: U.S. options are limited by U.S. power; that is, the U.S. cannot flare into reprisals as easily as nonnuclear powers. The country's international aims, needs, and responsibilities enjoy the backing of a superbly varied armament which is available to persuade, tempt, or occasionally force the acceptance of policy goals. Only some goals, of course, as no arsenal is unlimited. Since World War II there have been (according to McNamara) a hundred and sixty-four outbreaks of violence, less than half of which were related to communism; American armament could not cope with a large fraction of these, even if policy dictated it. What, then, were possible rules for selected intervention? Yarmolinsky suggested a few: When in doubt about the nature of an outbreak (say, civil war or external aggression) don't intervene. When possible, apply force rather than violence. (This is the "Schelling distinction," which has to do with forcibly preventing outbreaks rather than augmenting them.) The third section of the talk contrasted the performance of the State Department with that of its instrument, the Defense Department. The State Department had been content to develop attitudes rather than policies. It identified nations as hostile, friendly or ones to be contained. It's as if a doctor were satisfied to say that he was hostile to high blood pressure and thought measles should be contained.

The speech had begun with the country as a pugilist enjoined from punching roughnecks in the street and ended with the country as a doctor at work on the world's ills. The transition was not, I think, the intended core of Yarmolinsky's speech, but it sank in the hearts of those of us who may be less attuned to the subtler ranges of arms policy discussion.

The question period revealed still greater distance between the technocrats of armament and the laity. Yarmolinsky's face—dark, rapid, ready for engagement—is full of spark and humor. He delights in skirmish, is quick to rebut the naive, sometimes with hints of unquestionable but classified knowledge from the horse's mouth. (In the courtroom he joked about hearsay evidence.) He is also quick to spot the lance headed for the theoretical chinks in his armor and to counter by admitting it. When pressed about the difference, say, between intervening "to prevent a blood bath" in the Dominican Republic and not intervening to prevent a much bloodier one in Indonesia, he shrugged his theoretical shoulders. One can't do everything; there are no formulas. (The State Department had just been rebuked for not working some out.)

Yarmolinsky's wit, energy, and confidence were those of the theoretical man turned decision maker; he carried the authority of a wounded veteran in a discussion of heroism.

A student asked him to comment on the present state of the military-industrial complex. Head darting, half-rooster, half-squirrel, Yarmolinsky erupted into an odd, even angry response. Eisenhower, he said, had always wanted to do what his master, George Humphrey, had said to do—cut the budget—and he'd tried and tried to slice the biggest chunk of that budget, the military, and failed because it would have been suicidal to succeed, so he made his farewell address in a fit of temper. As to growing military influence on policy, he, Yarmolinsky, could answer as Holmes did in commenting on the power to tax being the power to destroy: "Not while I'm on the court."

Some of us in the little courtroom had the gloomy feeling that the monster which the puzzled, stymied general-president had in his stumbling way pointed to in his farewell gesture had now recruited and absorbed the Yarmolinskys, the brilliant planners whose intellectual discoveries are made within the bounds of arms policy and whose not unboastful assertions that such policy has nothing to do with morality bring them uncomfortably close to the scientific technicians of the nuclear bomb. Many of these men had spent years regretting their absorption in the techniques of destruction. One did not feel that there was much prospect of such second thoughts on the part of the urbane and learned Yarmolinsky and the fellow social scientists who joined him on the floor to congratulate him. Out in the cold air along the Midway, some of us thought that the military-industrial complex had acquired a brilliant warhead. The cannibalistic monster had further domesticated itself in the American world.

REFLECTIONS ON THE STATE
OF THE UNION

A Nation that makes an unjust War, is only a great Gang.
Benjamin Franklin

JOHNSON: There is but a shallow stream of thought in history.
BOSWELL: But surely, Sir, an historian has reflection.
JOHNSON: Why yes, Sir; and so has a cat when she catches a mouse for her kitten.

That wise and saintly Hibernian panda, Daniel P. Moynihan, counted forty-nine outbreaks of applause during President Johnson's State of the Union address (January 1968), the loudest coming after the "crime in the streets" proposals. Sump-low as the congressional level at which the President dumped a speech (which, for sheer content, could have been shaped for Aristotle or a crocodile), there is a gleam of true gold in that forty-ninth rush of applause. The gold is the unignorable distinction between direct and indirect evil, between evil which injures on the spot and delayed, circumambient evil. The mugging victim, the Congressman, and Dr. Johnson understand the difference. The terrible emptiness within the other Johnson's reflections on the state of the union was the failure to acknowledge the other direct evil, the one whose nightly telesight troubles millions with the fear that the American nation, eight years shy of its two hundredth birthday, is becoming Franklin's "great Gang."

That the rootage of the Vietnam war is at least as intricate as that of a Washington stabbing or of that "murder by mail-order gun" which put the—at that point—swallowing, silvery President where he had stood no one will doubt, but acknowledgment no more sanctifies the silence in his address than mutual acknowl-

47

edgment of rape sanctifies it. The congressional country lawyers cheered the President's call to put out the fire in the streets before checking the defective wiring, and we nervous Nellies of the world waited for him to put out the fire in Vietnam.

On the NET discussion of the state of the union, the sensitive Mr. Moyers, perhaps prematurely hardened by exposure to diplomatic intricacy—an arteriosclerosis spottable in the eyes of many an old *chargé d'affaires*—praised the omission on the grounds that it would have endangered the delicate negotiations he was sure were taking place over the world. But how would the world have suffered if Lyndon Johnson had said, "The bombing stops tonight. We will be at X in four days. We hope to see President Thieu, President Ho, and the NLF representatives at the table. We will press for an immediate cease-fire, the guarantee of minimal safety for all parties and individuals, the gradual broadening of suffrage and representation of all political units"? Would delicate diplomatic antennae have transformed such music into noise? The excellent men who discussed the state of the union need not have yielded to Mr. Moyers' veteran knowledgeability on this point.

Happily, they did not yield much elsewhere. Indeed, the state of the union looked reasonably well as much because of the exchanges between these men as because of the proposals they debated. Except from the eye-batting, teeth-flashing, voice-dipping, almost maniacally flirtatious William Buckley (whose popularity one must link with that of Mrs. Oswald and Al Capone as another instance of American *Schadenfreude*),* one heard a lot of clear-headed stuff. Milton Friedman is an excellent spokesman for that powerful feeling which leaps political fences to join Goldwatered Jeffersonianism to vital, Whitmanian anarchism. (Though Moynihan gave him too much credit for the negative income tax proposal. This economic illiterate read

* I've since been told by a mutual friend that the man's a charmer. His journal does show up a more modest, responsible, and driven man than the one who looks half-mad on television.

about it in Pound's old *ABC of Economics*.) His thesis, hoary but backed with at least debatable evidence, that government agencies corrode the objects of their repair lost its abstract nostalgia when it met Moynihan's description of the overgoverned young or even Walter Heller's proposal to send tax money back to states and municipalities. Arthur Schlesinger lucidly sketched the revitalization of city government and in the spirit of the new conservative-liberal fusion said that centralization in the affluent society was a New Deal hangover.

Moynihan praised the administration's measure-by-measure attempt to control the automotive miasma and joined with the Buckley-harassed, nobly patient mayor of Cleveland, Carl Stokes, to pick fine features (hard-core jobs, home construction) out of the crime-heavy presidential description of urban problems. It was a terrific endorsement. But what a Moynihan giveth, he can take away. Sputtering like a radiant strawberry pop tart, he described the reactions of the young studio cameraman to the proposals that a hundred new FBI agents be hired to search out narcotics takers and sellers, and suddenly the distance between the huge, silvery President and the country's *menu peuple* and *tiers état* gloomed like 1789.

Still, the NET discussion altered the feeling one had after the President's catlike reflections on the state of the union. One felt that if the good will and energy of Moynihan, Moyers, Stokes, Schlesinger, Friedman, and Heller could bring policy out of debate, when 1976 rolled around we could celebrate the two hundredth anniversary of the United States as a great nation rather than as Franklin's "great Gang."

ON CAMERA

In what one of his interrogators on *Meet the Press* called his "valedictory mood," Secretary McNamara quoted four lines from Eliot's "Little Gidding":

> We shall not cease from exploration
> And the end of all our exploring
> Will be to arrive where we started
> And know the place for the first time.

Never in public had the Secretary seemed more human. The lines helped him search for the innocence of expiation. He talked regretfully of his sponsorship of the Cuban invasion, which ended in the Bay of Pigs, and would perhaps have recited other errors but for the restraining influence of his immediate neighbor, the Secretary of State. Once he turned toward Mr. Rusk with a laugh which found no answering smile. That famous egglike surface permitted no departure from public impassivity (except perhaps for an eye gleam and tiny smile at a rapid put-down of Roger Hilsman).

One wondered about this impassivity. Is it diplomatic cool? Does it conceal a hunger for the quick, uniform, high-souled brutality which military action best supplies? Does it enforce the suppression of what might lead to the relaxed privileges his seat neighbor was beginning to take? Asked by Peter Lisagor of the Chicago *Daily News* about South Vietnamese indifference to the government of President Thieu, Secretary Rusk said of course there were villagers in South Vietnam who only thought of crops, healthy babies, and protection from marauders.

What connection was there between that answer and the poverty-stricken Georgia boy who threw lumps of coal at trains in the hope that firemen would throw enough back to heat the family home? How close were we to the adolescent who put on the military uniform which masked that poverty? The impassivity erased the distance.

In "Little Gidding" there were other clues:

> There are three conditions which often look alike
> Yet differ completely, flourish in the same hedgerow;
> Attachment to self and to things and to persons, detachment
> From self and from things and from persons; and, growing between them, indifference
> Which resembles the others as death resembles life . . .

Did that famous face (which looks like its own death mask) exemplify lethal indifference, or was it only a fatigued exemplification of Lord Acton's terrible maxim on power?

Four years after the return to the Pedernales plow, Johnson (and those of us who hated his presidential guts) has settled down. "I made every mistake in the book," the gentled Cincinnatus tells his public Eckerman, Walter Cronkite, and he lets out a notch of the famous private tongue: "You can tell 'em all to go straight to hell. But will they go?" A trillion tears and ten million quarts of blood watered these blooms of retirement. Time has reduced the Great Monster to "a man like you, a man like me." Which does not mean the abolition of judgment, only the reminder that everyone needs: "The sun makes shadows of us all."

"Winds whip the summit." Who knows what wind-breakers you and I would wear to keep warm up there. Down here, the best we can do is keep our binoculars clean and get ready the occasional rescue squad.

JUDGMENT DAYS

It is for Providence to make moral judgments.
Dean Rusk,
Foreign Relations Committee hearings,
March 12, 1968

A city that rules an empire holds nothing which is to its own interest as contrary to right and reason.
Thucydides on the decline of Athens

Consider Muhammed bin Tughlak. Eloquent in Arabic and Persian, possessed of extraordinary memory and knowledge, devout and charitable, he personally attended the sick of his realm. In the year 1326 some citizens of Delhi threw abusive papers into his audience hall. Muhammed marched to the Deccan and ordered the abandonment of Delhi. "The city," reports Ibn Batuta, "remained a perfect desert." Trouble bred trouble. The Mongols threatened and were bought off. Muhammed invaded Khurasan with cavalry and was repulsed. He struck brass and copper with silver insignia to pay the debt. The currency collapsed. His nephew, Bahau-d din, rebelled, was captured, skinned, and his flesh boiled with rice and fed to elephants (who refused it).

Senators McCarthy and [Robert] Kennedy will not be fed to fussy elephants, but the fury displaced from them will apparently fall on Vietnam. The presidential talk after the New Hampshire primary * has been colder and fiercer than ever. To cite another eminent leader: "The man who is to make the final decision must not let himself be moved by the misery and the horror that war brings to every individual on the front and in the homeland." †

The man of good will who becomes a tyrant is one of the world's horrors. The man himself is unaware of it. His course seems dictated by others, by conditions. The opposition is his martyrdom. He suffers.

> The wicked man suffers constant, consuming, inward pain, and finally, when all the objects of his will thwart him, he quenches the fiery thirst of his will by the sight of the suffering of others.‡

Our society is so clearly open and rational, the exchange of opinion so constant, the norms of behavior so widely accepted, it is almost impossible to think in terms of wickedness, tyranny, and evil. We leave our moral judgments to Providence. To think of men who have worked hard for many noble ends as new ver-

---

* But before the withdrawal of his candidacy at the end of the month this was written.

† Hitler to SS General Wolff, April 1945. Dulles, *The Secret Surrender.*

‡ Schopenhauer, *The World as Will and Idea.* New York, Modern Library.

sions of such human curses as Muhammed bin Tughlak and Adolf Hitler makes even the fiercest opponent of the war suspect himself of irrationality, makes him afraid of his mind's treason. Yet even those who do not want to say to Secretary Rusk and President Johnson "No, gentlemen, it is not Providence but men who make moral judgments" may use memory and analysis to prepare for what otherwise might seem a most irrational course: the ever fiercer destruction of Vietnam, the ever fiercer attacks on "those who serve to disunite the nation."

2. A Little Dose of Hellebore, or Revolutions and Gestures

I'll concentrate on things like health and wealth . . . but before that I've got a lot of hard work to do, straining my eyes to read books in very small writing . . . and of course there's no hope of ever becoming a Wise Man unless one takes three doses of hellebore.

Lucian of Samosata
Dialogues of the Dead

hellebore a plant of the genus *Helleborus,* particularly *H. niger,* the black hellebore or Christmas rose; a drastic, hydragogic cathartic, possessing emmenagogic powers, in overdoses producing inflammation of the gastric and intestinal mucous membrane, with violent vomiting, vertigo, cramp, and convulsions which sometimes end in death. *H. viridis,* the green hellebore, a native of Europe, is naturalized in the United States.

Century Dictionary

This section begins with a revolutionary who succeeded and ends with one who died young. Between are a handful of the better-known, more or less revolutionary gesture makers of the last few years.

THE REVOLUTIONARY TEST

"Neither the agricultural nor the industrial problem has been resolved," said Mao Tse-tung to André Malraux in 1965. "Still less, the problem of the young . . . The young must be put to the test." The *antimémoiriste,* from the hindsight of 1967, sensed the formation of "a new revolutionary action comparable to the one which raised and then repressed 'The Hundred Flowers.' "

Since, of course, the Red Guards have shaken the state "as a madman shakes a dead geranium," the students of Prague turned out the Stalinist rascals; * the followers of Dutschke, Savio, Carmichael, and five hundred other leaders at five hundred other places put many a place to many a test.

Are what a cynical friend of mind called "the revolting young" unique to these times? In most ways, surely not. The University of Paris was shaken apart in Abelard's time; Cambridge was started by rebellious Oxford students; the young Harlan Fisk Stone, assisted, it is said, by young Calvin Coolidge, led an Amherst "riot" which toppled a college president.

There have been deeper juvenile trenches than these. The Camisards tore southern France apart for years. They sprang righteously from religious suppression and broken official promises; the atmosphere was, as always, apocalyptic; there were

* The mayfly dies the day it is born because it has no digestive system; its significant existence is larval. The Stalinist rascals are mostly stomach; they returned and they—all stomach—gobbled.

Paul Goodmans (Jurieu) and Che Guevaras (du Serre); children, called *petits prophètes,* went from village to village spouting quotations not from Chairman Mao but from *Revelations;* the army commander, Cavalier, was a seventeen-year-old baker's boy; and such injunctions as the following were issued: "We demand that you throw out all the priests and missionaries within three days or be burned alive with them." *

A few years ago Mr. and Mrs. Opie showed in their *Language and Lore of Childhood* that a Davy Crockett rhyme thought up in Topeka could show up within a week in Brussels and Tasmania. Now the politics of youthful action travel with as great speed. A twenty-three-year-old German house painter (that fatal profession) is inspired by the Martin Luther King assassin to shoot Rudi Dutschke, and within a month students are in the administrative fortresses of Columbia and Grenoble.

Although the FBI and Deuxième Bureau will find portraits of Chairman Mao stuck up in both places, they should not think they're dealing with the old type of conspiracy. The "breath" is there, but it is that contagious, classic breath of the revolting young.

Of course, many of these young and not-so or professional-young are tuned in and set up for planetary revolution. Distributing leaflets on the "green swards of their seminaries," they might do well to think on Chairman Mao's revolutionary notions. Fifty years, he tells his French visitor, is a very short time:

> Khrushchev seemed to think a revolution finished when a Communist party comes to power—as if it had something to do with national liberation . . . Lenin knew revolution only began then . . . You remember Kosygin at the 23rd Congress: "Communism is the raising of the standard of living." Oh yes! And swimming is putting on a bathing suit! . . . Everything is yet to be done! The thought, the culture, the customs which led China where we found her must disappear.

* Closer to the Chairman's home is the teen-age founder of the great T'ang dynasty, Li Shih-Min.

No, it is not the matter of civil injustice, military brutality, or bureaucratic stultification which concerns the revolutionary. It is everything. "I bring not peace but a sword," said another revolutionary whose pure advance was quickly muddled by the old human slime.

THE COWSILLS AND OTHER
DEMOCRATIC FAMILIES

With our best youlldied greedings to Pep and Memmy and
the old folkers beloy and beyant, wishing them all very
merry Incarnations in this land of the livvey and plenty of
preprosperousness through their coming new yonks.

Joyce
Finnegans Wake

It is not, then, by interest but by common associations and
by the free sympathy of opinion and of taste that democracy unites brothers to each other.

Tocqueville
Democracy in America

The program says: "It took America 500 years to create the
Cowsills. Five hundred years of mixing nationalities, races, phi-
losophies, beliefs, and democracy within its borders." We're in an
immense, gold-armored cowbell, shafts of smoky light for clap-
per, the ugliest auditorium in the Midwest. It blacks out, then on
stage, out of a corolla of electronic song, the Cowsills.

Five thumping, pumping, pounding American children, Susan
(9), John (11), Barry (13), Bob (17), and Bill (20), with
toothy, miniskirted Barbara. "We call her Mom."

From the maddened heights of Insull's Civic Opera House,
the wail of adolescent desire: "Barry, Barry, Bar-oh-Bar-oh
Barrrrry." The spotlight converts Barry into three-buttoned
blue boy; he sucks the microphone, he rocks, his Mom and sis
and brothers rock: "I-I-I wanna, wanna hol' you tiight." Electri-
fied guitars, organs, drums. Mom and Susan, Barry, Bob, John,
and Bill. The American family in song crosses the chill yardage
which distanced Swifts, Palmers, Fields, and Armours from

Verdi melodrama, Viennese intrigue. The utility magnate's Palace of Strut is the electronic love funnel of a giantess.

The Cowsills. They take over here as they took over a mansion in Newport, twenty-two bare rooms, the money from Dad's naval pension spent on guitars, amplifiers, drums. There, *en famille,* Dad drilled them in the songs, the patter, the pelvic thrusts, the electronic hay-licked version of International Beatle that sees them, this Chicago night, on the verge of—maybe—making it big.

The Jeremiah of *Capital* (whose abandoned daughter ended operatically in the Thames) wrote:

> However terrible, however repulsive the break-up of the old family system within the organism of capitalist society may seem; none the less, large-scale industry, by assigning to women, and to young persons and children of both sexes, a decisive role in the socially organized process of production, and a role which has to be fulfilled outside the home, is building the new economic foundation for a higher form of the family and of the relations between the sexes.

Tonight the Cowsills are guaranteed fifty-five hundred against a cut of the house. Only a foot in the door of Big Money, but tomorrow they are off for London and a visit to the Pope. With luck, they will return to twenty-five-thousand-dollar-a-night houses. The twenty-two rooms in Newport will fill with furniture; the grass, "grown to a height of 3 feet," will be a lawn, and the wire cage in which Clyde, John's miniature monkey, was frozen dead the night it arrived will be warmed and filled with a new Clyde.

If it works out, it will mean that these kids and Mom have gone beyond new strata of adolescent love and suggested a "higher form" for the dying democratic family.

Not just Liverpool and Tulsa dropouts, but good American families over the land can play and stay together.

Jamming.

A VOYAGE TO CYTHERA

> Quelle est cette île triste et noire? C'est Cythère,
> Nous dit-on, un pays fameux dans les chansons,
> Eldorado banal de tous les vieux garçons . . .
> Où la jeune prêtresse, amoreuse des fleurs,
> Allait, le corps brûlé de secrètes chaleurs . . .
> > Baudelaire, "Un Voyage à Cythère"

"Baudelaire," she'd said years ago, answering the question to whom of the Great Dead she'd long to talk, "Baudelaire and Diaghilev." Wife of the driving Senator, she was already the Queen of Opulent Surprise. The biggest surprise was that her gift became the delight, almost the justification, of baronial America. In its Great Funeral, she fetched again from an unlikely spot (a Broadway musical) the nameplate for the thousand days.

Camelot.

Selma, the Alianza, the Bay of Pigs, Viet-Nam, the face-down of Khrushchev were converted into dreamland.

Now it was the week of the Greeks: in Mexico City, the Olympics; in space, Apollo.

On the heartland, meanwhile, only gloom. Camelot was in Modred's grip. One by one, the knights had been killed off. Wicked dwarfs threatened furious succession.

Queen Guinevere, genius of behavior, took off on Olympic Airlines for Cythera. And for its unlikely ruler, the Greek from Smyrna and Buenos Aires, from Liberia, Panama, Paris, and Skorpios, Master of Tongues and Currency, Philosopher, Pirate.

Queen of Surprise, in a bad time

> > donnez-nous la force et le courage
> De contempler nos coeurs et nos corps sans dégout!

REVOLUTIONARIES AND COMEDIANS

On his deathbed Lenin asked Krupskaya to return the book he'd borrowed from the local library.

Hours before he was shot, Che Guevara corrected the pronunciation of the La Higuera schoolmistress.

In Chicago these days [Spring 1970] North Side hostesses boast of Abbie Hoffman's unrevolutionary behavior. "He's so polite. And he leaves the bathroom cleaner than George does."

Revolutionaries, it seems, are as orderly as the best of us. Aren't they after "new order"? Abbie, though, is no classic revolutionary. Day by day, he sits with his more classic companions in the Dearborn Street courtroom. But he is of another tribe: Abbie is a comedian.

Revolutionaries and comedians are cousins. Both live from dissociation and subversion. The revolutionary makes the bomb that looks like a watch, the comedian the bomb that is a watch. The revolutionary takes to the streets, the comedian to the theater. The revolution is open to all, you need tickets for the comedian.

Abbie sits in the courtroom because he confused the genres. "Theater," he said, "is anything you can get away with." For a bit, it looked as if he could turn the street into theater. Pigasus for President worked nearly as well as telling the old lady to hold his money while he went into the store to steal some more.*

Nearly.

Reverse Marx: What begins as farce can end in misery. That's the pit under comedy. Make your Modest Proposal in the Biafra of 1970, and you're a monster. Abbie is a social comedian in a strange time.

In that pastoral America Henry Adams described as a time

* Abbie Hoffman, *Revolution for the Hell of It.*

"when every American, from Jefferson and Gallatin, down to the poorest squatter, seemed to nourish an idea that he was doing what he could to overthrow the tyranny which the past had fastened on the human mind," Abbie might have looked like the American version of Voltaire. But from President to tube watcher today, it is the present which appears tyrannical. Its complexity, its technical mystery, the insecurity of its elites, the surrealism of its entertainment perplex and frighten. That *Mann ohne Eigenschaften,* that President in search of a character, Richard Nixon, has supposedly understood the general insecurity, and he labors to appear the champion of familiar simplicity, clear-cut athletic decisions, Algerism,* the deserted village, the sweetness of pastoral quiet, the comedy of Fields and Lloyd, the religion of Billy Graham. The Gallup polls [Spring 1970] confirm his instinct.

The man who was brought in to modernize *The Saturday Evening Post* and modernized it out of existence says that if he had to do it again he "would keep Norman Rockwell on the cover." That is the world that counts for most of the audience Abbie tried to reach through the tube.

Professor Fiedler praises the hero of the Kesey novel who fished from the wall of the hydroelectric dam. Like Abbie, he wants people to camp out among the machines. But the tube watchers and workers know that if that generator breaks down, it's not going to be fixed with a fish hook; and if it breaks down, they're in trouble. You can't catch fish in the Chicago River, and anarchist Abbie has to eat, drink, and take baths with the rest of us.

So Pigasus for President didn't stay funny for lots of people. Even juxtaposed with Chicago's mayor: after all, Daley does more or less run the city. Abbie hasn't even run a successful road show.

Along with his sober brethren, the gadfly comedian sits in court with a shrinking grin. The other day he compared himself

* Horatio, not Hiss.

to the hero of *Farewell to Arms:* "They throw you into this game and then kill you if you break the rules."

That old lady outside the supermarket was probably FBI in drag.

THE PLAYBOY REVOLUTIONARY

> I, for instance, would not be surprised if all of a sudden a gentleman with an ignoble, or rather with a reactionary and ironical, countenance were to arise and, putting his arms akimbo, say to us all: "I say, gentlemen, hadn't we better kick over the whole show and scatter rationalism to the winds, simply to send these logarithms to the devil, and to enable us to live once more at our own sweet foolish will!
>
> Dostoevsky
> *Notes from the Underground*

Who knows where the true notes from the underground are being written? As for those false notes which periodically announce their revolutionary passion, just try the supermarket.

The everyday rhetoric of revolution is scarcely a perturbation "on the plane of the feasible" (Samuel Beckett), hardly "a modulation toward the theater" (Ezra Pound). It is *hors d'oeuvres*. It is a cocktail hour topic. It is an aphrodisiac.

Home from squeezing human oranges on business avenues, the Playboy Revolutionary puts on a turtleneck, lights up the latest snake root, and warms himself with Revolutionary Sentiment. Sometimes with, sometimes without that sweetest of chasers, Self-Contempt.

How just that the magazine which has most fattened on the Circean pleasures of Consumer Land should most systematically dangle the official eccentrics and official revolutionaries in its mammary cleavage. And what Playboy is cool enough to distinguish in that sleek warmth the Tax Exile, J. Paul Getty, from the Police Exile, Eldridge Cleaver; or separate the fine Whitmanian dribble of Allen Ginsberg from the cloudy slaver of the resident *philosophe,* that Condottiere of the Quilt, Professor Hugh Hefner?

The Revolutionary Pages which close out the homicidal luxury of the 1960s are in the hands of literary culture's Most Official Revolutionary, Leslie Fiedler.

Everyone knows and almost everyone likes Leslie. He's the circuit-burning charmer, the Automatic Nay Sayer who publicly suffers apocalyptic monthlies: the End of This, the Birth of That, No in Thunder (and pass the hat).

One of the great persons in Italian villages is the woman with black dress and blacker voice who is paid to mourn at funerals. Italians love theater, but do it right, cradle to grave. At funerals there are genuine corpses in the coffin. Leslie is more refined; either he ghouls up' dead cats and rag dolls or wails over nothing at all.

In the December *Playboy* he trumpets over the following pile of nonbones: "The age of Proust, Mann, and Joyce is over, just as in verse, that of T. S. Eliot and Paul Valéry is done with." And for the literature which came after the work of these corpses, Leslie calls for "a new new criticism, a postmodern criticism appropriate to postmodernist fiction and verse."

No easy job, of course, Playboys. Criticism is "natural" to an age of analysis and rationality, and the new age is "apocalyptic, antirational, blatantly romantic and sentimental; an age dedicated to joyous misology * and prophetic irresponsibility." In short, an age made for the sentimental, apocalyptic, reason-hating, blatantly romantic Bad Man of the Culture Boudoir, Yours Sincerely, L.F.

Swindling's a trade of tricks. To pass off shacks as palaces, you work up fancy trim and a few props. Leslie furnishes his critical slum with names and titles, the famous—for panache—and the little known for snob appeal.

This month's villain props are those antiquated practitioners

* Plato traces misology to the resentment of those who have no worldly understanding.

of an antiquated craft—Saul Bellow, Bernard Malamud, James Baldwin, and the like. The heroes (or wavelets; Leslie is a Wave Charter) are a French jokester named Boris Vian, a new novelist named Seelye, and such better-known victims of the Prophet's revelation as Thomas Berger, Leonard Cohen, John Barth, Norman Brown, Marshall McLuhan, and Philip Roth.

Victims, because by the time Leslie gets finished throttling them in his pigeonholes they may wonder if they shouldn't exchange the typewriter for a gun.

For Leslie, Berger, Barth, and Cohen are masters of the "new Western" (species: Pop Pastiche) and can be taken almost as seriously as those geniuses of adolescence, Frank Zappa and Bob Dylan. Dylan writes "a kind of pop surrealist poetry, passionate, mysterious, and quite complex—complex enough, in fact, to prompt a score of scholarly articles on his 'art.' " (Study that "quite," that "in fact," and the quotation marks around "art." Then ponder Leslie's ultimate certificate of "art," the scholarly article. Is the true prophetic text *Modern Philology*?)

As John Barth will surely crow with delight at his old neighbor's praise, consider the pleasure that that "laureate of masturbation," Roth, will take in learning that he is "a master of the 'thin' novel, the novel with minimum inwardness," and that "his book has no more meaning than any other dirty joke." When Leslie pins the Order of Merit on you, you bleed to death.

Like most of the road-running John the Baptists of Life and Letters, Leslie knows that the ultimate trick is buttering your stale wafers with religious bilge. Smear it on, and you advertise your depth, your seriousness, your dissatisfaction with the trivial (though you have been booming trivia for two thousand words).

Here's Billy Graham-Cracker at work in peroration:

> But in a time of closing the gap, literature becomes again prophetic and universal—a continuing revelation appropriate to a permanent religious revolution, whose function is precisely to transform the secular crowd into a sacred community, one with each other and equally at home in

the world of technology and the realm of wonder. Pledged like Isaiah to speaking the language of everyone, the prophets of the new dispensation can afford to be neither finicky nor genteel; and they echo, therefore, the desperate cry of the Hebrew prototype: "I am a man of unclean lips . . . in the midst of a people of unclean lips."

Oh Leslie! We Playboys shiver at your gorgeous labial sewers. We are grateful for that critical flame on the outer edge of Edge City. (And thank you too, noble Hugh, for speeding us to heaven on these ecstatic cylinders.)

Bravo pop, bravo primitive wildness, on wild men, on Indians, on "holy disturbers of the peace of the devout." (The devout! Poor rats who sit under lamps with thick books and lose themselves in the fates of those rattier than themselves.) Burn on, Leslie. Scorch these antique hutches. Bring us the hot future in the aluminum covers of The Funny-Bunny Gospel.

THE BOOKS IN FRED HAMPTON'S
APARTMENT

A few days after the lethal predawn police raid on the Chicago apartment of the young Black Panthers, I went down with other perturbed, inquisitive history sniffers and shrine makers to see what was what.

A beautiful December day, sunny and clear, though a haze of translucent filth hung over the Loop.

The apartment house is on the near Southwest Side. A slum? Not from a car. Largish stone houses with wooden trim (red curlicues, fluted columns, beige and gray), the streets oddly flushed and clean. Only the open lots, ulcers of urban renewal, bespeak slum, their mud valleys thick with glass bits, cans, old newspapers. Two schools, a large, gray pile of 1910 classicism— *William McKinley*—and a few blocks away a pile of parti-colored boxes from the 1950s—*Victor Herbert*.

A little after eleven a bearded, young white man, lawyer "for the Panthers and the Hampton family," admitted the day's visitors to the apartment. We walked single file through the steamy gray rooms where nine people had passed most of the night a few days before.

Violent death does not make for good housekeeping; nor do lawyers, pathologists, tourists, and guides, but it was clear that this apartment had never been an idyllic place to either live or die. The gray walls were undecorated except for slogans in red spray paint ("Dead Pigs Are Good," "All Power to the People") and, now, gaps made by pistol and shotgun fire. The stuff of life was piled in corners, on wall tables, in cartons of Cold Duck Sparkling Wine and Old Taylor: shirts, skirts, Panther news-papers, bottles, gauze curtains, uneaten hamburgers in wax paper, a can of Johnson's Pledge Wax, a portable phonograph, a copy of *Time* (Lieutenant Calley on the cover), folded hideaway beds, some clothes in a closet, a few pots, one with hardened spaghetti fragments, and in the back room a double bed with a Supersoft Restone Mattress which bore the horrible relief map of Hampton's blood. An ugly, characterless, nameless place, the rapidly assembled nest of people who would not be here long, people who did not sink their passions into furniture.

Characterless, to me, except for one thing: a few books scattered here and there in the apartment, some open, as if reading had been interrupted and were to be resumed the next day.

To a bookish man the books changed almost everything, for much more than the hamburgers, the few unlovely suits in the closet, the Supersoft mattress, and far more than the slogans sprayed on the walls, they were clearly the objects of choice. (Imagine being lost in woods, stumbling into a shack, finding cans of beans, a loaf of bread, an oil heater; and then seeing by a lamp an opened copy of *Dubliners*. That would mean *connection*.)

The books in the Monroe Street apartment spoke of self-improvement, of purposive learning, of curiosity. Here are the titles I wrote down: *Introduction to Embryology;* Chabod, *Machiavelli and the Renaissance;* James T. Farrell, *The Face of Time;* Hannah Arendt, *Imperialism* (a paperback selection from *The Origins of Totalitarianism*); *Black Rage;* Ashley Montague, *The Direction of Human Development;* Linus Pauling, *No More War; Vertebrates; Calculus;* Struik, *The Origins of American Science; American Political Dictionary; Abdominal Exercises* (one of the women was pregnant). Science, history, politics, a dab of literature.

There were people here who wanted to know how the body and the body politic were put together. The emphases were on origins, development, form, and social interpretation. "What is there and how is it thought about?" And then perhaps the famous nineteenth-century question: "What is to be done?"

"The precious life blood of a master spirit embalmed and treasured up on purpose to a life beyond life." Milton's gorgeous praise of "a good book" had an overtone in this apartment where guns and blood and wild words sounded with the study of embryos and Machiavelli. A book man like me who feared, hated, and only partly understood the violence of hunters and of hunted felt it meant that the blood which lumped the mattress and stained the floorboards was in part the blood of the books as well as their readers. If it didn't make that fierce nest a shrine, it lifted its meanness and its anonymity.

3. The Records of Truth and Fiction

For me alone Don Quixote was born and I for him. His was the power of action, mine of writing. Only we two are at one . . .

> Cide Hamete
> in Cervantes' *Don Quixote*
> translated by J. M. Cohen

It is theory which decides what we can observe.

> Albert Einstein,
> cited in Werner Heisenberg's *Physics and Beyond*
> translated by Arnold J. Pomerans

it was thought she was a woman and was turned into a cold fish for she would not exchange flesh with one that loved her; the ballad is very pitiful and as true.

> Autolycus in
> *Winter's Tale*, IV, 1

This section examines the problems of making up careers out of lives, lives out of detail. The last essay goes further (the theory hater can say, "The more air the higher the balloon"). It aims to show that the writer not only helps to "make up life," but that in making it up he makes up the sense of passage, of aging and changing. The section moves from a look at the contrivance of history by one of its more obvious "makers" to a look at the contrivance of time.

ON THE JOHNSON LIBRARY

In a dispatch from the Washington *Post,* Don Oberdorfer reports (December 8, 1968) that Lyndon Johnson's presidency will be the most scrupulously or at least most completely recorded of all presidential administrations. There are enough personal and official papers to fill two thousand four-drawer filing cabinets, histories of every federal department and major agency, a collection of photographs of the President at work and play which in the administration's first seven weeks included more than eleven thousand shots (the eight-year total for Eisenhower's administration was ninety-five hundred), and newsreel coverage of the President and his family which resulted in a monthly documentary prepared by a special naval detachment of twenty men. All of this plus the President's "countless memoranda," Mrs. Johnson's diary, and whatever comes afterward will be * stored in the Lyndon B. Johnson Presidential Library on the campus of the University of Texas. Oberdorfer quotes an official saying that "nothing like this has ever been done before . . . the value to history is likely to be priceless."

For years historians have bewailed the dearth of documentation in the time of the telephone and jet plane. Oral history projects compensate for the historical vacuum supposedly left by the resistance of modern political figures to pen and paper. It is surely true that fewer political arrangements are made by letter in our time than was the case in the eighteenth and nineteenth centuries. Nor has there been a President who matches, say, John Quincy Adams for interrogating his conscience and putting the results on paper.

It was the history-soaked Harry Truman who revived the presidential memoir (which had accounted for such first-rate works as the autobiographies of Grant and Van Buren as well as the splendid papers of the early Presidents now being edited in Cambridge and Princeton, Chicago and Virginia). Truman's volumes were followed by Eisenhower's, and surely the history-minded (dominated?) Kennedy would have added his own version to those which he suggested people as varied as Paul Fay and Arthur Schlesinger should write.

When, though, did the gigantesque element creep into this Respect for history? When did presidential action itself include the simultaneous recording of that action? Those who watched the political conventions in July and August [1968] saw in October that the nominees had allowed the filming of their reactions to the nomination. As they experienced victory, so they experienced the recording of their experience. In July we watched Romney congratulate the Republican nominee from the convention floor but refuse to say what the nominee told him; by October we saw the nominee thanking Mr. Romney for his call. In August we saw Mrs. Humphrey smile in her convention

* 1972: are.

box; in October CBS showed Mr. Humphrey kissing the image of his wife on the glass screen.

The Adams family seems to have acted in private as in public. Their dignity was generally of a piece. They would probably not have been ashamed of being observed at any time, but it is most unlikely that they would have tolerated it. Their self-confidence was intimately connected with a sense of privacy.

Naturally, one cannot expect the "communications media" to starve for presidential news. Modern Presidents have learned to regard "the media" as important conditions of their administration. Crises rise and—in the case of Khrushchev's key dispatch in October 1963—settle with their aid; elections are won and lost "through" them.

The pressure of events and the hunger of men to know about them quickly is not something new. Wordsworth, a contemporary of John Quincy Adams, discussed it in the preface to his poems of 1800:

> . . . a multitude of causes, unknown to former times, are now acting with a combined force to blunt the discriminating powers of the mind . . . The most effective of these causes are the great national events which are daily taking place, and the increasing accumulation of men in cities, where the uniformity of their occupations produces a craving for extraordinary incident, which the rapid communication of intelligence hourly gratifies.

It is not, therefore, only McLuhan's tribalized electronic society which hungers for that being-in-the-know which "news" gratifies; but the ubiquity of news-recorders creates the special conditions of these times.* The news today turns out to be the wrapping of a package which may not be opened for weeks or years.

The enormity of the materials is a demand for justification. The materials constitute an externalized, (thus false) conscience.

---

*When asked by reporters what he was thinking of as he ran toward the goal line, the San Francisco receiver Gene Washington said: "I was thinking what I was going to say to you about the way I felt."

Few public men will let themselves be photographed doing something wrong. A huge mass of material, therefore, declares that there was no time for the President to act badly. It is not only an externalized conscience but evidence of a clear one.

How deformed are decisions conditioned by the presence of History? Are the coat and tie on the neck of the decision as well as on that of the decider?

I suggest that the deeper the historical culture of the man recorded, the less he needs and the more he will reject the presence of the Historical Justifier at his elbow. The mountain of physical evidence to be scaled by future historians may be the sign of the historical flatness of the actor.

The contrast between the petty secretiveness of President Johnson and the mountainous frankness of his record is less paradoxical than may at first appear. Both spring from that mixture of egoism and uncertainty which is common to the powerful weak.

FARMING THE TUNDRA

The rapid, cigar-chewing little radio man Chicagoans call "Studs" has drawn seventy "noncelebrated" fellow citizens into the sort of self-revelation that until very recently could only be heard from the mouths of poets. For most of history the ordinary man's interior was a tundra of silence. In the eighteenth century autobiographers and novelists began making the maps by which the mute Jean Jacqueses and Myshkins discovered themselves and their voices. First individual discovery, then social revolution.

In our century popular analysis enables every man to see himself as a complex, fluent character. Who knows if this isn't the noblest expression of modern opulence. Or the second noblest, for in the past few years something else has happened: self-awareness has become self-revelation. Sympathetic men with tape recorders have revealed the extraordinary ordinary man as sage and poet. And the poetry and wisdom of the tundra are systematically farmed and then gathered into marvelous collections like *Division Street: America.**

Reviewing Oscar Lewis' *La Vida* for *The Nation* (January 2, 1967), Elmer Bendiner wrote:

> Is it possible to know a person by listening to a tape-recording of his autobiography . . . ? I doubt it. The art of knowing a person demands an ability to pierce the self-pretense which uses language to disguise rather than to reveal . . . Those with a taste for people and for life may wish that a novelist—without a tape recorder—would take up where Oscar Lewis left off.

This is intelligent stuff, but it seems to me off the mark. My view is that we do "know" the people in Terkel's, Dolci's, and Lewis' books as we do those in novels, in histories, or in our lives,

* Studs Terkel, ed., *Division Street: America* (New York: Pantheon).

through appropriate and differing conventions of knowledge. The conventions of tape-recorded autobiography include such props to the guided monologues as "self-pretense" and "disguise," as well as the monologist's sense of his own typicality and how far the occasion and the interviewer allow him to depart from it. So in *Division Street* none of Studs' people, no matter how violent or asocial, comes within miles of saying what Joyce has the mild Bloom say to himself, let alone what Dostoevsky has a Verhovensky say to a Stavrogin. None of these remarkable Chicagoans approaches the enchanted complex of even a good minor character in a good novel. A meal in Laperouse is one thing, a roadside apple is another; both delight, and "those with a taste for people and for life" will find immense pleasure in *Division Street* and in much of Lewis.

Is *Division Street* more than a pile of good human apples? Is it, in other words, a real book? Once again, this is too large-holed a net for the fish. A book like this has little to do with build-up, careful collision, *scènes-à-faire*, brilliant climaxes, a coherence whose every line reveals a single mind. It is, though, a carefully arranged collection of selected and well-edited materials. The old, the middle-aged, the young, rich, poor, Negro, Mexican, Wasp, the broken and those who break them, city strays, John Birch cabbies, brilliant Negro businessmen, gentle Irish police and their brute colleagues, teachers who save and teachers who ruin, all pour out their witness to the workings of the city, the death of neighborhoods, the threat and promise of machinery, the war, the mayor, God, buying and selling, delivering, conning, dropping out, rescuing. Without dominating opinion into coherence, Studs exhibits a great spectrum of distinctions. If no Chaucer, he is at least the good host Harry Bailey.

The book is not dominated by its topics or its facts. It's a treasury, not a ledger. The treasury is of articulate energy engaged with concrete experience. No matter where Studs' people stand on the scale of usefulness, narcissism, triumph, defeat, or despair, if they have expressive power they triumph here. The heroes are those who construct their lives or opinions with power.* A miserable, self-serving lout outlasts a useful, self-denying bore. It is the masters of the concrete who survive in what the Indian, Benny Bearskin, calls here "the abstraction of the city."

Studs, a good man, is on the side of those who love outside their own skin, but he is an honorable host and lets his guests have equal say. "Each of the subjects," he writes

> is, I feel, uniquely himself. Whether he is an archetypal American figure, reflecting thought and condition over and beyond himself, is for the reader to judge, calling upon his own experience, observations, and an occasional look in the mirror.

(Wrote Saint Augustine about only one archetype: "Do I then measure, O my God, and know not what I measure?")

Here are some of Studs' "subjects":
Kid Pharaoh, 37, who's found in front of the hot-dog stand he owns:

> A guy goes to school, what does he want to be? A doctor? A lawyer? These are the two biggest thieves in our society. One steals legitimate, the other kills legitimate . . . Guys like me they want to put in jail. Because I'm dedicated to one principle: taking money away from unqualified dilettantes who earn it through nepotism. I work at this and I'm good at my trade. I don't labor. Outside of being a prize-fighter, I took an oath to God I would never again labor. But there's a million people on the street that want to be taken and should be taken, and they're gonna be taken.

Sister Evelyn, 26, a Glenmary nun who works with Appalachians on the near North Side:

> We are not married. Is this simply an attempt to avoid the pain and ambiguity of a sustained human relationship? If

* The book is dedicated to three Chicagoans who made beautiful, useful constructions out of contemporary, local materials: Ring Lardner, Louis Sullivan, and Jane Addams.

so, this is a travesty of what it means to be a Christian. A Christian must be involved in sustained human relationships, because there is where Christ is found.

Lucy Jefferson, 52, who isn't going to raise her children "on Aid" because she "just don't like doles":

They call you by the first name, the students, everybody. You see, this was the policy to keep the Negro in his place. But I happened to be the kind of Negro that became controversial, because I read such things as *The American Dilemma* and I walk around with the book in my hand, see? I defied them in so many ways. I almost terrified 'em . . . Let's face it. What counts is knowledge. And feeling. You see, there's such a thing as a feeling tone. One is friendly and one is hostile. And if you don't have this, baby, you've had it. You're dead.

Phil Eagle, 55, who built up a large business with his wife, then after eighteen good years got sick and was told by her to get out and sell newspapers:

When she suggested I be eliminated, it gave me incentive. The medical profession credits my hundred percent recovery to my will power. I latched onto an idea. The idea is contained in the book, *Folk Medicine*. The book is almost a hundred percent concerned with apple cider and vinegar and honey and water and eating fish. And using Lugol. L-U-G-O-L. A solution which can be bought for pennies, enough to last for a year . . . Which everybody should have a drop or two drops a week. Following this book and changing my diet, eliminating sugar from my life and pop and orange juice, I recovered my health. That's one of the things that helped break up my home . . . The only thing between her and all this wealth is my heartbeat.

Charles Landesfahr, 34, a copy chief:

It takes a great deal of con to sound honest in this world.

An American Nazi in jail for defaming a Negro celebrity:

To me, one of the most beautiful things in the world is an Oriental rug or a flower. They're the epitome of whatever they are, the peak. I don't mean something should be perfect. I wouldn't want anything to be perfect. I like that one little flaw . . . It's the opposite of the order I was looking for. It's the human touch.

Again and again, the life heart is shown by such indirection; again and again, one's expectations are cracked by such unexpected feeling and intelligence.

The Cubists found new eyes in African sculpture and children's art; two French physicists, Abele and Malvaux, constructed the theorem of summary velocity out of Piaget's insights into children's notions of duration and speed.* So, I think, new forms of history and fiction will spring from such collections of "naive" narrative as Terkel's. Their variety and energy derive from a confidence which before was seldom shown or, if shown, shown only in trial reports or rogues' confessions. The new democracy of art, in which camera owners think that they are doing Leonardo's work, hi-fi possessors that they are fusions of Beethoven and Edison, "candid camera" characters that they are brilliant performers, the subjects of interviewers that they are dispensers of wisdom (and this while they step from the shattered store window, television sets in arm), this is the source of that confidence which is pouring as much new material into the hopper of modern narrative art as urban realism poured into that of the nineteenth century.

* *Vitesse et Univers relativiste* (Paris: Edition Sedes, cited in Jean Piaget, *Six Etudes de Psychologie* (Geneva: Editions Gonthier, 1964), pp. 97–100.

THE POSTLAPSARIAN MARILYN

After the international shock (with those of Hemingway and Hammarskjöld, in the Sixties' mode of the ambiguous suicide), after the *mea culpas* and *j'accuses,* after the essays on her significance, and then after what seemed the "real thing" (*The Misfits, After the Fall*), does that beauty fallen from the air supply enough for the day's menu?

This distant admirer of that body, that face, that expert self-parodist and self-displayer, this consumer of the gossip, the interviews, the essays, thought not. But a "reporter's biography" * supplies the necessary spice, new detail.

Every biography, every analysis, professional or personal, every "understanding" is a reduction for purposes of handling, packaging, dispatching. Fictional totality is an illusion secured by limiting characters to narrative function, but real people, even saints and heroes, function in too many ways and for too many people to be "definitively" understood. There is no such animal as *the definitive biography*. A Marilyn Monroe, whose mass of fact was endlessly complicated by private manipulation and public enquiry,† will never supply the clear view craved by "seekers after truth."

Edwin Hoyt offers the girl with the bad teeth who semi-annually failed to get beyond the early rounds of the Miss Western Fashion beauty contest; Johnny Hyde, the corpulent agent who wanted to marry her on his deathbed and to whom she was faithful except for a session with the visiting playwright she later married; Miss Emmaline Snively of the Blue Book Model Agency, who planted the fake tip about Howard Hughes' interest

* Edwin P. Hoyt, Jr., *Marilyn: The Tragic Venus* (New York: Duell, Sloan and Pearce).

† 1972: The "mythofacture" engaged in by a few famous women whose public history is "private in nature" might be a good subject for *Ms.*

in Norma Jean Dougherty which led to a walk-on screen test and the first of the cul-de-sac starlet contracts which gave her the small means to pursue an undisputed technical mastery of appearance (she studied a volume of Vesalius for poses).

Young as Moll Flanders, Norma Jean discovered that her capital was on her bones, but in the starlet days she learned how much more was required to be what she'd long wished. She took dramatic lessons (from Michel Chekhov, Natasha Lytess, the Strasbergs), went on magpie searches for verbal formulas, made a serious study of feelings and how to convey them. She prepared herself with the undivertible rigor of all good artists.

But for a world which permitted no masterpiece. Only that "self" worked óut of her by directors, reporters, photographers, commentators, fans. The "self" was a novel shade of human being, a small power able to alter ambitions, desires, voices, looks, responses. This composite of kook, international pacifier, wise and delicate woman, this ever more beautiful, ever decaying product of hard work, nature, and mass dream, still generates some of the force suggested by Hoyt's subtitle, *The Tragic Venus*. For though classical gods are beyond tragedy, Marilyn, like their successor, is incarnate in the sort of fact Hoyt supplies, and thus can still, after the fall, move unjaded remembrance.

COACH LOMBARDI

In his book *On Aggression* Konrad Lorenz writes: "The instinctive need to be the member of a closely knit group fighting for common ideals may grow so strong that it becomes inessential what these ideals are and whether they possess any intrinsic value." Such postpubescent groups are inspired by what Lorenz calls "militant enthusiasm," a feeling which makes one ready to abandon all other ties. "All obstacles in its path become unimportant; the instinctive inhibitions against hurting or killing one's fellows lose, unfortunately, much of their power . . . all reasonable arguments against [such brutal] behavior . . . are silenced by an amazing reversal of all values." There is physical expression for militant enthusiasm: in chimpanzee and man, every attempt is made to make the body appear "bigger and more dangerous than it really is."

Four conditions figure in a "militant" group's arousal: (1) the group feels that it is endangered; (2) its enemy is nearby; (3) there is at hand "an inspiring leader figure"; and (4) many other individuals, "all agitated by the same emotion," are present.

The outstanding "inspiring leader figure" of a "closely knit group" of physically magnified postpubescents in recent American history, Vincent Lombardi, was the son of an immigrant wholesale butcher in the Sheepshead Bay section of Brooklyn. Driven by the ferocious work-prayer-reward ethic of the industrial epoch, Lombardi moved from coaching a New Jersey high school through secondary positions at West Point and New York (offensive line coach of the Giants) to the Green Bay Packers. Short, solid, terrifying, he walked among his padded charges flailing, fining, cursing, weeping, embracing. Face lined with the suffering which older generations saw on the faces of martyrs, his days consumed in the technical frenzy formerly ascribed to great artists, Lombardi, more than any of his players, and perhaps more than anyone in America between 1960 and 1970, appeared to be the "representative man." The country's official leaders looked more like conniving spouters than heroes. Lombardi's obsessive devotion to team perfection and triumph stood like an inspired response to the impersonality and decay of institutional life. "The great drum of triviality" (Kierkegaard's term for urban publicity) boomed his virtues; and the obvious fact that it was triviality's drum enabled the most prostrate of worshipers to maintain that sense of superiority which is the ultimate sliver of American independence.

In *Representative Men* Emerson exhorted ordinary men to "Serve the great. Stick at no humiliation. Grudge no office thou canst render. Be the limb of their body, the breath of their mouth. Compromise thy egotism. Who cares for that, so thou gain aught wider and nobler?" The Packers gave Lombardi breath, limb, and ego. "He treated us all alike," said the linesman Henry Jordan, "like dogs." But wit preserved, and the gains— celebrity, wealth, influence—were generally deemed "wider and nobler." Especially when buttered with that intense communal religiosity with which Americans like to cover their fiercer enterprises. In the dressing room before a game that could not alter the team's league standing, Lombardi told his players: "If you give me anything less than your best, you're not only cheating yourself, your coaches, your teammates, everybody in Green Bay, and everything pro football stands for, you're also cheating your Maker, who gave you that talent." Spelled out, that speech says Failing Me Is Failing Your Maker.

In a way, this fierce little whipper was their maker. It is said that one chimpanzee is not a chimpanzee; it is no less true that one football player is no football player. Lombardi took strong individual talents and fitted them into a love machine of ritualized assault. In electronic America, he became a saint of the Old Warmth, the Old Togetherness.

Twenty-five hundred years ago, Pindar dedicated an ode to an athlete named Theron of Agrigento. It begins with a question to his fellow "kings of the lyre": "What God, what hero, what man are we going to sing about?" The poet always has this problem. In more recent times he has mostly sung about himself. In even more recent times the heroes, with the aid of equally untuneful followers, the As-Told-Toers, have taken up the lyre and sung about themselves. The results have not been fit for the eyes, ears, and minds of serious men. The books of Kramer, Lombardi, and Tarkenton have amusing moments and interesting inside accounts of strategy and performance, but there is a built-in drone to their story that makes one understand why the history of football is still largely in the hands of statisticians.

Between the trivial and the magniloquent falls the statistic. It isn't enough. We can no longer use so thumping a celebrator as Pindar, but we need something more than the low-note heroes and their idolatrous hangers-on. Perhaps a prose Ariosto, a comic writer of epics who could both evoke the tyranny and sentimentality of a Lombardi and place him and his fellows in that comic perspective where those of us who pour a thousand hours of our shortish lives into observing and cheering them also belong.

IN COLD BLOOD

The most famous murder of these murderous years * took place four years and one week after the slaughter of the Clutter family and was followed, two days later, by the murder of the murderer, an event which made forever impossible the sort of account which Truman Capote has given of the Clutters, their neighbors, their friends, and their killers—Perry Smith, the stunted, half-Cherokee autodidact who pulled the trigger, and Richard Hickok, the loving, thieving son who planned the abortive robbery and rape which led to the murders. *In Cold Blood* † lives on the minds and worlds of the two remarkable killers, and it is no small part of Capote's accomplishment that he could get from them what has converted the stuff of a good police report and some local color into a fine book.

For years now Capote has been—like his own "Miss Gorightry"—a "top banana in the shock department." In the intervals of exercising his famous charm on the world's famous people, he has written a couple of novels, some stories, plays, movie scripts, and reportage, everything but a memorable book. Fiction was not his suit; his imagination is gooey with nostalgia, reverie, or fantasy. His reportage is better; but reportage is limited by what's reported. Not every grain of sand contains a world. Urged by Shawn of *The New Yorker* to cover the Kansas murders, Capote finally hit on what seems to have been new for him, an appropriate and almost ready-made subject, an orderly, unspectacular world torn open by one night of spectacular disorder. Capote stayed in this world until order was restored to it; his book constitutes a part of the restoration.

The "nonfiction novel" is no novelty. Discounting the ten thousand mixtures of truth and poetry which followed Rous-

---

* The assassination of President Kennedy.
† Truman Capote, *In Cold Blood* (New York: Random House, 1965).

seau's *Confessions,* there is in our time the long endeavor of *The New Yorker* to obliterate the bounds between fiction and nonfiction. Hersey, McNulty, the Nabokovs (Nicholas and Vladimir), Roueche, Kahn, and how many others, including Capote, have written *The New Yorker*'s nonfiction using devices developed by the novel: the revision of the story's chronological and spatial lines, shifting viewpoints, the progression of effects, varied texture (letters, diaries, dialogue, expository summary). More recently, fine "documentary novels" have come from such social scientists as Oscar Lewis and Danilo Dolci.

None of these narratives can be sustained for long by the reader's consciousness of their factuality (no matter how sensational the facts); their flavor and resonance derive from careful arrangements of the scrupulously accurate observations of the participants. When these defect—as they do here in Capote's reconstruction of the Clutter family's last day, or to a lesser extent in the renditions of all but two of the women in the book— nothing is left but the writer's own powers as sensory organ, thinker, and stylist.

Oddly enough, Capote is not strong here, but he does have other powers, and they make his book. He is able to reproduce the ferocity, comedy, misery, pathos, bravery, and terror of the killers, to make of their flight across the country a fine picaresque and of their interrogation, trial, and deathwatch fine dramatic narratives. In these sections of the book the power of fact is released without waste.

Even better, Capote's controlled, tactful sympathy gives fair hearings to victims, killers, judges, sheriffs, friends and passers-by. This openness underwrites the book's chief effect, the depiction of the Clutter murders and the killers' execution as a ritual element of the springtime of "wind-bent wheat" and impending marriage which—out of factual chronology—conclude the book.

Capote has done two of the great jobs of literature: he has fought that imaginative mononucleosis which saps comprehension (and thus forgiveness) of the alien* and—what he has never managed before—has perceived and rendered a pattern as complex and beautiful as the lives which compose it.

*God and literature fuse in Pascal's great maxim: *Tout comprendre, c'est tout pardonner.*

EVENTS, HAPPENINGS, CREDIBILITY, FICTIONS

Every now and then critics conclude that a species or genus of an art has been exhausted or superseded.* The most recent object of this *genrecidal* criticism is prose fiction; here, from George Steiner, is a typical burial service:

> It is not only the traditional scope of fiction that is in doubt, but its entire relevance to the present, to the needs and idioms of our consciousness . . . As is now becoming generally understood, fiction has fallen well behind sociology and reportage.†

Such genrecidal conclusions as Mr. Steiner's—whose own fiction tends to document his thesis—are almost always worth careful study, for they almost always testify to a special sort of artistic crisis. The crisis goes to the source of the art, the methods, and conventions used at a given time to render the actualities which are their sources. The crisis seems to occur when new techniques appear to take over some of the older genre's function. So, a hundred years ago, photography exerted enormous pressure on painting.

The fictional crisis described by Steiner is more complicated than that old crisis in painting. The reason is that the verbal medium serves such a variety of masters. Indeed, fiction is not the only form of licensed lying. When we study its crisis, therefore, we'd better look first at the matter of credibility.

In various systems of thought and action the problem of credibility is signaled by such terms as "image," "propaganda," "cover story," "camouflage," "hypothesis," "legal fiction," "credit," "myth," "illusion," "dream," and "fantasy." Such terms stand

* William Hazlitt's "On Modern Comedy" and Edmund Wilson's "Is Verse a Dying Technique?" are well-known elegies of this sort.
† *Book Week,* 1967.

for ways of dealing with actuality. They are protected because they operate within isolated systems; when they leak from
their systems into areas where their degree of utility or fidelity
becomes unclear, they usually conceal public mischief or individual sickness. We then speak of such things as a "credibility
gap" or hallucination.

Likewise, when an element from an open system—nature,
actuality, the world—is introduced into one of these closed systems, the result makes for trouble, or at least excitement. If a
speaker explodes a firecracker on the stage, the audience shivers
or otherwise expresses recognition that an element from an open
system has threatened the security of the closed system, the
public lecture. Talleyrand, hearing that Napoleon was dead at
last, said: "That is no longer an event. It is a piece of news."
Dead, Napoleon belonged to print, to a closed and controlled
system, and Talleyrand was no long in even remote danger from
the man who had once called him "shit in silk stockings." Talleyrand's awareness of the distinction between the open and closed
systems is that of the artist.

Artists consciously employ the distinction all the time and
from the beginning seem to have made it a subject of their work.
One need not haul in such latecomers as Mallarmé or Joyce for
evidence here; Homer seems to have been on to it. In the eighth
book of the *Odyssey* the disguised hero listens to the blind bard
Demodocus sing about the heroes of the Trojan War (it amounts
to the *Iliad* *), but unlike the delighted listeners at Alcinous'
court, he cries. What was a closed system, a fiction, or at least
an artful story for them was a heart-rending, still existent experience for him, a form of event, not news.

This brilliant Homeric anticipation of the famous modern subject of the story of the story, the play within the play, is given
perhaps its ultimatè statement at the end of this part of the poem.
To his unknown guest the king says: "Tell us why you wept so

---

* Vergil and Cervantes are the two most famous imitators of this
Homeric strategy of self-referral.

bitterly and secretly when you heard of the Argive Danaans and the fall of Ilion. That was wrought by the gods, who measured the life thread of these men *so that their fate might become a poem sung for unborn generations.*" This royal claim that reality exists for the sake of art marks the limit of artistic solipsism: the closed system embraces everything. Wordsworthian recollections or *fin-de-siècle* boasts of art's superiority to life are dwarfed by it.

One can, I think, subsume all distinctions between art and actuality—even this extraordinary one of King Alcinous—into an even more general distinction, that between *being* and *having-knowing-picturing-remembering-loving-possessing-converting. Being,* and its alternate mode, *doing,* are not aware of existing or performing. A baby exists, unaware of existence. The beloved does not enjoy what the lover enjoys in her: she *is;* her lover *knows, enjoys, possesses* her. (When she herself enjoys, she is lover, knower, possessor; the greatest sweetness of love is this reciprocity.) The doer does, the observer sees, the witness and artist chronicle and convert.

One of the recent alterations in the equilibrium between art and actuality is the discovery on the part of many "do-ers" and "be-ers" that they are also characters; more, that they are or can be their own chroniclers, analysts, even poets. Max Scheler wrote that "feelings which everyone nowadays is aware of having in himself once took poets to wrest from the terrifying muteness of our inner life." Scheler only marked the effects of the novel of analysis and perhaps of psychoanalysis. These had given the silent lives of the world mirrors, but the tape recorder, the camera, the roving anthropologist, the reporter, the psychological caseworker, and the social surveyor have shown the "do-ers" and "be-ers" of daily life that they are not only specialized segments of opinion but proper subjects of biography, actors in potential newsreels, amateur sages, and semiartistic performers in events, in happenings. It is in part this transformation of characters into self-conscious actors and then into storytellers which makes critics feel that professional inventors of stories are "irrelevant to the needs and idiom of our consciousness." When everybody bakes bread, who needs bakers?

The doer who tells his story, the reporter who puts it into a new context, the historian or sociologist who provides a more elaborate frame for it are artists, as the Greeks would have said bakers are artists. They assemble divers materials into useful, beautiful, and delightful objects. Yet we must distinguish their works of art—Susanne Langer calls them works of practical art—from works of imaginative art. We can do this by examining the sort of event mentioned above, the intrusion on the closed system (the firecracker-menaced speech). Such an event has come to be known as a happening.

A happening is an artistic performance in the guise of an event. It is a situation which attempts to incorporate into a closed system as large an amount of uncontrolled, *actual* material as possible. Delight in a happening rises from the contrast between the special security of art and the potentially uncontrolled pressure of (intensified, rigged) actuality. And too, a successful happening is unrepeatable; a happening's success grows out of shock or surprise. (Happenings did not originate in the 1960s. They've always existed, particularly in times of leisured opulence. Johan Huizinga, describing the fifteenth-century Burgundian festivities which featured motet-singing bears, pies filled with orchestras, and forty-foot towers, called them "applied literature.")

Many happenings spring not from festive energy, Dadaistic wit, and opulent ennui but from social and artistic contempt, emotional rigidity, shallowness, cruelty, and perversion. Few national histories fail to feature tyrants who converted human beings into the subject matter of art. Such happenings have been examined by historians, social psychologists, and anthropologists, but they may be studied just as fruitfully by estheticians. (When art and nature are confounded, no specialist is privileged.)

Happenings are of interest to the arts because they stand for a desire to alter the relationship between art and actuality. Many, perhaps most, artists want to shake up an audience by violating its preconceptions about what belongs to art and what doesn't. The first-night performances or exhibitions of many fine works of art resemble happenings. The premières of *Hernani, Playboy of the Western World, Marat/Sade, Le Sacre du Printemps,* the first days of the Fauves exhibit, even some early reactions to *Les Fleurs du Mal* and *The Waste Land* exhibit the violent reactions characteristic of happenings. The violence springs from rage at the broken contract between actuality and art, the crossing over from an open to a closed system.

There is another artistic side of happenings. Art forms may be said to originate in happenings. When an old religious ritual was altered by a figure stepping from the laymen's section of respondents, Greek drama began; and when someone altered a kind of hunter's memorandum in a Cro-Magnon cave,* it was the beginning of mural painting. More recently, when Andy Warhol decided that the manufacturers of Campbell's Soup failed to realize that their product was as pleasing to the eye as it was to the stomach and signed his name as an artist pledge of the observation, he fused a happening to a new sort of sculpture.†

What takes place in these instances is that an action or object which belonged to the realm of *being-doing* has been appropriated for the world of *knowing-appreciating-loving.* The appropriation is usually bold, primitive, and shocking. The shock is one of transition; the consumer, the worshiper, or hunter has been converted into the spectator or appreciator. He has postponed the satisfactions of appetite for those of amusement, delight, emotional involvement in a nonworld. The shock itself, the happening element, can't be repeated. If Warhol went on to sign

---

* Recent studies make ritualistic, sexual discriminations of these old paintings. See Alexander Marshak's *The Roots of Civilization* (1972).

† See Hugh Kenner's brilliant discussion of this in *The Counterfeiters* (Bloomington: University of Indiana Press, 1968).

a can of Heinz Soup, he'd be called either an epigone or a bad promoter. He has to go on either to other happenings or to the exploration, elaboration, and development of his insight into a form. He has to relate it to some traditional system of materials.

An artist makes works which are not exhausted by initial performance, works which do not depend on bold shifts between art and actuality, which validate themselves in an artistic tradition and do not require validation by shock.

The claim that such works of literary art are no longer relevant "to the needs and idiom of our consciousness" ignores not only the crucial distinction between such works as happenings and imaginative art but the difference between these and such works of practical art as the reportage of Truman Capote and John Hersey, the wonderfully edited autobiographies assembled by Oscar Lewis and Danilo Dolci, collections of heart-breaking letters like those found in the mailbags from Stalingrad, and hosts of fine memoirs, biographies, reports, essays, and histories.

In my view, no matter how splendidly assembled, how fascinating in detail, or how rich in linguistic, expressive, or speculative power, these works are by nature limited in the same way all works of practical arts are limited, and that is by the necessity to conform in sequence, place, number, and character to actuality. Our delight in works of practical art is crucially conditioned by our feeling that they are true. All of us know that the cameraman selects, the camera angle determines, the reporter shades and dramatizes, the sociologist has a thesis. Nonetheless, we invest emotionally in their credibility. If we find that we have been taken in, our reaction is—properly—rage; and despite his skill we arrest the forger of Vermeers, we throw away the text with beautiful but inaccurate blueprints, we don't lie down on the handsome but backbreaking bed, and we refuse to buy the fake reporter's glittering work on the Bohemian massacre.

Works of practical art must be true; indeed, they usually begin with a statement of their credentials. Here are a few of them:

1. The tape recorder, used in taking down the life stories
   in this book, has made possible the beginning of a new
   kind of literature of social realism. With the aid of the
   tape recorder, unskilled, uneducated, and even illiterate
   persons can talk about themselves and relate their observations and experiences in an uninhibited, spontane-
   ous, and natural manner . . . most of the recording was
   done in my office and home . . . Occasionally I recorded
   at [the home of the Sanchez family] in the Casa Grande
   . . . I used no secret technique, no truth drugs, no psy-
   cho-analytic couch. The most effective tools of the anthropologist are sympathy and compassion for the
   people he studies.
   Oscar Lewis, Children of Sanchez

2. The editor believes the thing to be a just history of fact;
   neither is there any appearance of fiction in it.

3. All the material in this book not derived from my own
   observation is either taken from official records or is
   the result of interviews with the person directly concerned, more often than not numerous interviews con-
   ducted over a considerable period of time.
   Truman Capote, In Cold Blood

4. Throughout our work on [this book], I have been con-
   tinuously impressed by demonstration of the extent to
   which that much abused term "total recall" can be literally true. . . . I retraced with her, time and again, the
   threads of many of these episodes, always from a different vantage point. Each time they checked out even to
   the smaller touches of phrasing, style, figures of speech.
   Carleton Lake collaborating on Françoise Gilot's
Life with Picasso

5. He left the custody of the following papers in my
   hands, with the liberty to dispose of them as I should
   think fit. I have carefully perused them three times:
   the style is very plain and simple; and the only fault I
   find is, that the author . . . is a little too circumstantial
   . . . this volume would have been at least twice as large,
   if I had not made bold to strike out innumerable pas-

sages relating to the winds and tides, as well as the variations and bearings in the several voyages.

Five editor-authors delivering the real words of real people. Surely a praiseworthy activity, whatever the motive—entertainment, enlightenment, moral exemplum, what have you. All deny that fiction is in their pages; the first and third speak here or elsewhere of new forms of literature, but all deny that they are making anything up.

Now of these five claims two are manifestly false. The second is the preface to *Robinson Crusoe,* the fifth some of the prefatory matter of *Gulliver's Travels.* How do these fictional claims differ from the truthful ones?

The two fictional claims are part of a different contract, an eighteenth-century convention of the art—revived now and then —which licenses departure from the real world while claiming to be a chunk of it. Readers of *Gulliver* will never be troubled as readers of Capote or Lewis may be—indeed, have been—by the question of the accuracy of their books. Capote and Lewis must justify their books in terms of the truth of their descriptions and renditions: the fiction writer justifies his book in a completely different way. Warhol would not be arrested if he sneaked into the art gallery one night, siphoned off the tomato soup from his six-dollar sculpture, and substituted soapy water for it; but the maker of the original seventeen-cent can would be. The artist Warhol is not bound to the same standard of credibility as the practical artist, Campbell's designer.

Talking of public opinion half a century ago, Walter Lippmann wrote: "A work of fiction may have almost any degree of fidelity, and so long as the degree of fidelity can be taken into account, fiction is not misleading." The "credibility gap" causes rage in the actual world,* not the world of imaginative art.

Yet the degree of fidelity should be known to the imaginative artist. The imaginative artist "does the same as the child at play;

---

* "Washington `(UPI)—Rep. Harley O. Staggers (D-W. Va.) announced Tuesday that his investigative subcommittee will study whether laws are needed to protect the public from 'factually false and misleading

he creates a world of fantasy, which he takes very seriously: that is, he invests it with a great deal of affect, while separating it sharply from reality" (Freud, "The Relation of the Poet to Daydreaming"). The imaginative artist is—at least in his art— distinct from the lunatic and the lover, and in direct contrast to the practical artist he works out techniques to separate his art from reality. Systematically, he violates at least some of the schemes or procedures of remembered actuality: places, ideas, characters, time schedules, meanings. His art derives in a measure from the dissociation of given materials. Even those artists who minutely reproduce their vision, who check their time schemes with almanacs (Fielding), their place names with city directories (Joyce), their memories of houses and clothes against personal or newspaper accounts (Proust) are only accumulating powder for fictional explosions. Far more than the tellers of romance, the cryptographic fabulists, the algebraic comedians, the heart-twitching parodists, these "realists" wish to assemble the world in order to control it. Whenever the remembered actuality will not suffer the explosive charge readied for it, it is thrown out. Those biographies which draw parallels between the artist's life and his fictional version of it are wonderful sources of such removals. (This is the case even for those artists whose lives are in no small measure consciously arranged to provide material for their work.) The components of the work of art are changed whenever the artist sees that the pattern of his felt insight demands that they be changed. And that changes everything. It exempts the fiction writer from libel suits, and rightly so. A work of imaginative art really represents only those mo-

---

filming and editing practices' in the making of television news documentaries . . . NBC complied with its subpoena for a film copy and transcript of 'Say, Good-by,' a program dealing with the preservation of endangered species of wildlife. The program is alleged to show a hunter killing a mother bear when in fact the bear was brought down with a tranquilizer gun. CBS was given ten days to reconsider the demand for unused documentary materials. The confrontation could lead to a contempt-of-Congress citation against the network and possibly a court suit . . ."

Chicago *Sun-Times*, Wednesday, April 21, 1971

ments of an artist's life which were expressible in that period of
isolation from the world in which he worked out what counts for
him; in the process of working it out, he alters it under pressure
of his insight and his form.* Places, times, and details which originally stimulated his imagination come to belong more and more
to each other, less and less to the world from which they came.
The result can be so overpowering that the artist may say with
Alcinous that the life was lived for the art, or at least that only
in art were the intensity and meaning of the life felt.

The art form helps provide this intensity and meaning, and
the art form constantly alters. As fiction altered its modes of
handling its special data, writers found that the modes and alterations themselves became fit subjects for their work. Since Flaubert and James, fiction—like music since the sons of Bach and
painting since Cézanne—has been in no small part about itself.
That is, it deals explicitly with its modes of representation. It is
perhaps in response to such incestuous concentration that the
new works of practical art have risen to put pressure on fiction,
as if to say, "Back to nature, boys."

Fiction writers have often been men of unusual emotional,
intellectual, and sensuous energy, and great works of fiction thus
contain reports from the borders of human complexity and intensity. If we are to see practical forms expand to include such
reports, all the better. Engineers follow in the wake of the most
abstruse theorists; and theorists arise from great works of engineering.† From penny-dreadfuls to *Ulysses, Ulysses* through
John Dos Passos to Hersey and William Manchester, and these
to something novel.

It is, I think, time not for fiction's funeral but for weddings
and births.

---

* I think one difference between a man of action and an artist is
that the artist does not have to "meet the occasion." He works on his
own schedule; and he revises. There is next-to-no revision for the man of
action. (DeGaulle contrasts the ease of speech with the strange labor of
writing. Cf. Malraux, *Les chênes qu'on abat.*)

† Degas and Vuillard used photographs to define what they wished to
paint.

A WRITER'S STRAY THOUGHTS
ABOUT TIME

At the beginning of a symposium of physicists on the problem of time, the cosmologist Thomas Gold defined the central question:

> We seem to derive the notion of a flow of time in the first place from introspection. We then use the introspective notion to classify observations in the physical world . . . Perhaps [the introspective notion] is only a deception of a biological sort which ought to have no place in physics. Is it really basic to the description of physical processes that time progresses? Or does the set of world lines of all the particles comprise a great pattern which represents the entire physical world without reference to passage of time or to any idea of flow? Must we think of the laws of physics as operating upon the present to produce the future? Or is it only through the details of the interrelations between events in space-time and the information within the brain, which are part of the great pattern, that biological mechanisms have devised a representation in terms of flowing time? *

Symposium participants discussed a variety of things: Gödel's conundrum that one can loop in time (that is, progress to the past); conditions in which time is immeasurable; the temporal dependence on the distinction between observer and observed (which turned out to be that between an apparatus which is comparatively stable and an emission which is *declared* active).

For someone like me, who not only *feels* that time flow is one of the two or three deepest agents of experience but who, as a worker in a time art, regards the representation of time flow as one of his basic jobs, the symposium had certain shock value.

That truth is *not as we feel it* is one of the sources of literature;

* Thomas Gold, ed., *The Nature of Time* (Ithaca, N.Y.: Cornell University Press, 1967), p. 3.

and the creation and delivery from illusion is one of its great patterns. Still, talk of time as a biological "deception" poses at least an intellectual problem. One of the great masters of mental tricks writes: "There is nothing in the id that corresponds to the idea of time, and—a thing that is most remarkable and awaits consideration in philosophical thought—no alteration in its mental processes is produced by the passage of time." * What, then, is time, and what does it mean for one's life, mind, and art?

Language philosophers supply a relatively easy out, namely the claim that different statements exist in different language systems. The feeling system is a subset of the biological—as that is of the physical †—and one cannot cash checks drawn on one system in the banks of another. For this nonphilosopher, this solution is the equivalent of getting out of a room by a small window instead of a door. (Though Kant gave this particular window beautiful stained glass.)

For man and writer, what looms is the fact—or, if illusion, one that kills—that aging is the chief mode of ordinary human alteration. One is born weak, grows strong, ripens, coarsens, dies. This is built into everyone; every human system accounts for it. Daily life is a web of commemoration and anniversary, hellos and good-byes; much that we know comes in season; our behavior —if not our id—is dominated by time measurement. By change. Which makes time for us.

Now my craft of letters involves a version of time which is not the scarcely felt (or unfelt) drift time of so many hours. The time arts intensify passage, so much indeed that one contemporary philosopher ‡ sees them as the symbolic expression of the artist's knowledge of feeling.

Feeling is known only in passage. The greatest work of mod-

* Sigmund Freud, "Dissection of the Personality," in *Works*, standard edition, XXII, p. 74.
† Professor Gold reverses the subordination.
‡ Susanne Langer, *Feeling and Form*. (New York: Scribners).

ern literary art, Proust's *In Quest of Lost Time,* represents and analytically destroys most major forms of human feeling by showing them dissolve in time.

An occasion is an attempt to impose intensity on drift. A baseball game (despite its theoretical endlessness), a church service, "a man on the moon by 1970," a lecture, these sieve time from the slag which year by year lowers us deeper into unfelt inanition.

Even the space arts have a temporal dimension. Novelties of depth and color ignite the sense of where we are, the way in which we relate to other objects. They satisfy, I think, a deep need to hold fast against the time hurricane. We invest in land, in stuff, in the things of the world, to mark that we are here, here now. Against flow, against change, this is what we see, touch, relish. Time is the chief source of human fear, though perhaps now, on the verge of worlds where some of the time laws we know may be altered, we may reacquire the space fear which dominated men before Columbus.

Space fear is for men of action. Observers, witnesses, the untranquil if relatively passive, the unsaintly, the unheroic, *most of us,* are gnawed by time fear.

> Ruin hath taught me thus to ruminate,
> That time will come and take my love away.
> This thought is as a death, which cannot choose
> But weep to have that which it fears to lose.
>
> Shakespeare, Sonnet 4

Fear of loss and the traditions of craft generate much literary art. Most languages have special tenses for narrative, special beginnings ("Once upon a time" or such space-time metaphors as *Nel mezzo del cammin*), special conventions of conclusion ("They lived happily ever after"). Story arts divide the time world. Drama deals with a select past jolted by appearance or remembrance in such a way that a single, inescapable future looms over the scene. Dance and music are sensuous varieties of this same drive toward the inescapable. Narrative orders *what has been* into an illusion powerful enough to derange the reader out of his lamplit present tense, perhaps permanently altered by the force of his felt understanding of that re-created or imaginary past.

By imposition of an artful time order via the scarcely sensuous codes of language and literature, the narrator, the writer, may be the one who supplies what is not present in the id, not present in "the set of world lines," the sense of meaningful passage which makes of biological data a felt form.

Which is what we mostly mean by "time."

PART II

4. Scenes

Tragedy glorifies the structure of the world, which it supposedly reflects in its own form. Metatheater glorifies the unwillingness of the imagination to regard any image of the world as ultimate.

Lionel Abel
Metatheater

Gentlemen:

The world is so nice in these our times, that for apparel there is no fashion; for music (which is a rare art, though now slighted), no instrument; for diet, none but the French kickshaws that are delicate; and for plays, no invention but that which now runneth an invective way, touching some particular persons, or else it is contemned before it is thoroughly understood. This is all that I have to say: that the author had no intent to wrong any one in this comedy; but, as a merry passage, here and there interlaced it with delight, which he hopes will please all, and be hurtful to none.

Francis Beaumont and John Fletcher,
"To the Readers of This Comedy,"
from *The Knight of the Burning Pestle,*
second edition (1635)

The imaginary interview is an old genre, a dramatic scene embedded in narrative. It's been used to sweeten doctrine (Plato), to arrange unhistorical debates between historical figures (Landor), for autobiography (Gide), and for satire (Lucian, Voltaire). For several decades the real interview has been a favorite form of criticism and reporting. Its easy shuttle between performance and gossip tends to fuse (confuse?) them. Only a well-fortified ideologist or one of those rare Machiavellian thinkers for whom cause and effect need not be cheek by jowl can bypass the resultant notion that events are determined by the length of Cleopatra's nose.

The little imaginary interview which follows was written one spring morning in 1968 (or 1967). It nudges the technique of several American and European journalists (hopefully into the drink).

AURELIA FREQUENZA REVEALS THE HEART AND MIND OF THE MAN OF DESTINY

I'd come expecting to detest Tao Thinh, I left detesting him, but for a strange moment in between, a moment that was of hours', perhaps days', duration, I experienced with him a devilish sympathy that made for an intimacy closer and in its way more disarming, even incantatory, than would have been possible had our natures harmonized.

We talked over a period of days. The tape recorder is a barnyard of false starts, awkward advances, gauche retreats. Only occasionally is there a clear attack, a progress toward the subject. Without violating the accuracy of his portrait in any essential way, I am preserving here only these authentic developments.

We spoke in, of all places, Bao Kim, the Vevey of Annam. Here the abstemious Thinh has a *pied à terre,* scarcely more than a pair of shacks linked by a courtyard in which is tethered the beautiful incarnation of the devil which may be the only form of nonvegetable life Thinh loves: Kho Tuy, the Leopard, for whom Thinh procures meat, drink, and, yes, sex, but who remains, in Thinh's proud description, "implacable in his hatred of me and of any who murder his liberty." This living icon dominated our talk, and now dominates my mind as I work to see Nguyen Thinh there on the planks of Annemese cedar angled from his shack toward the mint-edged lake in the almost alpine semicircle of the Ran Chieu Hills, these hills which, for Thinh, have each a personality so powerful that he jokes about assigning them telephone numbers and putting them in the Military Directory. "They know me better than any man. You might wish to interview them about me."

Since his deposition in the coup of May 8, Thinh has stayed in these hills, usually with his marvelously beautiful Japanese companion, Daibata, and their child, a two-year-old boy as beautiful as his mother, as spare and wired as his father, but sightless. The interview as printed will not reveal Thinh's extraordinary feelings about his only recognized child. (There are supposedly five children whose mother is the Thai princess to whom he was married nine years but about whom he not only would not talk but whose name made him suddenly vacant as if he had been asked about the hobbies of the chairs we sat on.)

Our talk was in French, which he speaks with a strong Annemese accent but with complete fluency.

AF: Mr. Minister—

NTT: (Breaking in easily, authoritatively.) Don't begin with your thumb in the soup. I'm no longer a Minister.

AF: I must call you something. Most men who've run countries prefer the distance of their most exalted title.

NTT: I thought you were of the world. My exalted title is the one my father gave me. Call me that if you want, or better, call me nothing. Ask your questions, I'll answer them. (Here he pulled the cork from a flask of a scarlet drink, a liquor fermented from a cross between a raspberry and a currant. He poured it into two tin mess-kit cups; it tasted like sulphur and vinegar. I spat out my first mouthful to his laughter. He offered nothing more; I had to ask him for tea, but that was later, and he called back to Daibata, who brought us a wonderful T'ang brew.)

AF: As you wish, though it seems anyone so sensitive to such minor conventions as titles could not last as long as you did in public office.

NTT: When I was in office, I swallowed ordure from breakfast to supper. Some of my colleagues not only adjust to such nourishment; they crave it. I ate in public, vomited in private. I thought you were a realist, *mademoiselle*.

AF: Enough to appreciate the courtesy of *that* title, M. Thinh. But down to brass tacks, if you will. To politics, life, money, to your wants, your dreams, your needs, to your mind. (His hand to the fine pale brown rectangle of forehead.) Do I disturb you?

NTT: Yes.

AF: You've consented to answer questions. Did you expect me to ask you your saint's day? I can look that up in Paris.

NTT: You disturb me because I think here is a handsome, lean woman with no behind and small breasts who sits by a beautiful lake begging a man she has never met before to come into bed with her by attacking everything he says, raiding every gesture he makes for her notebook, feasting on—

AF: We will see about my desires later, Mr. Thinh. The only invitation issued and accepted has to do with other matters. Why not proceed? Why divert me with this journalist's portrait of the journalist?

NTT: Continue.

AF: For seven years now you have fought alongside, perhaps even within, the forces of the United States. Before that—

NTT: I know, the French. And you want to know why I—

AF: Perhaps you should conduct the interview. Just as you apparently reverse the roles of patriot and invader by siding with the colonial powers.

NTT: Miss Frequenza, your breasts would need to be twice their present size to escape the consequence of such a line of questions. (As my breasts have now twice become a fact of the interview, I had better go on the record to say that they have not been found wanting on the occasions to which they have been called.)

AF: I have been told that Vietnamese men prefer the small breasts of Vietnamese women, and that only those Vietnamese whose taste was corrupted by the milk-and-meat fed West were obsessed with mammary gigantism or its steatopygous equivalent. Is it the case that you sent your consort to Tokyo for breast-and-buttock enhancement?

NTT: I am suspicious of vocabularies like yours. They are either the fortifications of fear or the clumsily handled weapons of cowardly belligerence. (Here a lean, mahogany arm shot out, a piece of meat somehow in its lean claw. The meat was arced toward the tethered Kho Tuy, whose ivory tools gripped it in midair. I removed my eyes from the brief sequel, though minutes later my ears and nostrils were treated to the consequence of his furious ingestion.)

AF: How do you see your future?

NTT: In the mendacious crystals beneath your eyebrows.

AF: If you read it there, you also see a gallows.

NTT: I see a divan of reeds. I see a white woman terrified, bound to the divan. I see black musculature aquiver over a too thin, too flat, aging, powdered body. I see—

AF: Too much and not enough.

NTT: The papaya genitalia of a black leopard stiff with specie-crossing tension. I close my eyes to the scene.

AF: Your mother owns the pedicab concession of the capital, your consort the race track at Ne Hai. Although you have never drawn more than an army colonel's salary, you own a jet airplane, four villas, a diamond belt; your consort's Bentley has an emerald license plate which is guarded by machine gunners who spend three-hour periods of duty in its trunk. There is a long list of those stupendous superfluities which have stripped how many thousands of your fellow countrymen of their rice, their shirts, their leisure. You claim to be a patriot, interested in nothing but the expulsion of the Communists—

NTT: And the white flesh that befouls our streets.

AF: And keeps your villas for you. How reconcile your piracy and your supposed patriotism?

NTT: Reconciliation is the job of a woman. And a journalist. I am a soldier. One who likes his comfort.

AF: You have been called a thief, a narcissist, a megalomaniac.

NTT: You are articulate.

AF: Trials are made with words, their consequences are deeds. Death.

NTT: Perhaps. But feline menace is only words.
    (I love hate. The men and women whom I interview work against the grain of my rational disposition, but they grip me. Deeply. Nguyen Tao Thinh, sitting before me with the coldness of a glacier—a glacier of brown sugar—drove through my hatred to some untouched organ of fear, hatred, and—I will confess it—lust. I rose from my chair, I walked to his. I have short, ugly hands. To distract from them, I have let my nails grow long and carmined them. On safari, in the jungle, the desert, lying under the moon on a mountainside, I tend these nails. Now I brought them against his throat. His eyes, anthracite bits, flamed. His 1920s mustache bobbed. His arms rose between mine, and with a single

move broke my hold. And then, not his beloved beast, but he himself—though clothed and, as I could tell, unextended—stood face to my face, lips open, tobacco-spattered teeth in grimace, nose against mine, lips on mine.

We stood there, unmoving in this extraordinary expression of intimate, unreconcilable farewell.)

Commissioned by Lincoln Center's Repertory Theater to write a play, I planned one in the winter of 1966 and wrote it the next summer. I'd written two other plays, a three-act comedy which had never been produced * and a television play which a young Chicago director † tried and failed to produce for NET. The Lincoln Center play was planned as a panoramic survey of public and private lunacy and was intended for performance on a large stage in front of an audience of urban decision makers. (Sprawling, it employed all sorts of things to pull it together: A survey of theatrical modes and an alternation between historical and contemporary scenes are two I remember.) The producer wanted it for the small theater, and they were having union and other problems with that. Then too, the play had lots of characters and precious little expertise. It has stayed in the closet.

Since it was written, news has overreached it. For instance, the scenes printed here deal with problems which no longer seem newsworthy; the DeGaulle proclamation about "Québec Libre" came a year after my version's trumpeting about Latin America. (These are the small, sour-sweet pleasures of the closet dramatist.)

The scenes printed here are not in the original order; they deal mostly with matters treated in more straightforward fashion elsewhere in the book.

---

* Printed in *Teeth, Dying, and Other Matters* (New York: Harper and Row, 1969).

† Bill Friedkin, director of *The French Connection*.

SIX SCENES
from Dossier: Earth: Twenty-four Blackouts From the Middle Electric Age

1

A room in a slum, two cots, children sleeping across them, a pallet on the floor, pictures from newspapers neatly cut and tacked up, old stove, broken pop bottles, one being brushed onto a newspaper by a girl—she sweeps it with another newspaper. In shadow, another bed. Grandmother and some of the kids are watching a small television screen out of sight on the right; it casts a spectral, even a sacred light onto the otherwise dark stage; it emits a rock song. A little boy is frugging in front of it; he swats a little girl.

GIRL: Stoppat Roger. Ah bust you.

GRANDMOTHER: Don' do that son.

ROGER: She bus' me first.

GIRL: Ah did not.

ROGER: You bus' me, ah bus' you.

GRANDMOTHER: Lissn de music Rog.

ROGER: Anybody bus' me, I bus' them.

GRANDMOTHER: Shh that, Rog. Don' you go off now.

ROGER: You bus' me, I bus' you. Ah kill you.

GRANDMOTHER: You really gonna git it, Roger. You gonna git it from *me*. (She gets up to swat the eight year old, but there's a knock. Everyone freezes. From bed in corner we hear Mother's voice: "Who dat?" A frightened whisper.) Godda-

mighty, git out Rafe, git out. It dee Aid people. (A man
shoots out of bed, is getting on trousers; Mother fixes herself,
kids stir. Knocking on door is louder.) Jessa minit. Who dere?
Voice from door: Open up right now, please. Right away.
Rafe is at the window, opens it and out. Grandmother opens
door and the Aid people, black man and woman, man in tie
and short-sleeved shirt, woman in dress and carrying pad,
enter, move quickly around, over at bed, find man's sock,
hold it up to a sudden spot; everybody freezes for a moment,
then woman writes in pad and says to Mother: "I'm sorry,
Eva. It's gonna cost ya." General freeze and
Blackout

2

Hirondelle les Quatre Eglises (where the dour villa of General
President de G. finds itself). We are in the salon, noise of thunder, rain, as a chime sounds. A servant opens the hall door to a
man garbed with an elegance that is almost a uniform; but under
dripping hat, coat, umbrella.

SERVANT (middle-aged woman): Sir?

Man hands her his things.

SERVANT: Sir?

MAN: St. Mailly du Brin.

SERVANT: Of course. Madame begs you to attend the President
(à la française) in here.

MAN: Hmm. (He walks up and down peering at things, surprised
at the lack of general distinction.)

MADAME (appears; a dowdy little woman): Ah, Monsieur. How
good of you to come to us through this frightful rain.

MAN: Chère Madame (kisses her hand). It was an exciting drive.
And it is so fine to see you here in the country.

MADAME: Your first visit here? Of course. Well then, perhaps the hours did not hang too heavily on your hands.

MAN (a bit taken aback): Not for a moment. The ride is not the most breathtaking in France, but between leaving the hurly-burly of Paris and anticipating my luncheon here, it passed like a happy dream.

MADAME: I myself find it tedious. But the tedium never fails to succumb to the pleasures of the country. Our own country.

MAN: The General must feel the same.

MADAME: You must ask him. He is coming in from his roses.

MAN: Even in such weather. One detects the husbandry of flowers behind the wisdom of the Elysée.
MADAME: Pardon me, Monsieur.

MAN: I mean that the sensitivity to sowing and fertilizing, the rapport with the seasonal rhythms to which the tender of flowers must be sensitive is apparent in the decisions the President makes daily with men and affairs.

MADAME: I understand. We have an excellent gardener here. A cousin of our cook's assistant.

MAN: It is not easy to find a good gardener.

MADAME: Nor a cook who understands that Frenchmen too can eat with simplicity.

MAN (shudders at the prospect): Yes, I have heard of the brilliant simplicity of Madame's table.
MADAME: From whom, Monsieur?

MAN: The excellence and rigorous refinement of Madame's household are bywords in France.

MADAME: My wish, sir, is that they would so enter the fiber of our countrymen that there would be no need to single out those who practice it.

MAN: I'm afraid that the President and Madame have been fated by the gods to be singled out.

MADAME: The *gods,* sir?

MAN: By God. Or the world. Or nature, Madame. What you will.

MADAME: What is willed, sir, but not by me.

Man inclines his head, breathes heavily.

MADAME: The President is coming. (The Man has heard nothing, but his body is transformed in attendance. The General— in civies—does come in, immense, near-sighted.)

PRESIDENT (to his wife): My dear. And my dear St. Mailly. How good of you to come.

MAN: President (slight incline of the head as he takes the offered hand). It is so kind of you to have me.

PRESIDENT: I hope the rain did not spoil your drive.

MAN: It whetted my anticipation. I hope that you have not been discommoded in the garden.

PRESIDENT: Sir?

MAN: Madame indicated you were with your roses.

PRESIDENT: Ah yes. But not in the garden. I was arranging some for the table. I have always enjoyed the arrangement of flowers. It is something too frequently left for women. Some are not without talent there, but I think that ultimate arrangements of nature are best left with those who best know the stress of division from nature.

MAN: You will alter the homes of France, President.

PRESIDENT: I have. We are ready, my dear?

MADAME: At your wish, President.

President indicates the way to Man, leads Madame a few steps into the dining room, stage right. Three places. Plainly set. Huge vase of roses in middle.

MAN: A triumph indeed, M. le President.

PRESIDENT: But not the President's, St. Mailly. Beyond a simple disposition of a grand offering.

MAN: Ah yes.

Madame has gone to her place. Man runs to pull the chair but is anticipated by Madame placing herself in it. The President too is seated and has put his napkin in his collar before he remarks St. Mailly, whom he then waves to a chair. The chair, though, is on the wrong side and there is no place set there. Nonetheless, St. Mailly goes there and sits while Madame offers a muttered grace, all inclining their heads.

PRESIDENT: You are planning to eat without food or utensils, *mon vieux?*

MAN: Stupid of me, President. I am near-sighted and omitted to bring my eyeglasses. (He goes around to his own chair. President and Madame have not ceased to eat. He too begins. It is soup, and the President eats noisily.) Ah, superb (it is not), Madame. One detects the earth in such potage. (Madame inclines her head, the General grunts; after a moment the man starts up again.) It is extremely difficult to find a decent soup in France.

MADAME: How unfortunate you have been. My family has never found nourishing soup a rarity.

MAN: Ah yes, the northeast, Madame. I am thinking of Brittany.

PRESIDENT: If you were unfortunate dining in Brittany, then I must blush for the crudities we offer here.

MAN: The potage alone ennobles the table.

PRESIDENT: It is your presence which ennobles it, cher St. Mailly (but the repartee is slow in coming and is preceded by noisy ingurgitation of the soup).

MAN: It is only a true nobleman who could so graciously displace himself. (Soup slurp from the true nobleman. Another pause. Soup is finished. The General contemplates the roses, Madame the window, where rain continues, and the Man the air above the roses. He tries again.) A propos of Brittany, I reread for the first time in years some Corbière.

PRESIDENT (perks up a bit): One of the jewels of France.

MAN: Gnarled and rocky as the Brittany shore.

PRESIDENT: Briny, convoluted.

MAN: The range of a Zola in the compass of an acorn.

PRESIDENT (shifting gear): St. Mailly. France needs a chief of mission on the Latin American circumference, an ear in North America and an ear and two feet in Latin America. (He reaches into the roses and plucks one.) Mon cher Mailly, the President has determined that this mission is yours. (He hands him the rose.)

MAN (controlling his rather dismayed astonishment): Monsieur President, I-I-I don't know Spanish.

PRESIDENT (a pause; this hasn't been foreseen): Where there is a will, there is a language.

MAN: I'm totally and absolutely unprepared for this. I had a vague notion that you wished to discuss the developments in sterling with me.

PRESIDENT: By indirection find direction out. My dear . . . (A bell is rung by Madame and the fish course is trundled in by the maid. St. Mailly's reaction is controlled disgust.) Absurd myths about frozen fish in France.

MAN: Naturally, I could not be more flattered.

PRESIDENT: You have not been flattered, but appraised. The absence of Spanish will cause you to sharpen every other sense until you learn it. It is not a bad method of choice for a long-range mission. (To Madame.) My dear, I congratulate you.

MADAME: President.

PRESIDENT: And may the President be permitted to congratulate his old comrade in arms, St. Mailly du Brin?

MAN: President (in the same meek tone).

PRESIDENT: Who would have thought turning out of the vortex of the capital while Jupiter Pluvius exhibited his deliquescent power that the course of America was once again going to be determined by the proper administration of slight forces on delicate balances? What was lost on the plains of Abraham, what was sold by Bonaparte, mapped by Cartier, La Vender-rye, Cadillac, and Père Marquette, and coaxed by French arms into ripeness, will now, once again, after the English stabilization, be opened to Latin flowering under the impetus of Frankish reason. The failure of the Americas to ripen together under the differential hegemony of decadent Spanish, Portuguese, and British currents will be made good by the very power which has created the European basis of what health they have. Lah-Mey-Reek-Uh. St. Mailly, I drink to you. (But there is no wine, only an empty glass.) My dear, we cannot drink in air, pure as it may be. Shall we open a small bottle?

MADAME: President. (Hands spread.) It's Tuesday. (A frown from the General.) Madame rises quickly, brings in a large bottle of grocery store *vino*. The cap is—yes—unscrewed; the General pours into Mailly's extended glass and his own, the glasses touch in a smallish spot, and they collect what's left of the fading light until the *

Blackout

* I wouldn't have written this scene after reading the DeGaulle portrait in Malraux's *Fallen Oaks* (Holt, Rinehart: N.Y.) 1972, but in 1966 I thought DeGaulle almost madly pompous. Malraux's DeGaulle is noble, modest, wise. (It's Malraux who's a boaster, an irrepressible buzz.)

3

Georgetown elegance, a glassed-in sun room, Renaissance appointments, Cypriot and Cretan statuary, elegant bar; in distance, beyond blooming cherry blossoms, the Washington Monument. Secretary M. and Columnist A. having a drink.

M: . . . whereupon the President said, "Just when Ah git their pecker on the choppin' block, that snotnose Nellie walks off to git the ax sharpened." Which wrapped up that session. I tell you, Joe, they talk of two-front wars. I'm fighting a five-fronter.

J (taking his glass for refill): Sentimentality, Robert. You think you're under obligation to feel everybody's pulse. Meanwhile, buying hardware, wiping senatorial butts, tucking generals into bed, answering the likes of me. The President is built into the job. "Purity of heart is to will one thing." Any diversion deflects you. Your focus is crystal clear, yet you blur it by trying out everybody else's eyeglasses. You'll end up like Forrestal.

M: It's all very well to sit in a Georgetown parlor and talk of single-mindedness, but this is one of the few hours this week in which I'm not having to say, "Five thousand here, fifty thousand there, contract us for this, lay off on that, double the May call." You know darn well, Joe, we're all full of doubts about this thing.

J: There's where I think you're off. It's the sentimentality which I suppose you grew up to think was American tolerance. You know, the frontier mixture, pragmatic tolerance of all types. Except when it came to deciding where the trail was or to shooting the bear. By the time you were born, there were no more trails and no more bears, so all that was left was listening to the other fellow till the sun went down. And you went with it. You didn't run things in industry that way.

M: Maybe, but what is, is.

J: Nonsense. You become what you need to be. That's what a ruling class is. Nobody worth a damn says we're a nickel's worth better than the Chinese. If anything, there's a good chance they deserve the kitty. They're more disciplined, better schooled, probably more intelligent—racially—quite beautiful. There's no doubt they're going to take the whole pot before long. But that's not our outlook. We've been about two hundred years nurturing this harvest, and we've got to reap it. Adams, Hamilton, Calhoun, Clay, Lincoln, even Wilson and Roosevelt—Cousin Frank as well as Uncle Teddy—they all worked those fields, and now you're cutting and making the sheaves and hauling into the barn. It's no time for moans that you're using steel blades. This has been a legitimate empire, no mass-produced, Fascist, overnight recipe, no miserable oversimplification of reality. This is the old dream of a pioneered new world run by a mixture of Anglo-assimilated Europeans plus spice from Africa and the Near East. Though the brew has gotten a bit overspiced. At any rate, it's the best thing going in our time, and you're its guardian. That's the single focus. The rest is shooting second-story men, hired killers, subduing the misguided, hoping to corral the miserable.

M: Well, you've got tomorrow's column out of the way. And you may be right. God knows it's more or less what's been the framework of what I do day after day. (Joe starts to speak, he waves him down.) I know both good and bad can flow from good and bad, but it may be no accident that the first sentence of Hanoi's constitution is quoted from the Declaration of Independence. We're still a model for national independence. OK, we're no longer revolutionaries. The point of our revolution, you say, is its success, enjoyment of the honey we gathered. But who is the "we"? The men who gathered the honey? You know damn well this country is overweight, indolent, and except for pockets of researchers, craftsmen, the serious young, and I suppose some of its cultural leaders, just about where Rome was in 250 A.D. Maybe revival consists in stripping down. You can make a good argument that these Wars of the Chinese Periphery are just ways of knocking out peasant economies so we can rebuild them into industrial markets. A rice paddy farmer doesn't buy much machinery. OK. China's doing this on her own, brutally. We and the Chinese may be after the same thing. It's clear we and the Russians are: in the long run ideology doesn't mean a goddamn thing.

J: Now you're sounding like me. Except that ideology is our dessert. No, it's more than that. You can't enjoy a thing if you're eating with bloody hands. Not unless you're a maniac.

M: Joe. That's exactly what's troubling me. I'm being made to feel like Macbeth. And with some good reasons. You can't single-mind me out of it.

J (taking his glass and going to bar): One more of these Bloody Marys and you won't care one way or another. (He calls.) Margaret. Dinah better be at her very best for lunch. The Secretary and I are feeling very much in need of a pick-up.

Woman's voice (beautiful and cultivated, calls back): Ready in five minutes, darling. In the sun parlor.
The men raise glasses very slightly to each other.

J: Life goes on, Robert. That's our agony quota for the day.
                    Blackout

                    4
On screen, Vietnamese schoolchildren playing in schoolyard, high noon, small noise of plane, increasing, teacher comes out, looks at sky, noise increases, she opens her mouth, children stop on sharp cue, look up or at teacher or each other, then flash of light and surprised horror on faces.
                    Blackout

5

Living room of Schillinger's apartment in Chicago, overlooking Outer Drive. Light, comfortable, mixture of the new and the homey. On tables, books, newspapers, magazines, dishes of candy, nuts, cigarettes. Josie is flipping the day's newspapers, one by one, *Sun-Times, Tribune,* New York *Times,* glasses on her large nose pushed up every now and then with forefinger. She's in slippers, robe, forty-two, on the edge of plumpness, but still a good figure.

Lou—gray, wiry, handsome—comes in, tying up bathrobe, yawning, looks at Josie reading, starts to say "Morning," stops, looks away, stands in middle of room wondering what step to take, goes to door at end of room, opens it, stoops and comes up with big handful of mail, comes back to table across from wife, pours himself coffee from electric maker, sips, sets mail down, sits and begins opening the letters.

LOU (reads, then drags over little dictaphone and turns it on): Number one. "Dear Señor Rotella: Sorry, but I am unable to send you a rundown of the American reviews of my books. The best I can do is a summary. As follows: 'Louis Metzger is full of delightful baloney except when he agrees with me.' I am sorry you had difficulty getting the book. I cannot remember the name of the Spanish translator, and I don't know enough Spanish to say whether he's doing a good or bad job. No, General Franco has never written me about my work, and, as a matter of fact, I have never written him about his. Yours . . ." (Switches off the machine.)

JOSIE (who has looked up from the newspaper and then witheringly stared at him during last half): Must that be the cock's cry every morning?

LOU: You know I've got to get the mail out of the way.

JOSIE: You've got the most beautiful office on the South Side.

LOU: That's for serious work.

JOSIE: I don't even have a desk.

LOU: I take care of your business.

JOSIE: I don't suppose there's anything for me.

LOU: Haven't checked.

JOSIE: Well?—

LOU (flips through letters, pulls out one, then a second; looks them over): Your brother. (Throws them to her.)

JOSIE: And the other?

LOU: Both from your brother.

JOSIE: Can't read this postmark.

LOU: The idea's to slit the outside. It's called an envelope. In Egypt it was baked clay. You couldn't do it. Now they make 'em of paper. It's easy. You'll notice a flap on the back. Insert your blade. Then, when open, you get to the heart of the communication, the letter itself. If it is in English—

JOSIE (finishes in his tone): It will be in a language which has been getting the better of you for ten years.

LOU: Don't say that.

JOSIE: You can add that to Señor Rotella's letter.

LOU (hoists the pile of mail): The scales are piled heavy enough against me without your glok, Josie. What's the great muckraker got to say?

JOSIE: First, three of yours.

LOU (opens an envelope): "Dear Mr. Metzger: The American Studies Association is hoping to sponsor another of its symposia at the annual meeting of the American Historical Society. Our hope is that we can offer a debate or discussion between former Prime Minister Macmillan, Jean-Paul Sartre, and yourself on the subject 'The Dreams and Realities of Power.' The hope—"

JOSIE: Next one.

LOU (draws the dictaphone to him, clicks it on): Moment. Number two. "Dear Professor—(looks at letter)—Messenger: May I suggest that you substitute former Premier Khrushchev for Monsieur Sartre? There seems little point in discussing these matters with mere speculators. In the event of such substitution you may—as always—count on me. If Monsieur Sartre has already accepted, may I suggest my distinguished brother-in-law Arnold Bruzak of the Political Affairs Council of the American Federation of Labor as my substitute? He has often filled in for me, willy-nilly. Ihr Ergebener." That'll fix the old Kraut.

JOSIE (opens the next one): Oof. What a fine hand. (Hands it to him.)

LOU: It's Croatian. Lemme see. Well. "Most honored Dr. Metzger: Duh, duh respond to the attack in *Borba* duh of Draja Trumbič, Secretary Serbian Culture League duh duh duh duh . . . duh duh. Most respectfully . . ." (Opens dictaphone.) "My dear Serlič: I have already seen the scurrilous nonsense spewed my way by this miserable intellectual hooligan. A rat's spoor would have made more sense. How will Serbia maintain itself if morbid assassins like Trumbič are permitted to desecrate the already enfeebled pages of *Borba*? I am honored by his attack. You may print this letter as my maximum response. Respectfully, transatlantically, not quite yet despairingly thine, Metzger." All right, let's hear what the great voice of the Labor Movement is after.

JOSIE: Letter two was a picture of MacDonald in his graduation robe. "Dear Joss—Was sorry Lou didn't give the speech at

Mac's graduation yesterday, but Justice Warren gave a bee-uty. I thought I was in Warsaw, but considering that Lou would have had us in the Kremlin toilets, it was a relief. Sorry you weren't there. I hope you'll find time to let MacDonald have a word from his only aunt and famous uncle-in-law as he moves into the world, General Hershey and his SAT scores permitting."

LOU: Names that Galacian kidney-dribble after a union leader to the right of George Humphrey and expects a fifty-dollar check from me, may his piss freeze in his pizzle.

JOSIE (reading): "Now, Joss, I want you to have no hesitation whatever in saying No to the following. As usual. But Jean and I thought we might take a small gang here up for a spell of country and where better, if possible, and if you aren't there that week, than Dune Acres. Any chance? Please telegraph collect if impossible. Otherwise, we're en route and we'll call you from there. Eight of us, a kind of conference, tax-deduc-tible, so we'll pay the utilities for that portion with no qualms at all. Perhaps you can drop in for Sat. afternoon. Maybe Lou too." (Looks up.) Age cannot wither nor insult stale that little old frater of mine. My God, if I had strength I'd telegraph him collect. (Lou is glaring, furious, silent.) Ten thousand words.

LOU (brings over dictaphone): "Dear Arnold: For reasons hav-ing to do with the new Internal Revenue Code, I have been forced to report to the commissioner each and every visit to our house in Dune Acres. Forgive me for failing to let you know before this that when I was questioned about the last six visits you paid there, I indicated that they were, of course, social in nature. The deposition I signed is already with the bureau's legal department. If your lawyers can wòrk out some honorable way in which I can be of assistance to you when— or more optimistically, if and when—your case is brought to court, please let me know. I am as always your (pause) understanding *beau*—or shall I say *laid—frère,* L. Metzger, LL.D. honoris causa Edinburgh, Les.D., Paris, Oxfordiensis, Harvard, Etcetera. LM." That'll rot his lymph. Oh, mail: once the gods' gift, the world's fecundity, the harvest after the long season, now the world's offal. Foul, daily deposit (hands up, orating, poeticizing). How the world punishes its few nectaries. Regard the bees. They visit forty thousand flowers, fly fifty thousand miles for one pound of honey. They pour in their enzymes, and then fan the drip out of the flower stuff. Id est: They travail. But here, in this human, this humanoid, this *menschlich allzu menschlich Welt,* forty thousand bees encapsulate fifty thousand pounds of shit into envelopes and drop them daily on us human nectaries. (Josie starts putting dishes away. Then gets out typewriter, takes up his dictaphone discs, plays them into earplugs, and types.) Said Nestroy, "When wolves come upon each other in the forest, they see each other's wolfheit and do not cringe. When two men come upon each other, they reach for their daggers." Frederick the Queer Great was richtig. Business without arms is Notes without Instruments. (He is up, orating.) Let us then take (he clasps Josie on shoulder; she throws off her earplugs and takes steno pad in hand) a man. All right: "Arnold (pause, looks at pencil) Eversharp began writting letters every evening after supper. A square but (pause) angular man of subdued, (pause) subtle habits, Eversharp . . ."

Blackout

6

The playwright sits in upholstered chair drinking Scotch and smoking; the interviewer, a pretty girl, regulates the tape recorder; the photographer moves around snapping flashbulb pictures.

INTERVIEWER: If you prefer writing fiction, why write a play?

PLAYWRIGHT: I prefer roast beef to mutton, but I eat both.

INTERVIEWER: There is something, then, to the theater?

PLAYWRIGHT: Certainly. Even an inexperienced playwright like myself can see that. I'd better emphasize the inexperience, although Mr. Kerr will do it more expertly than I.

INTERVIEWER: Write the play?

PLAYWRIGHT: No, supply the emphasis. What I mean is, you sacrifice—I mean the fiction writer has it all—or most of it—in his own hands, but there's none of that ready emotional cash you get on the stage—a word, a look, a cigarette. (He threatens the interviewer's eye with his; the interviewer emits a small shriek.) See. A walk. (He stalks the interviewer.) You have all that going for you. It enables you to skip around, cover ground more quickly. I mean, I think.

INTERVIEWER: So you find the technique of playwriting exciting, and you wish to exploit it.

PLAYWRIGHT: Yes.

INTERVIEWER: But the play itself. Your play. Can you talk about its—its meaning, its theme?

PLAYWRIGHT: Meaning?

INTERVIEWER: I mean what it adds up to, not just a series of gestures and speeches.

PLAYWRIGHT: Oh yes. Well you know that bromide about meaning? "Meaning is what the burglar throws to the dog as he rifles the safe."

INTERVIEWER: That's rather cryptic. You mean there's no meaning in your play?

PLAYWRIGHT: No. No, no, no. But telling it is the name of the baby, not the baby. The real meaning is in the connections, the synapses, the progress, the unfolding, the whole being. The baby. The production. The Logos and then the, well, what followed. (He pauses in profile, extending drink and cigarette during the "Logos" bit.)

INTERVIEWER (to photographer): Get that.

Photographer fumbles a bit with equipment. Playwright has started to shrink from pose; then, what the hell, that's the game, he holds it till the flash.

PHOTOGRAPHER: Got it.

A screen shows the newspaper blow-up of the photograph with headline of interview: SAYS PLAYS SHOULD BE MEANINGLESS LIKE LIFE.

Blackout

PART III

5. Some Versions of Oneself

... almost ten percent of Rembrandt's ... output in painting consisted in likenesses of himself ... in the beginning his
face often served as a convenient model for studies in expression. Thus he may have come into the habit of looking
at himself with a painter's eye ... one feels certain short-
comings in this early work. The transitory nature of the
emotion is not sufficiently brought out, and the result is
a somewhat frozen grimace, resembling a snapshot photograph ... Although Rembrandt ... displays a good deal
of showmanship ... The painting does not lack that element of mystery which belongs to all his best works ...
Rembrandt realized early that the half tones are best suited
to the suggestion of psychological content. Only within the
half tones can one slip subtly from the distinct to the in-
distinct and play that game of veiling and disclosing which
Rembrandt employed so masterfully in suggesting content
of a less tangible nature ... in the self-portrait of 1640
in the National Gallery in London ... the strongest accent
of the picture ... lies in the man's critical, almost mis-
anthropic expression which seems to contradict the emphasis upon his rich attire. This is the phase of Rembrandt's life in which the first symptoms of inner crisis appear. We detect that uneasiness which frequently fore-
shadows profound change.

Jakob Rosenberg, *Rembrandt: Life and Work*

The tone depends on not explaining Nechaev or the
Prince.

Dostoevsky,
The Notebooks for The Possessed,
edited by Edward Wasiolek

In "On Vanity," Montaigne, the most constant and least vain autobiographer, mentions an unexpected dividend which comes in writing about oneself:

> Sometimes there comes to me a feeling that I should not betray the story of my life. This public declaration obliges me to keep on my path, and not to give the lie to the picture of my qualities, which are normally less disfigured and distorted than might be expected from the malice and sickness of the day's judgments.

Regular self-scrutiny, particularly published self-scrutiny, requires strength, and not merely the strength of vanity. Many writers have to wean themselves from the timidity natural to most of us; psychoanalysis or regular confession of some other sort helps the weaning process. A less regarded form of help is the questionnaire. Most contemporary writers are questioned about themselves with some regularity. (The usual questioning is like talk in an elevator, a way of overcoming awkward silence.) Even those who don't wish to exhibit themselves, or who wish to only under those fictional disguises which exaggerate some and omit other bad traits (partly for artistic, partly for personal reasons), are often drawn into public self-appraisal by such requests. The well-known duckers often get the most attention; a true ducker learns to throw strategic sops.

The following statements were all supplied on the request of those named in the notes.

STERN, RICHARD (FEB. 25, 1928) AMERICAN NOVELIST AND STORY WRITER *

My parents were the children of immigrant German Jews whose sagas had brushed by failure and, supposedly, great fortunes (a grandfather who sold Morgan the rights to the tungsten filament for a thousand original shares of General Motors common stock, "nowhere to be found" at his death) to settle into Manhattan apartments with their English-named children, dinosaur-clawed furniture, and Germanic pot roasts (served up by Finnish, then Irish, and finally Negro maids). My parents were large-minded and puzzled enough to permit their hard-nosed little *Wunderkind* to set up his cave of books and records amidst the aunts and roasts, suffering a temper which sent him at six under the bed for days, at twelve into occasional weeks of silence. To everyone's surprise, the phenomenon was refused admission to Harvard and Yale but was taken, all sixteen angry years of him, to Chapel Hill, where he first learned that the New York system was not universal and that there was news that went unprinted in the *Times*.

After Chapel Hill, I proved incompetent in three jobs, one with an Indiana department store, a second in a Florida radio station (where my fiancée's mother rode me out of town), and a third at Paramount International Films in New York. Not foreseeing the statistical inferno of "university writers," I quit for a year of graduate work at Harvard, where I wrote a Bowdoin Prize essay on John Crowe Ransom. The next year I taught at the Collège Jules Ferry in Versailles, from which I shifted—no longer a bachelor—to an assistantship at the University of Heidelberg and a night job as cable clerk with the occupation army.

* Written for the revised edition of *Twentieth-Century Authors*.

The third European year was spent in Frankfurt teaching illiterate soldiers and trying to wangle European jobs (with Churchill —"the Prime Minister regrets that his staff is complete"—and Fiat—I'd had lunch with an Agnelli in Cambridge and on its small strength proposed to sell Fiats to fellow occupiers). In 1952 I returned with a diaper pail, Biedermeier desk, and enough money for a doctorate at Iowa. There the notes, drafts, botched chapters, and plans of ten years began to make some sense. One day in that first hot September, my wife waited outside the Quonset hut with a letter from the subject of my Bowdoin essay accepting my first story for the *Kenyon Review.*

For eleven years now [1965], with fifteen months out to teach in Venice and Rome, I've been at the University of Chicago, another cave, in part of which there is the necessary isolation, in the other part of which are the woes and sweetness of mid-century institutional life. My novels and stories rarely deal directly with this life or with my own. A few friends, fellow writers, occasional readers, and critics sometimes see in what are for me very different works certain recurrences, an absorption in great inventors and their hangers-on, the free women and the energetic, coreless men who are the source of so much disorder, the Europe-America axis, and the use and abuse of narrative conventions. I grant but cannot imagine being governed by these or other recurrences. It is enough being governed by what more and more seems the noblest of habits.

STATEMENT FOR THE
NATIONAL INSTITUTE OF ARTS AND
LETTERS EXHIBITION, SPRING 1968

> . . . some autobiographical data or some general reflections
> on your own work, or a brief sketch of your next project,
> or perhaps some intimations of your own long-range
> plans (if any) . . .

Raised out of harm's way in Manhattan, badly educated in four
or five states, snuffling up the moveable feast, thirteen years a
respectable, scarcely visible Chicago burgher. Within, since God
knows when, that writing tapeworm, so endlessly consumptive
that clearer heads wonder why any host stands it long. And another wonder, why is there so little to show for it? Trollopes,
Simenons, Joergas * (fourteen hundred books, forty-two thousand articles and reviews, his worm a whale, and also a senator,
indeed a premier of Rumania, father of ten children, graphoma-
niacal brother of the great Victorian fornicator of *My Secret
Life*). Are there some who never waste pages, blot lines? (Pile my
own waste pages, and Joerga would give me an inch or two of his
nutty throne.) As for the next rescue from those waste pages, another novel, one that discards most temptations to show itself
being written, one that still hews to the standard narrative illusion.† Long-range plans? The burgher superstructure has little
but long-range plans, but the vermicular infrastructure has its
own process, untranslatable outside.

---

* The good Mircea Eliade—himself a strong fount of novels, stories,
and critical scholarship—told me of his fellow Rumanian.

† The result was a short novel which did exhibit its process (*Veni,
Vidi . . . Wendt*) and a novel which was reduced to a long story (*Idylls
of Dugan and Strunk*). *1968* (New York: Holt, Rinehart and Winston,
1970).

IN RESPONSE TO A QUESTIONNAIRE *

1. Do you feel that the situation of the Jew in America has altered in the past fifteen years? If so, has this had any influence on your present attitude toward your own Jewishness?

The situation. *The* Jew? One might collapse Mississippi Negroes or Algerian colons into useful singulars, but no longer American Jews. The unembarrassed and unfearful chameleonizing of the Jew in America has given him nearly as much elbow room as the white Anglo-Saxon. With of course the attendant loss which the American Jewish writers have been chronicling since the last war. Literature says "Here we go," as well as "Good-bye": the next ten years may see as many Jewish Eugene Hendersons as the last have seen Augie Marches, the twenty before that, Asa Leventhals. As for me, I like to think that my own attitude is my own changing, not time's. Twenty years ago, on the Saturday I should have been "bar-mitzvahed" but was not, because one wasn't in our family, I hid out in the Paramount Theater ducking the friends to whom, on Monday, I conjured up my ceremony. Five years later, in college, I claimed to be half-Jewish, partly to avoid Hillel functions and partly to try my luck on the other side of the street. Today, being a Jew is like being a Chicagoan, except that I pay no taxes (there may be hidden ones). I'm glad, rather than not, but I don't spend thirty minutes a year congratulating myself, or indeed thinking of myself as a Jew. Would this —what, lassitude?—have been possible in 1920 or even in 1945? Not even for the most assimilated of Jews, in this one's opinion.

2. What are your feelings, if any, about the generation of Jewish intellectuals whose socialism pro-

* Written for the *Commentary* symposium of April 1961.

> *vided the basis for their more or less antagonistic relation to the Jewish community in America and elsewhere? Do you believe there are viable elements in the tradition they represent?*

I imagine that there have always been "accepting" and "denying" Jews, as there are will and won't reactions to all "penalties of medium severity." There were certainly Jewish socialists who remained Jewish in ritual, community feeling, and self-consciousness, just as there were many of the sort the question describes. I think that Jewish socialists, from Lassalle on, have been, by and large, a first-class group, one which kept closer to humanism —again, by and large—than their Christian comrades. The group of American Jewish socialists of the 1930s didn't play nearly so important a role as the earlier Europeans, and I think that many of their notions were essentially poetic—e.g., their view of American popular culture as something especially vile and especially contagious I stuff in the barrel with the distributists' vision of the twelfth century or the agrarians' of the old South. Yet my heart goes out to them. Their intellectual belligerence showed up a lot of messes. That tradition is, I hope, viable. If it involved attacks on Jewish parochialism, that did not, and does not, deaden it for me, though such attacks would seem gratuitous today.

> 3. *Do you think that your experience as a Jew is importantly relevant to your experience as an American? Do you feel that Jewish culture—in the broadest sense of the term—exerts a significant influence upon American life? If so, how would you define this influence?*

When I think of my "experience as an American," I think of being identified as the holder of an American passport, and thus happily distinguished by an aura of purchasing power or, in Germany, of occupation force *mana*. Since I haven't been a winterer in Miami Beach, "my experience as a Jew" has not been similar. The noticeable identifying moments have been on the order of contributing to this symposium or being asked by a severe Jordanian border guard if I'd ever heard of the Stern gang. As for "Jewish culture—in the broadest sense," the influence on every form of American life is immense. Beyond calculation. The masochism of Jewish song writers and comedians, the emotional Woolworths of the Louis B. Mayers, the occult austerities of hundreds of physicists and composers, the Brandeis–Frankfurter–Ben Cohen form of the Second New Deal, a shape here, a phrase there, concepts, feelings: Who can number or define the influences? Just as a shot in the dark, I'll suggest this: harsh rebukes, open love, self-abasement, all of which individualize and color. Since the American "myth" pivots on individuality, perhaps Jews have tended to give new fuel to the myth at a time when it was really needed. Italian Americans could have added the same sort of fuel, but I don't think they've poured in a tenth as much.

4. *Considering that you are at least partly a product of Jewish tradition, do you feel any obligation—any sense of historical reverence—to that tradition? Does this obligation include an involvement in the Jewish community, or extend to transmitting the values inherent in Jewish tradition to your children? Or do you perhaps see no merit in the claim that the Jewish people have created or preserved certain special values?*

5. *Have you ever considered the possibility that your children may convert to another religion? If so, how do you feel about this possibility?*

Any obligation, *any* sense? I feel whips over a "no," though "reverence" supplies a little advance salve. I was taught as a seven year old to say "I am an American Jew." It was said mechanically, but the mechanism was worked by pride. I'm not proud of being an American or of being a Jew. Lucky? Mostly. Content? Mostly. Certainly there is a continuity, a history, which serious men can examine and generalize about, but "obligation," "sense of reverence"? I want to say "N-O!" writ large and with an exclamation point to drown out what may be some shameful doubt. As for getting involved in "the Jewish community," there is a tattered allegiance which involves such self-examination as this symposium response, but little more. In an emergency I might not be the last one to the hose. As for my children, they are half-Jews to the extent that I am Jewish, and they know about that, and about what would have happened to them if they had lived in Munich in 1935. They are probably a bit better informed about Passover than Rafferty's children. As for the claim that "the Jewish people have created or preserved certain special values," I think this is mostly true and mostly glorious. It is also true of the Nepalese Sherpa and the Catalonians. (I better add that I don't know if it's true of the Jews as a "people." How about the Falasha Jews in Abyssinia?) I don't think that one transmits Jewishness to one's children, as one sends them to a good school for what it can bring them. The transmission of Jewishness means the transmission of a consciousness, and that should not—cannot—be too artfully induced. If my children have or get it, splendid, or if they "convert to another religion," or rather take up another religion, also splendid.

> 6. *Do you feel any special connection with the state of Israel? Does it, in your opinion, exert a legitimate claim on your sympathies? Would you say that it embodies the values of Jewish tradition more clearly than the American Jewish community does?*

I'm particularly conscious of it, as I am, say, about Sammy Davis, Jr.'s conversion. I'm more interested in it than in, say, the presidency of Gabon, but think I might be anyway. A "legitimate claim" on my sympathies? If anything, it has what I regard as an illegitimate claim. As for the embodiment of Jewish tradition, who can say what best embodies so ancient and complicated a phenomenon? Perhaps some Mormon sect in southwest Utah. Israel does seem at least a mirror fulfillment of a prophecy, but then even Nostradamus was "right" once in a while.

THE NOVELIST ON HIS WORK:
A PARTIAL AUTOBIOGRAPHY *

1

You have, as I understand it, been considering the role of the Jew in contemporary fiction, both as subject and as writer. Jews should perhaps subdue their joyous pride † at the astonishingly disproportionate place they have occupied on the world scene in the past century, for it is of course fatally easy to exempt oneself from activity by pointing to the success of those with whom one identifies. But who, Jew or non-Jew, can be anything but amazed at the prominence of Jews in the twentieth-century worlds of intellect, art, and affairs? Everyone aware of his own partial identity as a Jew considers in his personal development the large measures of possibility to which these men point. And today a Jew who is a writer, particularly a writer of fiction, no longer measures fellow Jewish writers by the touching but sporadic brilliance of a parochial literature, but by the books of perhaps the finest active writers of prose in the Western world. Even when the subject matter of a novel by Saul Bellow, Bernard Malamud, or to a somewhat lesser degree Norman Mailer or J. D. Salinger is Jewish, the treatment of that matter is not private; it takes root not only in the minds of Jewish readers but

* A talk for a synagogue series on Jewish writers, (about 1961).

† Jewish modesty has a tough time of it in the tide of post-Hitlerian analysis of the "Jewish problem." One of the noblest analysts was Karl Barth:

> We find it uncanny that the Jews live among us and move like shadows through world history with that unmatched historical permanence, yet without roots, without security; without roots because they are sustained by the free grace of God . . . the Jews tell us . . . that we, who believe ourselves to be secure on the bank, are in fact not so . . . ("The Jewish Problem and the Christian Answer," *Against the Stream* [New York: Philosophical Library, 1954].)

in those of readers everywhere. Their achievement is comparable to that of the American Southern writers of the previous generation and that of the nineteenth-century New England writers.

Any man who talks of work he presents to the public as an objective exhibition is somewhat presumptuous; for a writer whose work has an almost nonexistent public, the presumption is immense. Nonetheless, the twentieth-century public has been intrigued as much by the process of creation as by its results. As more and more of the human interior has been mapped, interest in the man whose strength consists in his ability to exhibit his own weaknesses is as great as it used to be in those men of an earlier age whose greater deeds were not accounted for by their perversities. The saints and heroes have yielded the stage to what Kierkegaard in *Fear and Trembling* called the least of the three types of significant men, the witness, the artist-writer whose significance consists in abstention from the action he reports and endurance in the creation of the report. So these last years have seen the publication of diaries, letters, autobiographies, notes, first drafts, and numerous other droppings from creative lives.

"Autobiography" is a fairly new word; according to the *New English Dictionary* it was coined in 1809 by Robert Southey.* Of course, there were many books written by men about themselves before Southey's day, but the invention of the term does bespeak an increased self-consciousness of the art, practice, and significance of writing about oneself. By the end of the nineteenth century autobiography, either unadorned or in more or less fictional form, was very common and the subject of quite a number of essays, the most famous of which may be Sir Leslie Stephen's unsigned essay in the *Cornhill* magazine in April 1881. The famous progenitor of both the *Dictionary of National Biography* and Virginia Woolf wrote:

* Southey was the poet whom Lord Byron fixed in acid with the epigram "Southey will be read when Homer is forgotten, but not until then."

> The autobiographer has ex officio two qualifications of su-
> preme importance in all literary work. He is writing about
> a topic in which he is keenly interested, and about a topic
> upon which he is the highest living authority. It may be
> reckoned, too, as a special felicity that an autobiography,
> alone of all books, may be more valuable in proportion
> to the amount of misrepresentation it contains.

I suppose that Sir Leslie meant by the last sentence that when
one knows how a man lies and what he lies about, one knows
something extra about his needs and character.

I do not propose to lie here, perhaps because I am not going
to unload a full autobiography on you. I restrict myself to the
way my writing may have been affected by my being a Jew. To
do this, I am going to have to use reminiscence and interpretation which will, I think, be exceptionally partial because of my
feeling that my writing has so far not been crucially affected by
it. If it turns out that I discuss work too inconsiderable to be
called even minor, I can only plead that nearly as much can be
learned about rocketry from an analysis of the missile which
melts on its own launching pad as from one which joins in
perpetuity the universe's own comets.

2

Every case is special, so I will not begin my description of the
assemblage and launching—or attempted launching—of my
work by pleading my own difference from other Jewish writers
of our day (as if they could be lumped together as a cake on
which I preened as the birthday candle). Yet my case is quite
different from those of the Jewish writers whom I know, and
these include the most brilliant, Saul Bellow (probably the most
important prose fiction writer now active), the finest bloom of
the parochial school, Bernard Malamud, and Norman Mailer.
I am going to approach my "case" via Rilke's poem "Archaic
Torso of Apollo":

We'll never see that wonderful head
in which the eye-fruit ripened, but the
body glows like a candelabrum
where, way down deep, the glance, retained,
shines. Otherwise the curve of the chest
wouldn't blind you, the soft spin
in the loins couldn't shift smiles
into the genitals which hang there;
otherwise the stone would seem defaced,
a brilliant plunge from the shoulders,
not aflame like the coats of wild animals,
not bursting out of its borders
like a star: for there's no place that
doesn't see you. You must change your life.

This poem applies to me in the following way: I conceive of my work as the headless torso which in some fashion glows, glows the way the eyes of a head glow. My Jewishness—so attenuated a fact in my life and consciousness—I analogize to the lost head of the poem. Yet, for all I know, the Jewishness might be the source of whatever glow is in my work. For who knows his source? Here is a book [*Golk*] which unlike many of the works of writers I've mentioned does not deal with a Jewish scene or background, yet it may well be that there is much in it that can be thought Jewish in quality, in tone, in things which its author— less than anyone—can see.

A reader may caution me at this point about the subject matter of this novel, *Golk*. Aren't two of the leading characters, Hondorp and his father, Jewish? It is here that I have to give a peculiar answer, namely "Probably." I say "probably" because on looking over the novel, not while I was writing it but after, it occurred to me that Poppa Hondorp is associated in my mind with people who are Jews. A character in fiction is not like you or me a composite of many identities. I am a teacher, a Jew, a native New Yorker, a father, homeowner, Ph.D., a bad tennis player, big eater, a member of this, writer of that, etcetera. You may be a Chicagoan, Anglophile, Methodist, plumber, wife beater, Elk, stamp collector, manic-depressive, and so on. A

character in a novel or story exists only in those identities for
which the author needs him, although the author may also
be filling in other identities which are not important to his
scheme but more important than he may know at the time
to the energy of his work. Now for Poppa Hondorp I wanted
(1) someone who was a fanatically devoted and domineer-
ing father, (2) someone who was maniacally absorbed in
television, (3) a comic prop whose growing deformity—a
lipoma—would be a laugh every time it showed up and thus
could be used to vary the tone of episodes, and (4) a man who
so much wanted something that its not being granted him by his
son would be a telling point against that son. These are Poppa
Hondorp's functions as seen in retrospect by his inventor. That
he has an accent which I think of as a German Jewish one is due
to my desire to achieve an effect of *warmth,* for my own literary
standard is both near and far enough from Henry James' so that
what James in the New York ghetto called "the torture-rooms
of the living idiom" is for me at least "the crazy house of the
idiom," a source of comic warmth.

At any rate, as far as characters are concerned and as far as
the narrative idiom is concerned, my novel is not Jewish. In
what ways if any, then, is it Jewish and can it be identified as the
work of a Jew? I had best preface an answer by saying what my
own status as a Jew is, and see if I can draw from the novel certain characteristics which may be related to that status.

I suppose that I knew I was a Jew about the same time I knew
I was an American, which was probably a few years after I
knew I was a little boy. Yet my Jewish-consciousness has always
been an impoverished one. I went but a little while to Sunday
school; I was not "bar-mitzvahed," and although I never had
anything but respect for things Jewish as a boy, there was no
tradition I observed which was Jewish except staying home one
day for Yom Kippur and Rosh Hashonah. This impoverished
Jewishness was part of the atmosphere in which I and almost all
of my friends lived. In my own case I can only try to ascribe it,

first, to that paternal grandfather who was orphaned early in Austria and who spent much of his energy getting to America and making his way in the world and, second, to a maternal grandfather who was an assimilated German whose energies were also largely devoted to being "comfortable." Jewishness, like hair color, was an accepted part of our house, but though it was more important than that physical trait insofar as it helped shape, say, the politics of my father, I cannot see that it particularly enlarged my own religious, intellectual, or moral consciousness. When I went to the University of North Carolina I was sixteen, and there, happy in a very different sort of environment, I became both conscious of my Jewishness and afraid of it. I did not join a fraternity because at that time I did not wish to be thought of as a Jew more than, say, someone from the North. I also tugged at my past to the extent of being attracted by manners, habits, and characteristics which did not seem "Jewish" to me. Although I always had Jewish friends, my closest friends then, both men and women, were not Jewish. By the time I graduated from college and went to work in a number of places around the country, I had lost most of my self-conscious embarrassment about Jewishness. I was now so involved in other things that it was almost never a factor in my life, and when it was, I accepted it as a minor, even a comforting fact. In part I attributed what I thought of as my artist's disposition to the slight displacement from ordinary life which being a Jew allowed me, just as I attributed my distaste for what I thought of as the mundane affairs of my family to my artist's disposition. I liked being a bit of an outsider, not a penalized outsider but a glamorous one, and my three years in France and Germany as a college lecturer and government worker were in part consistently pleasurable because I enjoyed my identification as that least penalized of outsiders of the early 1950s, the American Abroad. When I came back from Europe in the spring of 1952 I came back to become a writer and professor.

It is of the writing career that I would like to say a few words.

My early writing was done under the influence of those fiction writers who had been established as The Masters by such textbooks as Brooks and Warren's *Understanding Fiction*. The principles of such writers are (1) to secure your efforts with a polished style, (2) to integrate all the materials of your story, and (3) to suspend the meaning of the story in the action as "naturally" as orange bits in jello. I wrote about ten stories between 1952 and 1954, more or less under such guiding principles, but more and more I was becoming dissatisfied with the results and with some of the principles behind them. In 1957 I started the novel *Golk*. This novel was written in the midst of writing another novel which I'd been working on since 1952 or 1953.* A month or so after I actually started writing the new novel, I met Saul Bellow, who at that time was writing his novel *Henderson, the Rain King,* the first of his long works which was not about a Jew. Now Bellow did a number of things for me: his own energies and regal view of the writer's life helped confirm my pass across the borders of well-tailored fiction. Although *Golk* may still be thought of as a careful book as far as construction goes, its freedom seems big to me, and its explicitness and occasionally rich prose seem to me to stand for fictional liberty. Bellow did more as well, although he had started to do that before I'd met him. He was the first major American novelist who was a Jew, and it seemed to me that his books were already as good as Hemingway's and the other American idols of my literary Pantheon. Of course, my favorite of all novelists, Proust, was a half-Jew, but Proust, like Tolstoy or Dante, is a man too great to be of help to other writers. If anything, such men hinder you as a writer as much as they help you as a man. But of the second rank, of a rank that might just possibly yield a Proust, Bellow was someone who spoke intimately to me about his work and plans. Now his life was much closer to a traditional Jewish life than mine was, and I learned from him some of the convolu-

* *Europe, or Up and Down with Baggish and Schreiber* (New York: McGraw-Hill, 1961).

tions of that life and its language—Yiddish—a language from which I had been cut off by assimilation. As I met other Jewish writers, notably Malamud and Mailer, and got to know my colleague at the University of Chicago, Philip Roth, I became conscious of my place not as a Jewish writer but as a writer who was also a Jew even though his material had never been explicitly Jewish. Now there were and are dangers here: think of yourself as a member of a school and you'll flunk out; think of yourself, or rather forget yourself, and do your job, and you may come to something. At no point did I seriously consider writing a work which would spring not from my feelings but from a school of fictional fish. I have written only one story * in which a leading character is specifically a Jew, and that's because the character's life is determined by his Jewishness. (He's a refugee from Nazi Germany.) If I look at *Golk* now to find out in what way it might be "Jewish," I'm stumped. Perhaps such scenes as the knockdown fight—or as it turns out, apparent fight—between Hendricks and Golk can be classed with others in "Jewish" fiction. One scene in the book was spurred by Bellow after he read the first version of the book, the scene in which Hendricks and Hondorp have it out before they separate. Before I wrote the Bellovian version of that scene, the breakoff between them was oblique and muted. Now they yell at each other, and the atmosphere is what I think of as Russian—open, frank, or to the point here, Jewish. Anything else? Perhaps. People have noted a certain coldness about the characters in the book, people who do not regard me as a particularly cold fish. Allen Funt, the inventor of the actual television program on which my "You're on Camera" is based, described the atmosphere to me as "Baudelairean," saying it was similar in that way to Mailer's *Deer Park*. There is, I think, a reason for this, perhaps a Jewish reason.

There are Jews who accept and Jews who deny. Marx, Freud,

---

* "The Good European." Teeth, Dying and Other Matters, 1972. There are more now.

and Trotsky are famous examples of denying Jews. In literature Mailer is one whose coldness may stand in part for a rejection of Jewish schmaltz. Much as I consciously deny this denial in my own work or life, something tells me this is my case. Hondorp is a conscientious denial of that notorious warmth and marvelous tradition of ethical accountability which I think of as Jewish. For me, there is perhaps a ray of hope: at the end of *Golk* Hondorp renounces his chilly way.

Perhaps I too, in my way, am renouncing my denial. At least I am now writing a book * which is about a man who is trying to reclaim what he has thrown away; and I am having emotional trouble with the book. My agent says that it doesn't sound like me. A colleague says that it is a sentimental book. I know something is wrong, but I have a feeling that I am both going to continue and going to pull myself up to the tone I want without faking it.

But one never knows. In the Rilke poem it says that if the body did not glow with the power reserved for the head, the statue wouldn't seem to burst out of its borders like a star. In German this goes

> und bräche nicht aus allen seinen Rändern
> aus wie ein Stern

Stern meaning "star." I shall conclude by saying that this Stern feels there's some chance he could not have broken out of his literary borders if the glow of his Jewish past had not somehow or other been transferred into the body of his work.

* *In Any Case.*

WORKING OUT A STORY *

In the theoretical table of organization which I believe serves as the basis of this course, the present talk will fall under the rubric "Efficient Cause, Parenthesis 'Genetic Fallacy'—One Week." If works of literature are one's subjects, then good Aristotelians rightly spend most of their time examining them and not their makers. Logicians rightly term fallacious a discussion of a work in terms of its designer, for who knows how remote the designer's intention was from the emergent design? If Shakespeare's diary were disinterred tomorrow and we read there that Hamlet was intended to be a portrait of Queen Elizabeth and Claudius of the Spanish Armada, I wonder how far we would go along with it. We would certainly read some things differently, but how many? (Would "Or to take arms against a sea of troubles" be a more significant line than it is?)

We have had scenarios, drafts, notes for projects from the hands of artists, and though we have become increasingly interested in these works for reasons which I shall try to discuss in a minute, more frequently than not they tend to blur our reading of the final version of the works. There are many reasons for this, but I shall now suggest only one: a man works on his design over, say, a year; he knows what he wants when he starts, but en route he discovers all sorts of things. A color which seemed fairly neutral when given to a distant barn turns out to be much brighter when seen in conjunction with a patch of sky above it. The relations are altered; the artist has to add a similar patch of the neutral color in the foreground. This in turn causes a spherical object on the ground to "take over" the picture. Then he has to . . . *etcetera ad*, not *infinitum*, simply *ad* whenever he sees *finem*. One day the work is finished, but it is not the work

* Talk given to a special humanities class at the University of Chicago (about 1962).

157

that he designed, although his design certainly bears some interesting relation to the ultimate work. The artist is at least the transmitter of the formal and telic "causes" of the work, and it is he who encounters the material, armed with these two—shall we call them?—tools. We can bear with him, no matter how loony his final pronouncements about his work, no matter how swollen with self-regard. But we will do better getting from him a longish story of the process of formation rather than an account of the work's genesis. Genesis is almost always permeated with hokum. It is after all an arbitrary point in a continuum, and only our theatrical urge makes us think it so important. Gibbon sitting on the steps regarding the friars walking in the Roman ruins, Luther meditating on the privy in the Wittenberg tower, Poincaré mounting the omnibus in Coutances, these are wonderful stories, and true ones, but they are as elliptic and hyperbolic as the first book of the Hebrew Bible, and perhaps the cosmological speculations of astronomer Hoyle or theoretician Lucretius.

In recent times we have become interested in the formation of artistic works and are less engaged by the glitter of genesis. Let me suggest reasons for this.

Kierkegaard talks in *Fear and Trembling* about three sorts of exemplary human beings: the saint, the hero, and the witness. The saint—his example is Abraham—is willing to sacrifice the whole meaning of the world—God's covenant—for the apparently contradictory injunction of God himself. The hero—K's example is Agamemnon—is willing to sacrifice his own happiness—in this case, Iphigenia—for the great cause. The third type, the witness, is much less exciting than the other two, and he sacrifices the life of noble action to record the noble actions of others; Melville's Ishmael is such a witness. Now for about two hundred years psychology, in the novel and in psychiatry has bored in ever closer to the actions and intentions of human beings. The great acts of heroism and sacrifice have been honeycombed with the analysis of *real motive,* of unconscious "intention." A man's great action may have more to do with his past than the demanding present; the hero may be a vicious brute, the saint a "pervert." Only the witness has not seriously suffered the onslaught. Why? Because he has not pretended to greatness of action, and so he has not minded his alteration from heroic self-sacrificer to wounded sublimator. The hero and saint have been crowded out of their niches, but the artist has grown— as a figure—in interest, and he is a frequent example of the anti-heroic hero. The artist's sketches, journals, diaries, first drafts, and letters are studied with the delighted absorption with which —as the Germans said of Goethe's—the Hellenes poured over the amours of Zeus. The "story of the story" Henry James called it, and so good a story was it that by the end of the nineteenth century Mallarmé could say that the only theme for a great poem was poetry itself, and Proust and Joyce could make the subject of great works the origin and formation of their own careers as writers.

The maker of a work reflects not so much upon the thing he wishes to present as upon ways of presenting it. Subjects usually "come." Especially if you're geared to watch for them by considering yourself an artist of a particular sort. Not being a sculptor, I don't look for the configurations of rocks, but for about seventeen or eighteen years now I have looked for stories, and so I frequently come upon story "material." More often than not, the material is discarded, or at least I think it's discarded. Now and then it turns up years later, sometimes in such altered form that I can't remember its origin.

The real job begins with working the thing out. Here's an example: A month or so ago I felt like writing about an uncle of mine who spent many lonely years living in an uptown New York hotel. His only diversion was a weekly poker game at the home of a man who, in Vienna decades before, had let rooms and lent money to Adolph Hitler. There were a lot of other things about my uncle that I thought could be pushed into a rather funny and pathetic story. But how to tell it, how to mine the story? I tried just rolling it out, but it seemed flat and episodic. I needed something else to get out the material. I then thought of another character for a story. This was a woman who put up postcards sent her by her employers and friends around the university. I thought one day a couple of weeks ago of putting "Miss Swindleman" and my uncle, now Harvey Mendel, into one story. Miss Swindleman was to be the tool to get the Mendel gold out of the mine. What happened was that Miss Swindleman took over the story. Mendel is still there, but Miss Swindleman proved—I think—to be the gold herself.*

Almost exactly the same thing happened to me a week ago. I've been thinking about another story,† this time about a wonderful dentist. I know the man, like him a lot, and find him both amusing and touching. How to mine his story? I thought at first of two possibilities: (1) a first-person account which would let the information about his personal troubles break in on a sympathetic but neutral narrator or (2) a subdued third-person account focusing on this man's relations with his father. Then, a few days ago, I found Miss Wilmott—perhaps an offshoot of Miss Swindleman—and now I see that the story is going to belong to her and perhaps to a Mr. Givens, a Negro house painter—vaguely modeled after an acquaintance—whom I threw in in one version of the story more or less for variety. (Whatever that means.) Though the story seems firm enough to me now, I'm having enough difficulty writing it so that it may well turn out to be something else. At least I feel as Joyce did when in sending a few fragments of what sixteen years later became *Finnegans Wake* to Harriet Weaver he wrote: "I work as much as I can because these are not fragments but active elements and when they are more and a little older they will begin to fuse of themselves" (*Letters,* edited by Gilbert, p. 204).

* See "Wanderers," in *Teeth, Dying, and Other Matters* (New York: Harper and Row, 1964).
† "Teeth," *ibid.*

THE WRITER AND HIS OUTSIDE JOBS

The magazine *Arts and Society* devoted a number to one of the era's standard topics, "The Artist in the University." I contributed the following brief, Shylockian statement. Since then I've given a talk on the subject, but it didn't work for this book. The talk dealt with the following topics:

1. Artists have almost always had professional lives outside their art.
2. In different eras writers have clustered in certain professions: the stage (after the public theaters opened in the 1570s); the pulpit in the early seventeenth century; the book world (printing, translating, editing) in the eighteenth century; periodicals and coupon clipping in the nineteenth century; teaching in the twentieth century.
3. Professional life has some effect on the artist's work:

my nature is subdu'd
To what it works in, like the dyer's hand.
Shakespeare, Sonnet 111

4. The effect can show in the development of genres: the Elizabethan-Jacobean revenge play (because of the success of Kyd's *Spanish Tragedy*): the complex private poetry of the seventeenth-century clergymen; the bookish books of the eighteenth century and then the length of the early novels (Shenstone said Richardson's *Clarissa* was long because the author was a printer); the self-confident scorn of the nineteenth-century rentiers and Bohemians (the Flauberts and the Rimbauds) and the sentiment and form of the great popular novelists (Dickens through Wells and Bennett); the philosophizing intimacy and genre testing of the twentieth-century teachers (Joyce of Berlitz, Pirandello of Bonn, Borges of Buenos Aires, Bellow of Chicago, and many others).

5. Unlike the earlier teacher-writers (Longfellow of Harvard, Herrick of Chicago, Moody of Wisconsin), the twentieth-century writer-teacher (beginning with Frost at Amherst in 1917) was hired as a writer. Since the writer's work—like the advanced researcher's in any field—is dissociative and even antiauthoritarian, the writer's presence in the university may have augmented the restlessness of the late 1960s, which may soon make the university an impossible haven for writers (who, like all researchers, need time and quiet—that is, laboratory conditions).

6. The doctor-writers—Empedocles, Rabelais, Schiller, Smollett, Keats, Jensen, Burton, Campion, Chekhov, Benn, Céline, W. C. Williams, Wang-Wei—and such doctors' sons as Flaubert, Proust, Sinclair Lewis, Auden, and Hemingway; the closeness of both professions to personal crisis, suffering, artful soothing, therapy and consolation.*

7. The relation of the immensely active public lives of Chaucer and Dante to their panoramic work.

8. The relationship of literature to the leisure of courtier, rentier, and more or less leisurely professional man; the change in professional standards (the effect on the professions) because of the writer-professionals.

9. The variety of writers' jobs: Van Brugh, architect; Prior, Perse, Dante, Chaucer, Claudel, *et al.,* diplomats; du Gard, paleographer; Corneille, Maeterlinck, Fielding, Boswell, lawyers; Aeschylus, Vigny (and many others), soldiers; Goethe, Malraux, ministers of state; Musil, engineer; Borges, Wilson, Mao Tse-Tung, librarians.

Statement †

Perhaps the artist who works more or less happily in the university should prod his ease as Kafka prodded his quiescent neu-

---

* This material has to do with the novel I've been writing since 1969.
† December 1, 1965.

rosis: "The deeper one digs one's pit, the quieter it becomes." This furred burrow one inhabits, is it too remote from the green world of change? Is one sleeping through one's time?

Who could say "No" with perfect assurance? Novel-writing lion hunters? Statesmen in pasture? The parson-poets of the seventeenth century? The actor-playwrights of the sixteenth? Fleet Street editors, nineteenth-century rentiers, Renaissance employees of Pope and Condottiere? Who couldn't "live" more by painting fewer walls, rhyming fewer lines?

Or is it that the college teacher's burrow is at a double remove, a burrow within a burrow? After all, the university has its special precincts, carefully chosen personnel; its lawns are tended by polite retainers; its meeting places command good behavior. Plus which the university artist is lapped in the institutional radiance of tenure and pension. What can he know of street wars, cutthroat trade, the reluctance of field and bone?

Yet.

In a university one can be lonely; one can cheat, love, be loved; one can even be heroic, villainous. One breathes, eats, works, pays, engenders. What the writer writes about—alteration, doubt, illusion, gain, loss, forgiveness—are not these in the university as in every human nutshell? And for those who work with "the times," what other twentieth-century institution is at once pulpit, seedbed, laboratory, marketplace, the crossroads of what's been and what's to be?

If one's need for isolation and rent money can be met, the university will serve as Shakespeare's theater served him. There is no paradise for the artist; and he can make whatever hell is necessary for him wherever he is.

On April 16, 1966, Robert Bly led a group of twenty-odd poets onto the stage of Mandel Hall at the University of Chicago to read poems in protest against the continuation of the Indochina war. I'd been invited to read something, had written my first poem in years and prepared a statement. When I arrived, Mr. Bly, a portly, well-dressed man, shook hands and said he was surprised to see me. (My name was on the program, though last and in smaller type.) "Here I am," I said, "poem in hand." "Well," he said, "go out in the audience. When the poets finish reading, there'll be an intermission, then anybody out there who wants to read can come up on stage." "OK," said I. Bly led the poets in single file onstage, made an impassioned address, read a poem of his own, and introduced Poet Number One (James Wright). Wright read briefly, was applauded, and gave way to Chairman Bly, who made another speech, read a poem of Cummings ("I Sing of Olaf"), and introduced Poet Number Two (George Starbuck). Thirty-five minutes. Nineteen poets to go. Plus eighteen pieces of Bly. I thought of enlisting in the Marines. Instead, I went home, tail not warming my legs.

Thus the following statement and the little version of Watts' Lullaby went unheard.

NOT PROTEST, BUT CELEBRATE

1

As usual, we poets are on the wrong track. As usual, we are ignoring our opportunities. For centuries we have been lumped with lunatics and lovers. Now, at last, we can mix wid de quality. It's poets after all who manufacture the crucial weaponry of this war, poets who are licensed to create fiction and distribute illusion. So our breed is expanding; for our new poets are in office;

masters of words, coiners of metaphor, skillful employers of abstraction.

With a difference. For our new poets realize their poems in fact. Look at the difference. Here is an old-fashioned poet's couplet:

> Forbear this liquid Fire, Fly,
> It is more fatal than the dry . . .

For this poet, Lovelace, the liquid fire is a mere conceit to tickle fancy. Compare today our poet General Westmoreland. He does not trifle with imaginative liquid fire; he employs the real thing. He *demonstrates* the power of the conceit, and not merely by tickling a fancy or two.

Another old-fashioned language poet, Dryden, wrote that he grew

> weary of his long-loved Mistris Rhyme.

There were

> Passions too fierce to be in Fetters bound,
> And Nature flies him [the poet] like Enchanted Ground.

For our new poets, there are few fetters and no enchanted ground. Their words crumble mountains and break nations. Talk of pity and terror. Our new poets, beginning with the same convictions of sacred office, the same desire to publish their work widely, the same devotion to illusion, the same linguistic tools, have gone so much further than we have. That's why I recommend that we substitute for the mixed delight of protest the earnest joy of celebration.

2

Perhaps you will permit this statement from one who has less right to be called a poet than anyone you have heard or will hear tonight from this stage. It deals with the special nature of the writer's protest to government policy. Discounting what counts most, the writer's protest as another point in the constellation of human disgust, hatred, and even fear of this almost unremitting infliction of pain, the writer's protest is against that leukemia of the imagination which disables men from comprehending the situation of other men and which, further, enables them to touch these others into abstractions, to convert men and women into *body counts.** The writer's protest takes in the apparatus of this slaughterer's touch, the deformation of language, rhetorical viciousness, the unconscious and the conscious misemployment of fiction. The writer believes fiction is reserved for the child at play, the daydreamer, and himself; in this reservation little blood is lost; there is no systematic obliteration of the ability to distinguish facts. The cover story, the daily handout, the corruption of fact by policy, the deformation of history by rhetoric, the dehumanization by enfeebled imaginative powers, these comprise the special objects of the writer's protest.

One can also say that we are still able to protest here; we are not clubbed down as were those who came to Baeza in Spain last February to pay tribute to the poet Machado; we are not imprisoned for our writings as were Andrei Sinyavsky and Yurii Daniel; we do not see writers assassinated as was Muhammad Massoud in today's Iran; we have not even had our exit permits canceled as were Manfred Bieler's and Günter Kunert's last month in East Germany (though Professor Hughes of the Harvard History Department has recently felt the cold air of Mrs. Knight † on his traveler's neck as have not a few others in these postwar years). But it is this very liberty from conspicuous tyranny which enables us to discern what threatens it.

I conclude with words written by Tolstoy in 1899 after the news that an American regiment participating in another "un-American war" had refused to advance to the town of Iloilo in the Philippines:

> The news is given out as something surprising. But the surprise is why such phenomena are not constantly repeated:

* Five years later the nation heard Lieutenant Calley talk of "wasting" the enemy.

† Head of the Passport Division, U.S. Department of State.

How could all those Russian, German, French, Italian, American people who have fought of late, at the will of strangers whom for the most part they do not respect, have gone to kill people of another nation, and to subject themselves to sufferings and death? . . .

If they do not throw down their guns and call out to their adversaries to do the same, it . . . is due to the fact that the people *believe* their governments, which assure them that all those burdens which men carry for the sake of war are imposed upon them for their own good. All the governments have with striking impudence always asserted that all those military preparations, even the wars themselves . . . are needed for the sake of peace . . . only when public opinion will brand the people who from fear or advantage sell their liberty . . . to become instruments of murder . . . will . . . a new era begin in the life of humanity.

The time is at hand.

We know of course it was not.

CRADLE SONG FOR A
VIETNAMESE CHILD
(AFTER ISAAC WATTS)

Hush, my Dear, lie still and slumber.
Holy Angels guard thy bed.
Heavenly blessings without number
Gently tumble on thy head.

Sleep, dear Babe, thy food and raiment,
House and limbs thy friends provide,
All without thy care or payment,
All thy wants are well supplied.

Milk—powdered—and lemonades,
A burnished silver Claymore bomb,
Licorice, wooden feet, bandades,
Salves to cool the gold napalm.

Soft, my Child, we won't chide thee,
Though thy lips bespeak small thanks.
'Tis the angels here beside thee,
Quaintly mounted in the tanks.

'Twas to save thee, Child, from dying,
Save thee, Dear, from bitter flame,
From the wicked northern lying
That these blond redeemers came.

Gentle Babe, so lapped in blisses,
Thou wilt never need wax old,
Touched so deep by silver kisses
Loosed from high in the blue cold.

STORM OVER THE UNIVERSITIES *

> If I were told I might write a book in which I should
> demonstrate beyond any doubt the correctness of my
> opinions on every social problem, I should not waste two
> hours on it; but if I were told that what I wrote would be
> read twenty years from now by people who are children
> today, and that they would weep and laugh over my book
> and love life more because of it, then I should devote all
> my life and strength to such a work.
>
> Leo Tolstoy, "Letter to Boborykin," July 1865

I gave the title of this talk over the telephone to Mrs. Stutzman
about ten weeks ago. She couldn't record the title properly, because her records were in the administration building of the
university, and at the time she had no access to them. The
building had been "taken over"—as the expression of the day
goes—by a group of students who were not going to leave the
building until their "nonnegotiable" demands had been met. The
university community was in a moderate frenzy of excitement,
compounded of fear, of pleasure in a break from routine, of pleasure in new contacts, and of the heady sensation of finding
oneself in the newspapers and on television. There were meetings of all sorts going on, days, nights, weekends. "Everyone"
became "concerned"; "everyone" searched for programs, reached
for analogies, found something in the siege situation which allowed him to express whatever rage or delight previously had to
seek more standardized outlets. The intensity of the situation
was increased by a sense that it was part of something much
larger. In the years since a thousand students massed to protest
the closing of the Bancroft Walk at Berkeley in September 1964,
student protests—which up to that time had often gone unre-
ported in the national and international press—were seen as and

*Speech given to a group of high school students visiting the University of
Chicago (April 12, 1969).

converted into an international student protest movement. So when students at Grambling College protested that famous little institution's overemphasis on football, or students at Prague Technical College massed to protest the inadequacy of the lighting system, the Doctors of Mediumology could classify them not as Football Troubles or Lighting System Troubles but as Student Protests, part of the Student Movement. The movement soon had pro- and anatagonists: Mario Savio of Berkeley, Rudi Dutschke of Berlin, Danny Cohn-Bendit of Nanterre/Paris, and Mark Rudd of Columbia became household words, villains to some, heroes to others, convenient pegs for the evening newsreels, spokesmen or foci for magazines. Against them in the Medium Game one found Grayson Kirk of Columbia and S. I. Hayakawa of San Francisco State.* The Gallup poll found that the subject of Student Protests was the most talked about in the country. No wonder, then, that when our own chapter was being written, many felt the enchantment of history in the making augmenting the rage and/or joy of response to broken routines. Biologists, mathematicians, theologians, historians, economists, psychologists issued thoughtful, impassioned statements, gave news conferences, buttonholed students, opened classes to this intoxicating subject.

So when Mrs. Stutzman asked for my topic, I—caught up in the general excitement, devoured by the general desire to investigate the remarkable events, and oblivious of my ignorance of the subject—said "Storm over the Universities." The title was adapted from the historian Hexter's account of the debate among seventeenth-century historians about the role the gentry played in the English revolution of the seventeenth century. Hexter's famous essay in *Encounter* went over the claims of one historian after another and showed that these claims had been based on peculiar emphases of selected data, that none of them had been

---

* A fine account of the San Francisco State ruckus is in *College Days in Earthquake County* by Herbert Wilner and Leo Litvak. (New York: Random House, 1972).

a full account of the seventeenth-century events, that his own wasn't a full account either, but at least it did a bit of historical dry cleaning, knocking dust out of some essays, clods out of others.

So my little talk to you today was to take some of the leading notions advanced by one side or another in the great student debates and show their limitations.

I began reading up: in Henry Adams' essays I found out about faculty-student relations at Harvard in his day and in his grandfather's. The trouble, thought Adams, was that people who give instruction shouldn't be meting out disciplinary penalties. Studies demanded social equality. Excellent for those gentlemanly days.

I went on to read about medieval universities, the town-gown riots in thirteenth-century Paris and Oxford, the troubles with foreign students, the clash of police with younger instructors, the disagreements of tenure professors with junior professors.

Then it turned out that every other magazine or newspaper— French, German, American, Italian, whatever—was full of interpretations, arguments, reports dealing with the great events. Presidents of colleges and nations issued statements; students of every stripe issued counterstatements. Scholars were assembling them all; the more assiduous or excitable were already issuing monographs and books. Each week one reads of new ones: the latest in my purview is Professor Lewis Feuer, who has leapt from seeing capitalists under every bed in the 1930s and Communists under every bed in the 1950s to seeing the Oedipus complex at the heart of every youth movement and expression (Nechaev, Sarajevo, Savio).

I wrote my piece one afternoon and, woe upon woes, saw that it would not have nourished a flea's shadow. I discussed the old student movements, dealt with ancient prescriptions about the young. Aristotle, for instance, saw that youth cared for action, not discourse, and said they shouldn't participate in political discussions, preferably not even hear them. Far be it from me to quibble with the antique great; they are most of what we know, one way or another, but I wasn't too confident about this particular gem. I talked further about television, its bringing to students such exciting capsules of complexity that most college instruction seemed dull; indeed, television could be credited with shaking up all sorts of old-fashioned hierarchical value systems. When a young man sees his President talking on Channel Five, then switches to the evening's rioter speaking into a microphone in front of the appliance store he's just looted on Channel Seven, and finds that after all there isn't *that* much difference in the wisdom of the two men, and indeed that the rioter is actually more fascinating because of his excitement and his clothes, well, it puts a bit of pressure on certain basic instruction.

So my piece went, going from history to the present and then zooming up to the finish line with a conclusion which at the moment escapes me, the psychic eyelid closing on what's unpleasant.

I am, thought I, not much of a thinker. If I'm anything, it's a story writer, somebody who gets at the truth in a roundabout way, by inventing people who feel intensely about something or other. Sometimes these people feel and act as I might, sometimes not. At any rate, the interest is in the coherence and amusement, the power of the story. Often the story can live only because lots of big things are left out, things that would crush the little things stories love to feed on.

So I was dissatisfied with my big overview piece. I decided then that I'd read this group a story. Well, I was writing a story then and I happened to finish it in time, but when I read it, it did not seem to relate in any way to the topic that had foamed from my excitement ten weeks ago. Besides, it was connected with other things I was writing, and it is not a good idea to count one of these little chickens before all the eggs get hatched. What I decided to do—finally—was to read a story which indirectly deals with the topic, a story about an imaginary teacher at this university written seven years ago. Whether it has any relevance —to use this grotesque word of the moment—to "Storm over the Universities" I don't know. I have purposely refrained from thinking about it.*

---

*I then read the story and, afterward, was rebuked by a teacher for avoiding the published topic.

A STATEMENT ON STUDENTS, DISCIPLINE, CURRICULUM, THE UNIVERSITY AND SOCIETY, WITH A POSTSCRIPT ON LOVE

In response to repeated requests by such eminent provocateurs as *The Maroon,** herewith one man's views about current topics.

Thought can connect everything in and out of nature, but only problems—defined perplexities—can be solved. Although the action which flows from definition usually overflows it, rational men can't advocate its dismissal.

Specifically, although the questions of discipline, curricular revision, student power, the university and society, and the deformities of national policy are connected, I see no rational way of dealing with them all at once. Therefore, a brief remark about each, beginning with the last:

I. National Policies: I favor the view that many of the policies and priorities of this and other states look like the products of madness or farce. Society is complicated, yes, but the schism between special and general interests menaces both. Among the national policies I'd like to see debated are (1) the dissolution of institutionalized brutality (such as the interplay of the so-called military-industrial-academic complex), (2) a guaranteed income geared to population planning and resettlement, (3) major revisions in inheritance taxes, gift arrangements, and the general tax structure, (4) "Manhattan projects" for air, water, food, clothing, and shelter, and (5) the dissolution of those allegiances which foster hatred and brutality rather than affection and invention (the end of invidious racial and class distinctions).

II. The University and Society: The Technological Utopia

* The University of Chicago student newspaper, which—submerged by statement in the spring of 1969—didn't print this one. It is a bit much.

(limned in I) will, in large measure, depend on the moral, historical, ethical, esthetic, and technical powers clustered in and transmitted by the universities. The training necessary to the creation and release of such powers flourishes when discipline (the mode of *studenthood*, a German philosopher might say) is a part of students and teachers. Every teacher studies, every student teaches, but there is a progress from learning to teaching to doing, complicated because each case is a variant. The educational, like the esthetic process comes close to the movement of life—birth, ripeness, decay—and there can be no perfected model. The best flourish in an atmosphere of affection, gaiety, high seriousness, courtesy, openness, and different sorts of respect for experiment and success, fallibility and failure.

Although every university undergoes constant redefinition (as its students and faculty change), I think certain elements of a good university are stable. A university which directly services particular ideologies or institutions is weaker than one which indirectly services many. In consequence, the sponsorship of projects, idea fashions, and research patterns should be frequently scrutinized and challenged.

III. Student Power: The strength and weakness of studentdom are identical: transience. As the world alters, so does the student body; alteration generates both repetition and innovation. To the extent that new students have the same or similar problems, the experience of sensitive tenure should be called on to cut Gordian knots; to the extent that new students have different problems, they should be registered, debated, and translated into reform. This involves a kind of organized student body—politicization?—a demonstration that students' thoughts and feelings can become elements of reformation.

IV. Curricular Revision: My view is that the present curricular pyramid should be stood on its pinhead. Every freshman should become—via small seminars—an assessor of evidence, an evaluator and definer of truths, that is, a scholar. Thus the new student will know the joys and difficulties of demonstrating complex truths. In addition, the distance between student and professor diminishes in seminars. The first year's curriculum should accommodate a great variety of specialized interests: so the lover of topology would spend, say, a third of his time topologizing, while the freshman gripped by racial problems would spend his time searching sources, examining contexts, devising therapies. Senior year should be breadth and connection.

V. Discipline: Student-faculty groups should handle disciplinary matters. In their first years students could deal with misdemeanors (pilfering, cheating). When the student becomes familiar with the university (its peculiar relationship to civil authorities, to its ancestors and siblings), he can function equally with the faculty on such matters as "disruptions." In my view, the university is a peculiar species of a peculiar social genus. Those who simultaneously employ and subvert that specialness are villainous. An explicit intent to destroy has more meaning in a university (where idea replaces action on center stage) than in the "outside world," and in my view should be—the debated—ground for expulsion.

Sentimental Postscript: One can love dogs, jello, books, can love what others think wicked or ugly, love what won't or can't return love. So this writer loves the University of Chicago, loves it even as he dislikes some of its elements, policies, and procedures, and hopes to help change them. Someday it may be that love will have nothing to do with consanguinity, the pleasures of the familiar, the pleasures of novelty, but now much of life's sweetness derives from such narrow affection. Let those who work against it make sure they have substitutes at hand or in mind.

6. Chicago Exhibits

. . . when one sought rest at Chicago, educational game started like rabbits from every building, and ran out of sight among thousands of its kind before one could mark its burrow.

The Education of Henry Adams

The two essays which follow were the most difficult to place in the book's table of organization, yet it seemed to me that they clearly belonged. The "I," about as adventurous as a piece of fly-paper, moves around and records. His opinions guide what he goes to see but not what he ends up seeing; what he sees is some of that moving scenery which alters his life. The report on the Modern Language Association convention is a bit too conventionally flip. Months later, one old friend, Ellison, told me angrily he did not go swimming with the bunnies, and we exchanged bad words, which kept us apart a couple of years. Another, Mailer, wrote a caviling letter to The New York Review *(where the piece appeared), which I answered in kind; since then we have not been on the old terms. (Writer-friendships are more fragile than grocer-friendships.)*

The Chicago piece was written for a Harper's *series on cities. (I remember Elizabeth Hardwick's fine essay on Boston.) It was written in a time of sunnier—blinder—politics. Mayor Daley, for instance, was accessible in those days. After the piece was printed, the* Sun-Times *(which reprinted it) brought me downtown to see the mayor again. I was told he'd liked the piece better than any which had been written about the city. In those days that didn't make me suspect I'd done a bad job. I liked Daley. He was calm; he knew everything you wanted to ask about taxes, water supply, city transportation, and more—the problems of juggling ethnic passions as he tried to "move the city." He didn't seem like Mike Royko's Boss, and I don't think he was. Then. A few years later, I sat next to him at lunch. I was wavering about him—he was up for re-election in 1967. I asked him about Johnson. He said he was a country boy who was learning very fast about cities. "You hear from him?" Giggle. "He calls every day or so." He was cool to Bobby, crazy about Ted. A political scientist across the room snottily told him to stop dragging the racial issue into the campaign. Daley flashed: "An issue meets you at every door in the city, you don't sweep it under the rug."*

179

He said he'd been learning plenty these last post-King-in-Chicago months. I voted for him again.

Then, that year, the new politics of television helped drive him back into the worst part of himself (the Ramapithecus who starred in the Democratic convention). A tongue that was never smooth got rougher and thicker. He'd blurt something and fire started in the street. When he was blamed, he hardly understood why. His press aide said he sat amidst the worldwide postconvention stories stunned and confused. Why didn't people understand? Didn't they know it was Stevenson who'd launched his career, that he was still a Stevenson man? I thought I'd write another piece about him. The press secretary said it looked like a good idea. I said I wanted to ask him about the claim Sandy Smith made in Life *that the worst Chicago police offenders at the convention came from mob-linked districts.*

I heard no more about doing a piece.

In 1972, unlike most of my university colleagues, I voted against Daley; though I didn't deny that Chicago was a prettier and pleasanter place for a professor to live than Buffalo, Cleveland, or New York, that the garbage got collected, that the middle-class streets were cleaned, and that Daley didn't scare people as much as Mussolini had.

INDIANS AND SETTLERS:
A LOOK AT THE MLA

The day after Christmas 1953 I broke out of the rippled aluminum siding of our Iowa chateau for three Chicago days of MLA.* City lights, city sights, old friends, old teachers, shop

* The annual convention of the Modern Language Association.

talk, and, first, a job to unlock the aluminum cage for good and all. On the Rock Island Rocket I sat beside the head of the Iowa Music Department, Philip Greeley Clapp, and remembered my friend Higgins, the pianist, stuck in Conway, Arkansas, at "the friendliest college in the South." Mr. Clapp was off for his own convention, he must be "hiring." By Moline, I was into Higgins' talents and misfortunes, sure that I could see rising in Clapp's gentle bulk the charter of Higgins' liberation from amicable Arkansas. I described Higgins' encounter with the Englishman who told him that he could not give recitals with such a name, not in England, couldn't even accompany a soloist, might, just might, get work pushing a piano onstage. "Names don't mean," groaned Mr. Clapp, "that much." There was no job for Higgins.

The job for which I'd come had been dangled before ninety-six other graduate students in the Midwest. We began assessing the choked stream that afternoon at the University Club, where the doorman pointed to the Illinois chairman's cold ambassador, a bulletin board upon which our ninety-seven names were linked by dashes to fifteen-minute appointments in various Palmer House suites. Chicago's wind had never bayoneted more fiercely through the overcoats, scarves, mittens, and fedoras which, like that bulletin board, buried us in featureless brotherhood. We saluted each other in the corridors, waited for interrogation by the professorial squadrons. ("How do you regard yourself, Mr. Stern?" "?" "Ultimately?" "?" "Writer or scholar?" "Mumble.") Our wire service reported that the chairman himself was talking in the grand ballroom with a man from Princeton, and later that the search for the fortunate fish had ended in that Eastern mainstream. We moved on to other suites, topping each other with gentle suavity: "Of course, I've always thought of the *Odyssey* as a picaresque." More and more frequently we met downstairs in the Polynesian Bar and Trader Vic's or across Michigan at the Art Institute in front of the strange peace of the *Grande Jatte*. The last day saw some of us on Clark Street, where girls with even bleaker futures than our own waved coffee-colored hips over our watered booze. "At least they don't wear badges." (The tall and myopic suffered neck pains after hours of MLA lapel gazing: "Excuse me, sir, I understand North . . . South Dakota's looking for someone in the eighteenth century.")

A dozen years later most of us were back in the Palmer House, though germane proliferations (American Association of Teachers of Slavic, the Mark Twain Society, the Linguistic Atlas) overflowed blocks into the Hilton, the Blackstone, the LaSalle. The forlorn brothers of 1953 now were soliciting the ultimate self-estimations of others. In those same corridors we remarked the same incidence of genteel theft from the publishers' carnival booths, roughly the same ratio of whiskey and amour, which puzzled the chambermaids: "What did you say this convention was?"

Now, though, it was a seller's market.* The appointments, worked out with numbered discs and a Domesday Dossier Book, were at the convenience of the young. Interviewers waited in suites while job seekers finished Manhattans at publishers' parties and came up to ask the questions: "You're still requiring a section of freshman English?" "What kind of medieval stuff goes on out there?" "How much did you say?"

Even the weather was mild, and small expeditions loped up to Jacques talking of yet finer restaurants in countries combed over on Fulbrights, Guggenheims, and ACLS grants. Overheard remarks went further afield: "In ten years they'll be teaching Swahili in the high schools." And staples: "They're hard to steal from California." Observations: "Nuns don't like to get out of elevators." And allusions: "They fret not at lonely convent rooms either." There were many more un-nunlike girls, readers of *Vogue* as well as *The Journal of English and Germanic Philology,* some attached to ambitious husbands as bait for the great. Pursuit was also allusive: "Do I dare to eat a peach?"

Conventioneers seldom admit the worth of papers in years they do not read them, but here and there one heard of "solid

---

* 1972: The pendulum has swung again; jobs are scarce.

jobs," of Professor Ehrlich's dazzling run through Gogol after the Slavic Teachers' dinner, of Professor Silverstein's attack on allegorical simplifications at the Chaucer section. Probably the same proportion of in-wit and pretense, sense and nonsense, to which historians were listening in San Francisco, scientists in Berkeley, philosophers in New York.

There was one change, though, that may mark a turning point for the MLA, and this was the heavy presence of poets, novelists, critics, and editors, mixed in painlessly with the old settlers. It looked as if the convention was the bonfire before which all American literature warmed its hands: New Directions and the University of Pittsburgh Press, *MP* and *The Iamb,* linguist, biographer, edition maker, teacher. There was not yet the scientist's fusion of experimenter-theorist and professor, but the congregation was at least similar to the American Political Science Association, whose membership lists Senators and professors, Truman and Hans Morgenthau.

As if to demonstrate the character of the 1965 convention, the American Studies Association invited John Cheever, Ralph Ellison, and Norman Mailer to talk about the relationship of the novelist to the country's power structures. The session was probably the best attended in the eighty-odd meetings of the MLA. Perhaps a couple of thousand professors of literature sat waiting the rare tidings under files of hundred-bulb chandeliers suspended from enormous carved pools of red lacquer.

Cheever began—nervous, small, elegant, rapidly, brilliantly witty. He machine-gunned a "parable of the diligent novelist" quitting a seminary, holing up in a slum, raping, knifing, buggering, becoming a spy, living, dying, writing on the roller coaster of experience; an undebatable swipe at the novel as document, the novelist as seared survivor. The audience, ablaze with pleasure, was largely unaware that the session's supposed subject, the novelist and power, had gone up in smoke. Then Ellison, who had arrived but an hour before, spoke, as usual without a note, about the attempt of sociologists to impose their statistical distortions of experience on the public and about writers who spread such ready-made anguish over the actual contours of their lives.

Mailer, in a fine blue suit, vest lapped in black silk, took the microphone like a bulldog and in a voice which gripped every throat in the room read a corrosive, brilliant, hit-and-run analysis of the failure of American novelists to keep up with a whirling country, their division into the opposed camps of those who fed titillating pap to the genteel and those, like Dreiser, who pointed American Julien Sorels to the doors of power (though *his* clumsiness could not open them). Down the road were "the metaphorical novelists," Hemingway and Faulkner, one of whom described the paw, the other the dreams of the social beast; then around a corner, where Dos Passos appeared as a genteel novelist (the author of *The Naked and the Dead* knows this corner well), to the real object of the analysis, *Herzog,* Dreiser's neurotic grandson, a triumph of sensibility despite its failure to depict society and its absorption in a character so foolish "you wouldn't have him in your living room."* If *Herzog* stood for the novel's failure, the absurd novel (whose finest creature was *The Magic Christian*) was the symptom of the country's failure.

Breathless with tension under the lacquer, the audience heard a final Savonarolesque call for the novel to redress the brutal inflictions of the times, Vietnam, psychotic rapine, "the motorcycled lions roaring across the land." The pretty, bespectacled miss beside me released a sigh for that one talent which would suffer no death today. The settlers thundered applause, their hunger for retail violence and perilous survival slaked by a master.

Upstairs, a press conference, largely devoted to Mailer and Ellison's explaining to the CBS man why they were glad their talks weren't taped, why television and documentary necessarily distort reality. A Viennese lady reporter requested information about literary influences and was escorted to the elevator by Mailer. Where too he was a delightful performer. In the carful

*As I have been in Mailer's "living room" at a party, I find this a very, very severe judgement. (Or was the "you" here some remarkably fastidious person in the audience?)

of goggling professors, sloshing his drink, he called out "Nine" as the elevator hurtled from Ten, and when released at Seven he fired genially at the uniformed auntie from his fortress of licensed clowning, "You Jew," and rollicked like a sailor down the mirrored corridor, leaving behind a small carnage of titillated shock. It was the right note for this MLA—the twitting of old mania, the domesticated recklessness, the comic flip to inertia. It was far from the queues in front of bulletin boards, the intellectual mob stirring in clerical treason.

Two hours later Cheever and Mailer * were off to Hugh Hefner's baronial nunnery, swimming, arguing with bunnies, eating dinner from a menu divided into à la carte and bunny sections: "Monday—Codfish Cakes, Green Beans, Rice Pudding."

In a few years the settlers may be trailing the Indians down here; the bunnies too wear badges, and the tent is getting bigger and bigger.

* 1972: The original had Ellison in here.

CHICAGO: MOSTLY A LOVE LETTER

1

I am too old now to think that love has much to do with reciprocity, though that used to be what distinguished it from liking. "You love what can love you," said my father, "and anything else you like. Don't say you love Brown Betty." But I did love that roasted, sugary apple stuff capped with the white hard sauce, and I love the unresponding thing I write of now.* Which is a difficulty.

My defense of Chicago bristles with the convert's paranoia, as my initial view of it—in June 1952—was compromised by that disease called "New Yorkitis": "provincialism, proud ignorance of the rest of the nation, and lofty condescension toward cities of lesser note."

Like most Chicago visitors since Father Marquette made portage here in the seventeenth century, I was on my way to some other place. Chicago was for me a standard composite: the stockyards, Colonel McCormick, the Capone syndicate, Seurat's *Grand Jatte* at the Art Institute (which in my sole art course was considered the goal toward which the nineteenth century moved), the university where Hutchins, Fermi, and the Oriental Institute were a bonfire in the menacing cold of the Midwest, and winds, physical and oratorical. But the view from my train window was something. Even in that odd time of the steel strike, with the smokestacks of Gary and East Chicago looking as remote as the heads of Easter Island, the exhibition of power was astonishing. At Whiting, the monster even stirred: Standard Oil stacks breathed rainbow fires, fat white drums gurgled repletion, gondolas rattled coke back and forth, and over all lay the indolent sweet smell of sulphur and oil. Then the track tangled with fifty others; we dove in the dark toward the LaSalle Street station.

* 1961.

I had something to do in Chicago between trains, and that was to call the father of a friend, who, like myself, had spent the last three years in Europe.

He serves as well as anyone for my first notion of a Chicagoan: a devoted reader of the World's Greatest Newspaper, a Republican for whom Senator [Robert] Taft meant thunder on the left. He arrived puffing, a two hundred pounder, took my elbow, and moved me out of the station under the elevated tracks toward State Street. There was something he wanted to show me. Past bars, chop suey and tamale joints, pawnbrokers, tattoo parlors, and what struck even my New York-trained senses as a remarkably diverse crowd, we came to State Street.

"There," he said, pointing. "What do you think of that?"

"That" was the display window of a men's haberdasher, where a sitting dummy sported a blue suit whose tag read $32.95 and a name something like Dacron. "Wash it, hang it up, and it looks as if the tailor had pressed it," said my guide, radiant at showing me what a first visitor to Chicago should see.

A year before, a friend in Iowa City had written that he'd gone into a clothing store there and asked for pants with a certain narrowed cuff that he'd seen in a *New Yorker* ad. The salesman informed him that "that hasn't even hit Chicago yet." This occult instance of the cultural lag, which my New York mind assumed without questioning, was confirmed by my guided tour of what counted in the city. A backwash of Eastern tides— that was Chicago; though perhaps when the factories were not on strike, it might be regarded as an arterial system for the Eastern heart.

On the train my seat neighbor advised me to get a drink before we crossed the Mississippi; no liquor was served in Iowa. After the river more than the liquor supply seemed cut off. The country was mortally ugly. It looked as if Chicago had drained the agricultural lands which had nourished its monstrous, materialist innocence; I sympathized with Mrs. O'Leary's cow, that incarnation of pastoral revenge.

2

Visitors are apt to come to Chicago to see what it lacks. The Ojibway Indians had turned their noses from the wild onion tracts whose skunky smell they called *che-ca-gou;* most assessments since have been heavy with elegiac distaste.

The elegists are former inhabitants who mourn the vanished glories of the opera—Melba, Mary Garden, and Louis Sullivan's wonderful auditorium *—the frame mansions of Prairie Avenue, the literary excitement and legitimate theaters of the 1920s, the camaraderie of radical politics in the 1930s, the energetic acquisitiveness of the 1880s, the frontier culture of the 1830s, anything which stands for the elegist's own vanished bliss.

These morticians were often English visitors (Chesterton, Kipling, William T. Stead, author of *If Christ Came to Chicago*); more and more frequently they have been, as I at first was, professional New Yorkers.

The best-known recent mortician was *The New Yorker* magazine's [late] A. J. Liebling, who complained in 1952 about Chicago's slow horses, feeble baseball clubs, fatigued strip shows, third-rate bars, the absence of the long-planned St. Lawrence Seaway, and the Hutchins Children's Crusade of twelve-year-old matriculants at the University of Chicago. Liebling concluded that the city had stopped around 1930 "as suddenly as a front-running horse with a poor man's last two dollars on his nose." His piece, which still rankles in those Chicago noses which sniff New York breezes for the local weather, was called "Second City." The name was taken over by the brilliant group of cabaret players who, from a remodeled Chinese laundry on North Wells Street, spread their new version of topical satire across the country.

Such sublimation is not uncharacteristic of Chicago. In fact, if cities have character—and have, therefore, what Nietzsche said men of character always have, a typical experience which recurs over and over again—then Chicago's experience might well be

* Now restored and in use.

the Great Bounce Back. The city made its greatest leaps after the Fort Dearborn massacre, the Great Fire of 1871 and the industrial sickness of the 1880s and '90s.

As for Liebling's complaints—those at least that could not be leveled at any megalopolis or were not indisputably matters of his taste—they seem to have lost their point. The St. Lawrence Seaway is built and Chicago operates as a world as well as a national port; the White Sox won the pennant in 1959; a Chicago horse won the Derby in 1960 (and another shares the record for the world's fastest mile *); and the University of Chicago filtered the hysteria and simplistic abstraction—if also some excitement—from the Hutchins system.†

Visitors come to Chicago with comparisons and blueprints; inhabitants feel for the city as they feel about their lives: Chicago is what happens to you here, and it is hard to separate what it is from what you are. Yet one looks for constants.

First, its history, though this doesn't go far. A list of arranged Chicago events tells as much about the quality of Chicago life as a furniture inventory about the family which slouches in the chairs and snores in the beds.

Fiction is more helpful, but in a sense too helpful. Chicago does have the longest line of fine realistic writers in the country— from Mrs. Kinzie to Joseph Kirkland, Hamlin Garland, Dreiser, Farrell, Algren, and Saul Bellow (whose *Augie March* is perhaps the greatest of all American city novels), but fine fiction lives in its particulars, and Carrie Meeber's Chicago is not Frankie Machine's, nor Augie's; one cannot distinguish the place from the artistic temperament that renders it.

Topography is more useful, but no constant. What counts here topographically, what affects life, has changed and changes now in every windy second. Like Amsterdam, Chicago built on reclaimed lake bottom, built canals, reversed the course of its river (a classic work of modern sanitary engineering), built in

---

* I have not troubled to check the next decade's record book.

† My biased guess is that it's as good a university as any in the country.

the last seventy years the famous creations of Sullivan, Wright, Holabird, Root, and van der Rohe, and is now [1961] building such works of scope and splendor as Goldberg's sixty-story twin cylinders, the Marina City apartments.*

One must stick with what one knows. For me it is a question of trying to square that first view of Chicago with those I've had of the city twenty-four hours a day for the past six years.

My first discovery is that the city's become manageable for me. It's not only that I can find my way around a twentieth of it, but I feel that in a small way I count for something here. In our time everyone is at least numbered; but *counting,* the official version of loving, is an activity: one is not only counted, one counts. One is, if not needed, at least potentially heeded, a minuscule but distinct existence on the roiled surface.

In a famous essay on cities, Georg Simmel wrote that Athens' greatness was due in part to its being a group of small towns as well as a metropolis. This is still true of Chicago.

In the New York in which I grew up neighborhood was a method of exclusion. Wandering around, you made your own. Now it is true that there are infernal neighborhoods in Chicago, great blotches of wooden flats put up after the fire but before the brick-enjoining ordinances of the 1890s, stony blocks of filth strangled by hang-dog little factories, terrorized by the entrepreneurs of policy wheel and heroin, but most Chicago neighborhoods are geographic centers of power and flavor †—Bohemian, Lithuanian, Italian, Chinese, Greek, Mexican—and reveal themselves in distinct cuisine, architecture, speech, gesture, physiognomy. It is their variety which points to what is crucial for a great city, the powerful suggestion of human possibilities.

The people in my own neighborhood, Hyde Park, came to realize some of these possibilities recently, as they pioneered a

---

* The finest buildings since 1962 are Mies van der Rohe's Federal Plaza and the Lake Point Towers apartments. The architectural tradition is the most vital in the city; perhaps the feeling for stone accounts for a certain stoniness of feeling about other urban matters.

† The neighborhoods continue to break up.

redevelopment program which transformed a crime-pocked swamp into one of the great neighborhoods of the country. The transformation involved a hundred million dollars of public and private funds and hundreds of dwellings. It was conceived, planned, fought for, and is directed almost entirely by the neighborhood's own inhabitants.* The result is more than improved visibility and safety. There is a sense here in Hyde Park of that "common life for a noble end" which is neither smug, cozy, nor intrusively collective, but which bespeaks the possibility of triumphant alteration and constitutes a psychological treasure for no small number of individual Hyde Parkers.† This sense saturates the first-class neighborhood weekly (the Hyde Park *Herald*), a hundred Hyde Park charitable ventures, art centers, concerts, speeches, and an alderman's election which here is a contest second only to the presidential one in partisan fury.

If neighborhood is a way of triggering variety and individual accomplishment for large numbers, it can easily become a fetishistic crippler of a major city. Even at best, there is a smack of provincial vanity in such local devotion and, worse, a straitening enclosure on more than space. Such feeling is opposed to the major general feeling I have about Chicago, and that is its openness—its apparent ability to grow unopposed west, south, north, and up ‡ (it was for Chicago that the skyscraper-hating Wright designed a mile-high building)—but always attached to the grandest sign of its openness, the lake.

No city that I know is so dependent for pleasure and usefulness on a body of water as Chicago is on the great lake which it amorously receives into itself. The lake is an immense resort, a supplier of water, a receiver of cargoes, a purifier of waste, and a harbor for the searchers of solitude—fishermen, sailors,

* Those of us who could afford it; this was the burgher blindness of 1962.

† The highfalutin' rhetoric was my burgher shield.

‡ Mayor Daley is anxious to have it grow east: he wants a third airport in Lake Michigan. Perhaps it can be called the *Circus Maximus Daleyiensis*.

artists, lovers. Chicago outlines the lake with question-mark-shaped beaches pointed at the tip with clumps of handsome museums and apartment houses whose glass skin reflects the outlying factory fires whose profits are their source.

Behind this spectacular façade the western plain erupts into what for me is little-known brush—small factories gripped by antique tenements, new apartments rising out of treeless pavement, pretty homes grazing in small lawns, or files of efficiency units which know the lake largely by reputation. Yet the lake counts for the west, if indirectly, for it mothered the marsh in which Chicago rose. Unlike rock-bottomed New York, Chicago's bottom is soft, and the result is that she's green. *Urbs in horto* is the city motto. For years she was known as "the garden city," and her park system is studied the world over. Even a slum, simmering in ash, sports its pair of cottonwood trees and plank of grass.*

To accommodate the green, Chicago built its streets wide—unlike, say, Harlem, where incarcerated eyes glare ten yards across the street to other locked eyes. Here eyes are at least veiled by leaves. (Nero, who knew the deadliness of propinquity, decreed that Roman streets must be twice as wide as their houses' height.)

The Chicago green may be as important as the famous $2.50 minimum wage [1961] which has drawn a great migration from Kentucky hills and Mississippi levees to the steel mills, although now and then a volley of automation sends it right back, or into domestic service in the new suburbs bubbling up continuously west and south.

Chicago has always had strong Southern ties, even after the building of the Erie Canal changed it from a city dependent on New Orleans river trade to a Northern link between the East and the West. It has employed Southern workers, supplied Southern factories with machines, money, and engineers; and in my view it has some of the ease of Southern cities today. This is

* And, on occasion, unwanted company.

due in part to the large numbers of poor Negroes * who discover the city's natural delights—the lake fishing, the ball parks (Wrigley Field is advertised as a good place to have a picnic), the free concerts in Grant Park, the free sailing lessons at the Sixty-third Street harbor, the Y expeditions to the woods and dunes. The poor Negro practices and invites an ease of life which he has rescued from the leprous exclusions of this country.† Such exclusion, and the new fellowship of the Negro with the equally displaced hillbillies, is supposedly behind the revival of blues singing in the tiny South Side Negro bars. It is only one chapter in Chicago's long Negro history, which began with the anonymous Indian's joke that Pointe du Saible, the "first white man" to come to Chicago, was a Negro.‡

3

Flavor and openness, roses and peaches in the street. Not quite. If cities have typical experiences, they may have typical vices. Perhaps Chicago's vice is a blinding concentration on the immediate and the future, accompanied by merciless abuse of its past. It's been said that the city's only genuflection to history is the turn that Michigan Avenue, Chicago's elegant showplace of the new, makes at the grotesque old water tower, the sole survivor of the Great Fire in the near North Side. Recently, Sullivan's beautiful, sagging Garrick Theater was ripped down, despite an agitation which should have raised a Lazarus, let alone

* "Blacks" was unacceptable in 1962.

† Few would hesitate to deride such an observation today; but there's truth here still, cousin to the more acceptable notion that the black talent bank is the greatest in the country. Survival rootage has already shown beauty and power above ground.

‡ This is the most antiquated section of the piece. When Martin Luther King set up headquarters in Chicago back in 1966, black misery found a tongue, and Mayor Daley showed the first major crack in his *urbanity*. From his initial misunderstanding of King to the convention of 1968, there is a straight line. Not, however, one which necessarily leads to disaster. Chicago knows it is and has been seriously ill. Whether or not in time for therapy is still moot.

the two hundred thousand dollars needed to buy and restore it.*
What Wright called "the declaration of independence for American architecture"—his Robie House of 1909—almost went the
same way, until a New York developer bought it as headquarters
for the Hyde Park Redevelopment Project.† The Indiana Dunes,
Chicago's "playground," is being whittled away by the vicious
rapacity of Indiana steel companies, despite the assiduous work
of Hyde Park's former alderman Senator Paul Douglas.‡

"Sweep away," says Chicago, confident in the metabolism
which grew it out of the onion marshes into the prototypical
city of industrialism in fifty years.

There are metropolitan sores which cannot be swept away.
On the South Side the Negro schools sink into a dark age of
violence. The city's transportation founders as the Illinois legislature—rural, Republican, and Chicago-hating—refuses it a
proper share of tax revenues. Meanwhile, the parasitic, con-
temptuous suburbs siphon the city's wealth and invest theirs in
their own backyards. In the city itself, culture is thin and gaudy
—statistics and clubs replacing the reading of books or the pride
in and patronage of local artists: young Easley Blackwood's sym-
phonies will probably be performed in San Antonio before the
brilliant Chicago Symphony (under Reiner, the best but most
conservative in America) condescends to them. §

Cynical indolence or fluttery naiveté clot serious standards of
criticism in the newspapers, ‖ and if it were not for *Poetry* magazine and the marvelous FM station WFMT, Chicagoans would
have almost no local source of serious contemporary opinion

* Sullivan's Stock Exchange Building is turning into scrap as I write
this note (November, 1971).

† It is now headquarters of the Adlai Stevenson Institute of International Affairs.

‡ Douglas is retired; the whittling continues, although there is a Dunes
National Park.

§ Under Solti and Giulini the orchestra is still the best. And far less
stodgy.

‖ 1972: The criticism is much better.

outside the university.* Chicagoans—like most Americans—resent paying as much for a fine novel as a fine steak, and such sniveling decadence of values is scarcely veiled by the self-gratulating, hard-boiled sentimentality which is the Chicago style.

Chicago does not satisfy those for whom New York's enfilade of sensation is the only barrier to ennui. On the other hand, for those who, like myself, need the variety of a great city but cannot exist in an unremitting eventfulness, Chicago's sores are those incidental to the pursuit of love.

To round off my notions about Chicago, I decided to talk with a man who somehow seemed emblematic of the city—its mayor, Richard Daley. I knew that he'd been born in Chicago about sixty years ago and that he lived with his wife and seven children in the same neighborhood in which he'd grown up. One of the most powerful politicians in America, he ate the hardtack of local Democratic politics without losing his capacity to distinguish it from better fare. Strong where weakness would lead to his extinction, yielding when refusal would mean loss of more than the immediate, enamored of his city, but more important, conscious of what its greatness is, Daley has for seven years been one of the best mayors in the world.†

As is almost always the case when you meet a man whose picture you have seen often in the newspapers, you're momentarily taken aback by the colors of face and clothes. The mayor was a flash of blue to me—eyes, tie, suit. He sat alone in a fine office—a stocky man whose features worked through a banquet luxury of flesh. Assured, patiently curious, extremely courteous, he waited for my questions.

I thought that I could relax him away from the manner of a

* This was itself a provincial view.
† I stick with this view but add only that Lord Acton's great maxim applies. "Between seven years and seventeen falls the shadow." Those who stay in power get testy, get abstract; their hangers-on grow indolent and vicious. The Daley I sat beside in 1967 was still forceful, sympathetic, and alert. He cared and he worked; but meanwhile the narrow intelligence bristled evermore with age and frustration.

public man by asking him about his childhood memories of the city, but very quickly these memories led into general talk about city problems. We talked for thirty-five minutes about the city's growth pains and wounds, its apparatus of therapy and salvage, the pile of continuous and everyday problems in whose details he was soaked without being drowned.

Of the public men I've met, none has seemed more in command of his own concerns than Daley, and the sympathy which I felt for him was all the more remarkable in that he and I could scarcely be more different.

In time I began to feel that I was holding up the settlement of a strike, and I got up. The mayor invited me to come back and talk things over as if he were a county JP lounging in front of a bellied stove, and I the first man he'd talked with in years. Temporary or not, the decency and warmth were immensely winning, and walking out of the huge Corinthian-pillared fortress of City Hall, I felt the mayor's emblematic quality was his essential high-mindedness.

That afternoon I took my children to the Point, a grassy South Side promontory jutting into the lake not far from the university. It is coiffeured now with three huge aluminum lollipops —radar gear *—under which lounge Hyde Parkers of every age, shape, color, and language. They come each summer day to swim, sun, read, talk, play casino, fry hamburgers on hibachis, and dispute the warnings of occasional policemen vainly attempting to enforce the "No Swimming" signs painted in yellow on the four-tier stone terrace rising from the lake. Petitions to the Fifth Ward's alderman, Despres—the council's only independent and second non-Democrat †—about the badgering policemen or the motorboats which swing their water skiers toward the illegal swimmers pass from hand to hand. The Hyde Parkers sign with the righteous ease of habitual public complainers and go back to the water or to the *Nicomachean Ethics*.

---

* 1972: The aluminum curlers have been removed. No longer can the Army track Michigan fleas.

† A few more have joined Mr. Despres.

Five miles away the summer's sixth gangland killing victim is being removed from a Cadillac on the Wacker Drive; twenty blocks south the police are keeping a "wade-in" demonstration against the stolid white burghers of Rainbow Beach * from becoming more than a demonstration. But here at the Point, the day's work done, an evening of hi-fi and a book or a trip to the trotters at Sportsman's Park ahead of him, the besummered Chicagoan takes in some of the grace, ease, and beauty of his city.

* There are very few white burghers there now.

7. *Others*

As he disappears from sight
his teeth glow with a soft uranium light
    and you can't make out his words . . .
    I think for years now he's been
having many sons
by beautiful, secret wives . . .
    Craig Sterry
    "No One Can Be Trusted, Something Tells Me . . . ,"
    from *Quickly Aging Here:*
    Some Poets of the 1970s
    edited by Geoff Hewitt

    I found no truth in one report at least—
    That if you tracked him to his home, down lanes
    Beyond the Jewry, and as clean to pace,
    You found he ate his supper in a room
    Blazing with lights, four Titians on the wall,
    And twenty naked girls to change his plate!
    Poor man, he lived another kind of life . . .
        Robert Browning
        "How It Strikes a Contemporary,"
        from *Men and Women*

The most remarkable people are usually those most remarked.
Not necessarily better, wiser, subtler, those who are called upon
for opinions, decisions, and actions are almost always better,
wiser, and subtler for their responses. The act of speaking out
alters people, as living in sun instead of fog alters them.

Few fiction writers spend much time on "historical charac-
ters," the remarkable actors and speechmakers of public chroni-
cles. When they do, the results are rarely triumphs. Historical
characters are often interesting as versions of "the real orig-
inals," known to readers from other sources. Seldom does fiction
transform an historical character. Shakespeare's Richards,
Dante's popes, and Tolstoy's Napoleon function in special ways;
at best, readers have new notions about the meaning of their
actions. War and Peace *required the vanity, pettiness, and uncer-*
tainty of its Napoleon (although Tolstoy is too grand to make
him a doll of these traits). For Richard the Third, *Shakespeare*
wanted a lyric ranter, an enchanting rat; the want contrived a
*Richard out of some of the historical clichés of the day.**

In Dante the characters simplify around the traits which place
them where they are in the Great Design. In hell they darken
around their sin:

ma giu s'abbuia
l'ombre di fuor, come la mente e trista
Paradiso, IX, 71

Dante meant that they could do little but think about their sin.
(In his physical, dramatic version of their mental difficulty they
act what they think.) It is true that powerful feeling simplifies us.
At least it enables us to deal with experience in one way. This
goes for love as well as agony.

Fictional characters are simpler than the simplest real person;
every day contains so many thoughts, impressions, and gestures
that the most complicated character in literature can never be

* Shakespeare's "historical characters" aren't historical in the modern
sense; expectations of accuracy have altered.

given a hundredth of them. (The sacredness of human life is no accidental sentiment.) The made-up characters of fiction and biography are made to appear complex and complete because they answer every—narrative—question asked of them. In life one can say "What if he'd gone to school?" or "What if we'd made love?" No sensible person asks what Hamlet majored in. One can ask, however, what Napoleon did in those hours his biographers don't treat; and this is the great threat to the grandeur of biography.

Sometimes, the historian-reporter-biographer takes poetic liberties * with "real people." Mailer's versions of the astronauts in Of a Fire on the Moon *look licentious. The map is more complicated than the terrain to which it's supposedly a guide. This doesn't mean that Mailer's versions are more complicated than the originals. The astronauts can swallow Mailer's view (and fifty others) and convert it to their own thinking and behavior. (I'd guess that Neil Armstrong took some of Mailer's description as prescription; Frank Borman, on the other hand, thought the book more lunatic than lunar.) An established artist develops an audience which knows how to read him. Mailer has established a Maileresque way of reading (or listening to) Mailer. By now his readers know the sort of investment he has in his "reports." Mailer is not only willing to accept the egg on his face; his next book usually starts with a description of it.*

Fictional complexity also comes under fire, I think illegitimately. Zola said of Stendhal's world: "Life is simpler than that." Yet one of the social jobs of literature is complicating what we think about and experience. Every few years literature creates another model which makes moving sense out of lively data, and, say—to use the favorite example of literary historians—the provincial housewife realizes she's Madame Bovary and kills herself.

A number of my friends are men and women whose work makes people interested in their lives. I've not written much about any of them. Since portraits are in a sense epitaphs (see

---

* In a way, he always does.

*page 40) and one wants one's friends around alive, even kick-
ing, one holds back. Anyway, alive they can digest your version
and turn it into something ridiculously inadequate. (The modern
saints—Gandhi, Dolci, and the like—seemed to enjoy shaking
up the plaster versions of themselves. The most pathetic people
are centerless bags of energy who constantly require commentators in order to know where they are.) Another reason for my
restraint is fear of retaliation. A man as full of defects as this
writer will be cautious.*

*The miniature portraits in this section were written immedi-
ately after hearing about the person's death. In their arrangement
here, the "other" increasingly dominates the small space. The
portrait-size made it imperative to conceal the poverty of "sup-
porting data," for what is wanted is a sharp impression.**

* I've fathered four or five of those literary mules, the interview.
There, portraiture should give way to drama. But it's the "interviewee"
who should arrange the drama. This happened with three of the interviews (Mailer, Ellison, and Lillian Hellman). The fourth (Borges) I
arranged myself; but it still remains "his" piece and I can only point
anyone interested in it to the Summer 1969 issue of *The American
Scholar.* (Mailer reprinted our interview in *Advertisements for Myself,*
Ellison his in *Shadow and Act;* the Hellman piece appeared in *Contact*
about a dozen years ago.) Of the few interviews done with me, I found
it difficult to manipulate opinion into drama; and the opinions are mostly
in this book, in one form or another.

A MEMORY OF FORSTER

> He traced his decomposition—his work had been soft, his
> books soft, he had softened his relations with other men.
> He had seen good in everything, and this is itself a sign of
> decay. Whatever occurred he had been appreciative, tol-
> erant, pliant. Consequently he had been a success . . . it
> was the moment in civilization for his type.
>
> E. M. Forster, "The Point of It"

Mr. Forster, eighty-four then in 1963, was next to me at table
(the maneuver of my friend, a fellow of King's College). It was
summer; high table was three sides of a rectangle in a small dining room off the Commons Room. Forster had been invited back
to this decorous Georgian quadrangle after World War II. It
was his home, he was its jewel, the icon of English literary
civility.

A long man, now stooped and rounded, Forster's lined face
was shyly forward, a wise old dog's face. His movements had
the slow grace of economy and security, the movements of a man
who has learned how to live a long time.

A man of old accomplishment and long modesty, Forster had
perhaps surrendered too early to self-criticism. Or had he
found, as years passed, that what he'd done survived much that
was more flamboyant? The man who had domesticated English
mysticism could not be surprised by odd survivals.

Extremely courteous, he had a tolerance founded in that persistent curiosity which saw his absorption in the newspapers, the
new books. He spoke of a fine review in *The Observer*, of the
day's menu, of Cambridge out of term. A small emanation of the
peculiar worked from the wit-sheathed gentility. There had been
a heavy burden of chicken in recent menus; he would scrawl a

note about it in the fellows' commentary book. He was so pleased the other day to receive a copy of the first book of his to be translated into Italian; he wondered why they bothered now. He enjoyed Santha Rama Rau's dramatization of *A Passage to India,* but again the success was puzzling. It sounded to me as if he felt that his work was a piece of antique family silver, brought out every ten years or so for some special turn in sympathetic nostalgia.

Alert to what went on, inoculated against the familiar gestures and self-willed eccentricity of this snug collegiate galley, the secret Forster was still at work; the Man of Sympathy who had invented unsentimental ways of conveying it.

At an age when most men are alert to others only from fear of being injured by them, Forster's alertness was ceremonious, inflected with his own rhythm and bite. Here is an instance: My friend had gone beyond the standard offering and bought a bottle of red wine. I drank, relaxed, conversed, grew jocular, expansive, illustrative, and swept the half-filled bottle onto the figured white tablecloth. Talk stopped. Forty eyes studied the small red sea. I ventured: "I wonder if anyone has ever made so clumsy a debut at your table?" There was a long and, for me, not unweighted pause. Mr. Forster was visibly reflecting, eyes back researching high-table debuts. Survey concluded, he turned to me, and in the slightly burred precision of his speech, said: "I'm not entirely certain of that."

Ah well, minutes later, in the Commons Room, digesting my clumsiness and my friend's rebuke, I looked up to Mr. Forster holding out a clipping from *The Observer.* "Here's that review," he said. "I hope you'll agree with me about it."

That summer I went up to his rooms two or three times. At least to the long, high-ceilinged room with the blue china, the family portraits, the leather chair and hassock before the fireplace, the cluttered table where he might be found writing notes. If I had a child with me, Forster would move slowly across the room to a cabinet for a box of candy, would offer it with enormous sweetness to the little boy, and then give him some book or trinket. To me he talked of life, letters, and—modestly—himself. He still got around a bit. He had a flat in London on the fifth floor of a walk-up; it had recently been burgled, his first experience of that. He spoke of the young policeman who had become a close friend, of the man's family with whom he loved to stay up in the north "where they make goods, not words." His personal talk had the direct warmth which is so much a part of the great English novels, a warmth which began flickering in his own work and, in different ways, in Bennett's, Wells', and Virginia Woolf's, and which burned out in the mockery and anger of the postwar years. The men who could "make you see the whole of everything at once" (*A Room with a View*) were hard to believe after 1945.

Last year [1969], age ninety, there was a ceremony for him at King's, a concert, a dinner. Forster relished the beauty of it; he was a man who had prepared for celebration as he had prepared for long life.

And apparently for what would come.

The year after I saw him at King's, a friend of mine volunteered to read to him. His eyes were too weak to read much and, oddly, no one seemed to ask whether he'd like to be read to. He was most grateful, and the next day my friend found a chair drawn up across from Forster's and a book by the table. "Would you mind reading *The Death of Ivan Ilyich?*"

"Now I am here, but then I shall be there. Where?" Ivan Ilyich sees it is not his vermiform appendix but death itself that is inhabiting him. He tries to avoid it, goes back to the law courts, tries talking with colleagues, goes through his redecorated house, when suddenly "he saw IT."

In the cold room with the fire lit and the eighty-five-year-old man drinking up the great preview of death, my friend began to cry. Mr. Forster reached over and touched his shoulder. "Don't worry," he said. "Don't worry. It's all right. It'll be all right."

THE POLITICS OF A MASON

Building and literature are the political arts, but builders have often had to be more politic than political. How else will they get sites, get materials? And it's *a fortiori* for classical builders, the designers of those "typical" buildings of the age which anonymities reproduce for the quick appetite of business. What were the politics of Callicrates, of Bramante, of Mies van der Rohe?

What are the politics of rocks?

Resistance.

In the farewell salutes to Mies,* I read no word of his part in the closing of the Bauhaus. Perhaps the story isn't known.† It certainly isn't known as well as it should be. I heard it from the genial—the *genialisch*—old fellow a year ago.

Four of us paid him a cocktail-hour visit in the old apartment next to the Pearson Hotel on the near North Side. A 1930s apartment, chambered beyond need, wary of outside light. Rather bare within, for there were no rugs, and the furniture was against the wall so Mies could wheel around the place. For decoration, marvelous pictures of his buildings—the Barcelona Pavillion, part of the great National Gallery not yet open in Berlin. And one of the clearest, most beautiful Picassos I'd ever seen, a Spanish cousin of Klee. Against the walls Mies chairs and non-Mies sofas, many covered with blueprints and ruled drawings, extraordinary in a glimpse for line, detail, and delicacy.

The builder himself, in his wheelchair, was—in seconds—not only presence but personage. A wonderful talker, ebullient, a fountain of ease, his great arched head tilting in the humor of things with memories, comment, hospitality.

* Summer 1969.

† A full version came out in the Sunday New York *Times* magazine a year or so later.

The memory I want to recall here is his of the closing of the Bauhaus. I may have some details wrong, but this is substantially what he said of it.

He'd been head of the school for a few months. It had moved from Weimar and Dessau to Berlin (or somewhere near Berlin). He said: "One day we came in and found it closed up. I went in to see Rosenberg to complain about it. He said to me, 'It's not me that's shut it. I don't want to close it. I'm an architect myself. I have my degree from Riga.' I said, 'If you're an architect, how can you sit at such a desk? If I were you, I'd throw it out the window.' He said, 'It must be the Gestapo who's closed it.' So I went over to the Gestapo. The head of it then was a young fellow, twenty-seven or twenty-eight, and I sat outside his office on a narrow bench, day after day, all day long. He kept avoiding me, going out the back door, but one day he came out to call someone, and I went up to him and asked what it was all about. He said, 'There's So-and-So in your group who keeps shooting off his mouth.' 'That may be,' I said, 'but that is not our business.' 'Well, all right,' he said, 'we'll let you open, but let's hope you can control things.' And the next day we came and it was open, and I called everybody together and said, 'They've given us permission to reopen. Now I suggest we close it.' And we did."

FLANNERY O'CONNOR:
A REMEMBRANCE AND SOME LETTERS

John Morgan, a philosophy student at the University of Chicago, called me the evening of August 3, 1964, to say that he had just heard from Milledgeville the news of "Mary Flannery's death." John and I would meet occasionally around the campus, and he'd pass on news about Flannery. He told me last spring that she'd been very ill, that he hadn't been able to see her when he'd gone home. I wrote her then and received a letter scarcely different from any other I'd received from her in the five years we'd known each other except that the signature was penciled and shaky.

Milledgeville
[April 14]
1964

Dear Richard,

I'm cheered my Chicago agent is keeping up with his duty to keep you informed on my state of being. It ain't much but I'm able to take nourishment and participate in a few Klan rallies. You're that much better off than me, scrapping Tuesday what you wrote Monday. All I've written this year have been a few letters. I have a little contribution to human understanding in the Spring Sewanee but I wrote that last year. You might read something called *Gogol's Wife* if you haven't already—by one of those Eyetalians, I forget which. As for me I don't read anything but the newspaper and the Bible. Everybody else did that it would be a better world.

Our springs * done come and gone. It is summer here. My muscovy duck is setting under the back steps. I have two new swans who sit on the grass and converse with eachother in low tones while the peacocks scream and holler. You just ought to leave that place you teach at

---

* I won't trifle with her typos.

and come teach in one of our excellent military colleges
or female academies where you could get something good
to eat. One of these days you will see the light and I'll
be the first to shake your hand.

Keep me posted what you publish. Since you've slowed
down, I might be able to keep up with you. I'm only one
book behind now and once my head clears up I'm going
to read it first thing.

Cheers and thanks for thinking of me. I think of you
often in that cold place among them interleckchuls.

Flannery

She'd come to the "cold place among them interleckchuls" in
February 1959, although she was frightened of Northern winters.
As if to certify her fears, there was a blizzard and ice storm
which forced her plane down in Louisville. She was put in
a bus and spent nine hours riding to Chicago. I met her at 2 A.M.
in the terminal building downtown. She was off the bus first, her
aluminum crutches in complex negotiation with handrails, helping arms, steps. Tall, pale, spectacled, small-chinned, wearily
piquant. I was to recognize her, she'd written, by the light of
pure soul shining from her eyes. Fatigue, relief, wit-edged bile
were more like it.

The streets were studded with ice bits. The walking was
worse than I'd ever seen it in Chicago. The difficulties drew from
her bitter snorts of fulfilled prophecy.

She was installed as Emily Something-or-Other in Residence
at a girl's dormitory. The girls asked her about "Christmas cus-
toms in Georgia." "Do they think I'm from Russia?" It didn't go
too well.

Out of the girls' lounge, she functioned splendidly. She'd
written a fine statement about her work as preface to her public
reading; and then she read her stories wonderfully, her voice
slightly less inflected than that of her characters but full of wry
strength.

She read to an audience of thirty, huddled, embarrassed, in the front two rows of a thousand-seat auditorium. "You ought to award them your crutches," said I.

"Lucky I don't flingem atem."

Flannery's idea world was the South, Writing, the Holy Ghost, and Bilge about all three, but her power was narrative.

Her printed stories were built bit by bit until she felt their form. And their sound, for she was a great ear writer. In fact, she had exceptionally alert eyes and ears, gifts which aren't much talked about but which both irrigate lots of her drier story matter and make her wilder creatures eat out of her hand. (Not that Bible salesmen, German DPs, and escaped "mentals" were less than facts of Milledgeville life.) Maybe that sensuous alertness was bound up with the disease which got to her so young.

The story she read was "A Good Man Is Hard to Find," and a few of the thirty people in that audience can remember the sound of her voice, and the angry-flamingo look behind her spectacles. Anybody there could tell she was her own element, not a derivative of Welty or Faulkner.

We passed those days at parties, dinners, and drinking coffee around town. It was a rather big social bite for her, but great relief from the sessions in the lounge. She talked some about her own work and about Milledgeville. We discussed the novel she'd just finished and a couple of new stories. I felt that they showed the pressure of trying to get certain things said more directly than she'd said them before. She thought not, but her late stories seemed to go back to her earlier manner. Maybe she relaxed after putting down what she was afraid she might not have time to put down. Though we never talked about this, and for all I know she didn't think much about it.

We corresponded off and on till her death. Her letters are usually typed on small sheets of paper, though for writing to Europe she used the airmail blues and sometimes wrote in ink. The first letter I find is headed "Hoover's Birthday 1959." I'd written her about a visit to Mystic, Connecticut, and I think there was a paragraph about the Mystic Power Company. "Dear

Dick," she wrote (though from then on she addressed me as "Richard"),

> Would I were at the Mystic Wax Works where something could be made of me. There is no place hereabouts to cool off except in my mother's deep frieze which is already occupied by last years turkeys. This is the season at which I pick up peafowl feathers as the dear birds shed. In the cool of the evening I am to be seen out in the pastures, bending painfully from my two aluminum sticks, reaching for some bright feather. I hope that this affecting picture touches you.
>   . . . Should you be in the region of Providence there is a good writer there name of John Hawkes. If you would be interested in co-authoring with me a book listing where good writers may be found, like Duncan Hines for restaurants, we might make us a little extra money. Since I have got my novel out of the house, my thoughts turn largely to finance.

She sent an envelope of peafowl feathers and renewed them a year or two later from the bird which was, she said, pictured in a *Holiday* magazine.

> Milledgeville
> 17 May 59
> Dear po Richard,
>   I am cheered to hear that the moths have not got into your peafowl feathers yet. I take this symbollically (sp?) to mean that my memory too is unmotheaten in your head. Your memory is unmotheaten in my head also.
>   . . . If I said my novel was finished, I was misinformed. I am still working at it madly and madly it needs it. Conversationally, I am untrustworthy.

She'd just won a Ford grant and she alludes to the amount given her and that given someone else.

> I reckon my 4 thousand a year looks to me like 8 thousand to him. Last week I made $50 reading a story at a nearby college and I am going to buy a vacuum cleaner with it and reform my life.

Milledgeville
10 January 60

Dear Richard,

One year it is more or less since I was tempted by you
to risk life and limberness to come to that place and be
questioned for a week by those creamy dormitory dolls
and all them other thangs that happened to me such as
riding nine hours on a—. It spoils my syntax to think
about it. We will pass on to other things.

. . . If you think it is pleasant to see yr novel in print,
it is not pleasant to see your novel in print. I have just
seen mine. The jacket: on an evil red-lavender background, the head of the hero, in black wool hat, peers out
from behind some clay-colored corn (The School of
Southern Degeneracy). The title page: a mess. The con-
tents; as I am responsible for these we will not go into
them. Anyway, I have not read the book.

My goose has laid two eggs already since Christmas
and I would send you one if I thought for a minute you
appreciated the finer things.

In a postscript to a handwritten letter, she alludes to something I'd written. "P.S. You caint finger one out of a rosary
neither. Your nurse corrupted you." And, to my defense,

Milledgeville, Ga. A Bird Sanctuary
2 June 60

Dear po Richard

Yessir, you can finger a decade but somebody is then
going to ask you a decade of what and you will have to
louse it up with some more words . . .

I am never going to Chicago or New York again but
am going to spend the rest of my life in Milledgeville.

It seems you are being reviewed exclusively in Catholic
magazines. This is what you get for being a Catholic
writer. Ha.

She also inked in capital letters an ad for the novel she mentioned: "READ GOLK AND END UP IN A PEW."

12 October 60

Me I am on my way to Minnesota but managed to get

a plane that I don't have to so much as get off of in Chicago as I wish not to set foot again in that airpot. I am going to talk at two Cathlick colleges and read at the University and get back as quick as I can to be with the chickens . . .

4 April 61

Dear Richard G.,

. . . You had better get yrself better established with the post office. This is disgraceful. Address me a letter to F. O'Connor, Milledgeville, Ga. and I get it at once. This of course proves that I am better known than you are, even if I didn't get the Nat'l Bk Award. Who is Conrad Richter?

. . . I ain't done nothing otherwise but write a story called "Everything That Rises Must Converge" to be in NWW in October. I think about another novel as if it were a trip to darkest Africa.

Me, I am satisfied with politics myself—a president after twelve years, or eight anyway.

Somebody invited me to Chicago this February and I said Ha ha ha ha ha ha ha ha.

Cheers,
Flannery

21 April 62
Milledgeville

Dear Richard G.,

Hoorray fr you. Rome or Venice yet. Go to see my friends the Fitzgeralds in Perugia and tell them howdy for me. Are you going to bring culture back to Chicago or what? I am coming to Chicago myself shortly to bring it a little culture from Milledgeville. I am going to talk at Rosary College—the thing you finger, son—in River Forest wherever that is and then I am going on to Notre Dame. If I can find a telephone at Rosary College, you can expect to hear my unformed tones over it enquiring as to your health. However, this may be a medieval institution and they may not have telephones.

. . . I just met Eudora W. at the Southern Litry Festival where her and me give a paper along with Andrew Lytle and Cleanth Brooks and then we all discussed Whut Makes Suthen Litratoor Great around a panel table.

I hope you get shut of the snow before I get there.

Excelsior,
Flannery

30 November 62

Dear Richard,

You are not the only one that's been somewheres. I just got back from Texas. I talked at East Texas State College, so don't talk to me about any University of Vienna. The first thing they showed me in Dallas was General Walker's house—a battleship grey, two story, clappboard dwelling with a giant picture window in front of which you see a ceramic Uncle Sam with a lampshade on top of him. Texas and U.S. flags flying on the lawn. I also heard a Texas joke, to wit: Texan calls up the White House, says, "Is President Kennedy there?" Voice says, "Nawsuh, he ain't here." "Well is Jackie there?" "She ain't here neither." "Well where is Mr. Lyndon?" "He done gone too." "Well who's running things up there?" "We is." (I am trying to make you homesick before your year is out.) . . .

Milledgeville
Georgia, USA
27 July 63

Dear Richard

What you ought to do is get you a Fulbright to Georgia and quit messing around with all those backward places you been at. Anyhow, don't pay a bit of attention to the Eyetalian papers. It's just like Cudden Ross says all us niggers and white folks over here are just getting along grand —at least in Georgia and Mississippi. I hear things are not so good in Chicago and Brooklyn but you wouldn't expect them to know what to do with theirself there. Down here is where all the writers come from and if you onct come you would never want to leave it.

What are you fixing to do, publish another novel? Do you want to be known as One-a-year Stern? I am doing my best to create the impression that it takes 7 years to write a novel. The four-hour week. You are not helping the Brotherhood. Examine your conscience. Think. Meditate. Shilly-shally.

Cheers anyway,
Flannery

PART IV

8. Novels

Yes, novels . . . work in which the greatest powers of the mind are displayed, in which the most thorough knowledge of human nature, the happiest delineation of its varieties, the liveliest effusions of wit and humour, are conveyed to the world in the best chosen language.

Jane Austen
Northanger Abbey

but he
Must struggle out of his boyish gift and learn
How to be plain and awkward, how to be
One after whom none think it worth to turn.

For, to achieve his lightest wish, he must
Become the whole of boredom, subject to
Vulgar complaints like love, among the Just

Be just, among the Filthy filthy too,
And in his own weak person, if he can,
Must suffer dully all the wrongs of Man.

W. H. Auden
"The Novelist"
Collected Poems

But for something to read in normal circumstances?

Ezra Pound
Homage to Sextus Propertius

The following pieces are products of a fiction writer's workshop. The opinions—some of them harsh—are those of someone who believes he knows what's going on. Others may regard them as infighting. There's undoubtedly some of that, but not as much as literary hard-hats would have you believe.

Unlike scientists, who can collaborate on all but the highest levels because they're working toward the mastery of what's really out there, novelists work alone because their best work means dissociation from the familiar. (There'll never be a Darwin-Wallace coincidence in the arts.) Novelists count only as they are distinct from other novelists.* Everything that is different about them becomes their stock in trade.

Novelists need each other the way countries need boundary lines: "That's X's way or place." Essentially, there's no taking over another novelist's territory. It would mean taking over his mind. (There's a certain amount of theft, some of it for parodic —or other legitimate—purpose.)

Most novelists can and often do admire their colleagues' work; but convictions about the way novels should be written, the way life feels, the way it is, blind you to some good work. Criticism helps relieve feelings and, better, enables you to spell them out in terms of the art.

---

* I think this is true for all artists, including those who programmatically reject a form of individuality. ("Neo-Plasticism aims precisely at representing nothing that is individually determined." Determined by "nature" and "the senses," said Mondrian and van Doesburg. OK. But then they added determined by "sentiment." Does this mean Mondrian would paint only what had neither appeal nor interest for him? Ridiculous.) For architects the matter is, at least theoretically, different. Mies could well have meant that he'd like all buildings built in the same nonstyle style. (Of course, it was *his* "nonstyle.")

PICARESQUE EXTRA CUVÉE

The Confessions of Felix Krull, Confidence Man (The Early Years) * derives from the picaresque as Dr. Faustus does from the biographical memoir: in both novels the ease and looseness of the traditional forms become components of quite formal works. "Formal" not in the sense of the classic French novel (The Princess of Cleves, Adolphe, Madame Bovary, The Plague), the novel which exhausts a single situation by means of extensive motive analysis and crucial scenes, but "formal" in the manner of the greatest moderns, that of thematic control.

Felix Krull is another extension of that most accommodating fictional form, a form which has served jest book Bildungsroman, travelogue, quest, and thriller. Mann makes use of most of its traditional materials—nimble hero, complacent partners, ferocious officials, sharpers, victims, rags to riches—as naturally in his pedagogical format as did Smollett and Lesage in their adventurous ones. Indeed, the form seems made for a writer of Mann's didactic inclinations; his return to these confessions three times in the last forty years shows he knew it.

Mann had never taken to the French form, although he had taken a great deal from it. (He reread Renée Mauperin three or four times while working on Buddenbrooks.) His style, with its distance, its internal, masochistic burlesque, its perpetual assertiveness, could never "forget itself" in the restricted outlooks whose divergence composes the novel of conduct. Mann's world is always at the far end of his prose leash; readers are much less involved with Hans Castorp than with Emma Bovary. Mann's narratives unroll almost as conspicuously as Thackeray's and Fielding's. In his last two full-scale novels, the style issues from

* Thomas Mann, Confessions of Felix Krull: Confidence Man (The Early Years), translated by Denver Lindley (New York: Alfred Knopf, 1956).

a narrator, a broad but limited intelligence whose presence in the traditional form of the two books constitutes their chief device and invention. In *Dr. Faustus* the expansive humanism of Serenus Zeitblom weights every page with that ambivalence which is Mann's trademark; in *Felix Krull* the Germanic formalism of the "great man's autobiography" is compromised by the situation itself—a swindler recounting his truancies—and by the carefully heightened version of the *Dichtung-und-Wahrheit* style.

Of all Mann's heroes, Krull is the one who speculates most consciously, most in the manner of Mann's essays, about his experience; and he has by far the most experience. It is the manner in which this experience is selected from and narrated that distinguishes this version of picaresque. Compare a brief portion of it with one from a work whose general arrangement is similar to it, *Moll Flanders*. *Moll* and *Krull* are both first-person accounts of criminal careers written post facto from positions of safety, Krull in weary retirement at the age of forty, Moll in repentent security at seventy. Both narratives are organized chronologically and scattered with edifying reflections. Here are Moll and Felix at their initial thefts:

> . . . and the devil, who I said laid the snare, as readily prompted me as if he had spoke, for I remember, and shall never forget it, 'twas like a voice spoken to me over my shoulder, "Take the bundle; be quick; do it this moment." It was no sooner said but I stepped into the shop, and with my back to the wench, as if I had stood up for a cart that was going by, I put my hand behind me and took the bundle, and went off with it, the maid or the fellow not perceiving me, or any one else.
> It is impossible to express the horror of my soul all the while I did it. When I went away I had no heart to run, or scarce to mend my pace. I crossed the street indeed, and went down the first turning I came to, and I think it was a street that went through into Fenchurch Street.
> *Moll Flanders,* Modern Library, p. 181

So great was the joy of beholding this bountiful spot completely at my disposal that I felt my limbs begin to jerk
and twitch. It took great self-control not to burst into a
cry of joy at so much newness and freedom. I spoke into
the silence, saying: "Good day" in quite a loud voice; I
can still remember how my strained, unnatural tones died
away in the stillness. No one answered. And my mouth
literally began to water like a spring. One quick, noiseless
step and I was beside one of the laden tables. I made one
rapturous grab into the nearest glass urn, filled as it
chanced with chocolate creams, slipped a fistful into my
coat pocket, then reached the door, and in the next second
was safely round the corner.

No doubt, I shall be accused of common theft. I will
not deny the accusation, I will simply withdraw and refuse
to contradict anyone who chooses to mouth this paltry
word. But the word—the poor, cheap, shopworn word,
which does violence to all the finer meanings of life—is
one thing, and the primeval absolute deed forever shining
with newness and originality is quite another.

Felix Krull, pp. 42–43

What Moll thinks is but a small part of what she does; the narrative moves into action. Moll says, "It is impossible to express
the horror," and she doesn't try. Mann's narrative, however,
moves toward commentary. Felix is around the corner in a second, and around that corner is an elaborate speculation, though
one as important to the movement of Mann's book as Fenchurch
Street is to Defoe's. In comparison, *Moll* (and, I think, all previous picaresques) seems a boundless, untreated flux.*

Every detail in *Krull* is part of a general notion; and it is these
which organize the novel. One can relate the incidents of *Moll
Flanders* and have an orderly action; if one tries this with *Krull*,
the relation will make sense only if organized thematically. The
digressions which Krull asks the reader to excuse are digressions
only from the traditional order; the accounts of the circus per-

* This is exaggeration for critical purposes; *Moll* is "treated" brilliantly, and *Krull*, though its events have an apposite, illustrative air, is
a good deal more active than garrulous.

formers, of a couple seen on a Frankfurt balcony, of shop windows, the speculations themselves, form the novel as the progression of incidents forms *Moll*.

Krull's themes are from the Mann warehouse. The dominant one is the nature of entertainers, artists, superior people, their relation to the world and, by virtue of a Mann *Vortrag*, to Being as well. In brief, these special people create themselves and their world: "Had I not instead the assurance . . . that my voice might quite easily have turned out common, my eyes dull, and my legs crooked, had my soul been less watchful?" Their talent for illusion—which is not so illusory—and for deception—which is craved—gives them entry to and power in the world, and leads to their overthrow. Their chief talent is for pleasure—"The Great Joy," Felix calls it. They gorge experience, and the novel supplies their feast. Their altar is the department store, which is also—for Felix—a university where he learns to discriminate clothes, jewelry, and women.

Krull celebrates a Dionysian bacchanalia. Words and their offspring, codes and laws, are the apparent villains. But words are what the weary Krull must now resort to in memoir. "Only at the two opposite poles of human contact, where there are no words or at least no more words, in the glance and in the embrace, is happiness to be found, for there alone are unconditional freedom, secrecy, and profound ruthlessness" (p. 83). These, final words from a writer, even one so notoriously ambiguous about the artist as Mann, are more than the Ironic German's playful literary suicide. Even the smugness of literary security doesn't hide the depth of uncertainty about power and culture which makes even the greatest works of modern German literature edgy, ambivalent, tremulously pompous, as if standing on tiptoe waiting to be turned into divine music.

Yet in *Krull* the questionable, unresolved feel of the action, the action which includes speculation, is what keeps the most didactic page fictional, eventful, controlled from outside, not, as in Fielding's inserted essays, from inside the novel itself. And

though the style is, in a sense, the protagonist mocking the world
he reveals, the style in this is Felix's, and Felix is not in control
of the novel as an autobiographer is in control of his confession;
the control of character and reminiscence in this book is incom-
parably greater than in that of the most aware autobiographer.

PROUST AND JOYCE UNDER WAY:
THE TRADITION OF AUTOBIOGRAPHY

Several years ago Mlle. Claude-Edmonde Magny protested against the publication of writers' discarded sketches, notes, and interim drafts. Of *Jean Santeuil,* the work which Bernard de Fallois assembled from the papers Proust left behind in an old *carton à vêtements,* Mlle. Magny wrote:

> Those critics who hope to learn by autopsy the mystery of creativity will find with satisfaction the themes of the *Recherche* already prefigured—but minus that essential, the intricate architecture of the work, the transfiguration of reality by style, the transfiguration of time by selected experience . . . the reading of *Jean Santeuil* can scarcely bring us anything but anecdote. More seriously still, it "comes off on," fades into, our understanding of the *Recherche:* many an unpleasant trait which had to this point remained in the shadow, in the background of the author and the person, is roughly illuminated, and by a lurid daylight.

One does not rush to disagree with such critics as Mlle. Magny, but here, it seems to me, her objection excludes a work which I for one would prefer to reread, even at the expense of reading her excellent criticism of it. *Jean Santeuil* and the remarkably similar early work of Joyce, *Stephen Hero,* are not distinguished by that "intricate architecture" which, since James' time, has been regarded as the source of our greatest literary pleasures. The pleasures they provide are possibly lesser ones, but there is no reason to throw them out; they won't ruin the literary palate.

R. P. Blackmur writes in his introduction to the collected prefaces of James that "Proust . . . wrote always as loosely as possible and triumphed in spite of himself. Joyce made only such sacrifices as suited his private need—and triumphed by a

series of *tours de force.*" What are these triumphs which triumph
in spite of the victor, and these "sacrifices" which suit the need—
the "private need"—of the sacrificer?

Proust scattered his views of form and composition all through
his work. One appears in *The Captive* (*La Prisonnière*). The
narrator is thinking about Wagner's operas:

> . . . I thought how markedly . . . these works participate
> in that quality of being—albeit marvellously—always in-
> complete, which is the peculiarity of all the great works
> of the nineteenth century, with which the greatest writers
> of that century have stamped their books, but, watching
> themselves at work as though they were at once author
> and critic, have derived from this self-contemplation a
> novel beauty, exterior and superior to the work itself, im-
> posing upon it retrospectively a unity, a greatness which
> it does not possess. Without pausing to consider him who
> saw in his novels, after they had appeared, a *Human Com-
> edy,* nor those who entitled heterogeneous poems or es-
> says *The Legend of the Ages* or *The Bible of Humanity,*
> can we not say all the same of the last of these that he is
> so perfect an incarnation of the nineteenth century that
> the greatest beauties in Michelet are to be sought not so
> much in his work itself, as in the attitudes that he adopts
> when he is considering his work, not in his *History of
> France* nor in his *History of the Revolution,* but in his
> prefaces to his books? Prefaces, that is to say pages writ-
> ten after the books themselves, in which he considers the
> books, and with which we must include here and there
> certain phrases beginning as a rule with a "Shall I say?"
> which is not a scholar's precaution but a musician's ca-
> dence. The other musician, he who is delighting me at this
> moment, Wagner, retrieving some exquisite scrap from a
> drawer of his writing table to make it appear as a theme,
> retrospectively necessary, in a work of which he had not
> been thinking at the moment when he composed it, then
> having composed a first mythological opera, and a second,
> and afterwards others still, and perceiving all of a sudden
> that he had written a tetralogy, must have felt something
> of the same exhilaration as Balzac, when casting over his
> works the eye at once of a stranger and of a father, find-

ing in one the purity of Raphael, in another the simplicity of the Gospel, he suddenly decided, as he shed a retrospective illumination upon them, that they would be better brought together in a cycle in which the same character would reappear, and added to his work, in this act of joining it together, a stroke of the brush, the last and the most sublime. A unity that was ulterior, not artificial, otherwise it would have crumbled into dust like all the other systematisations of mediocre writers who with the elaborate assistance of titles and sub-titles gave themselves the appearance of having pursued a single and transcendent design. Not fictitious, perhaps indeed all the more real for being ulterior, for being born of a moment of enthusiasm when it is discovered tᴏ ᴇxist among fragments which need only to be joined together. A unity that has been unaware of itself, therefore vital and not logical, that has not banned variety, chilled execution.

The Captive, Modern Library, I, pp. 211–13

There are a good many things to remark in this excerpt; but our chief interest is the attitude that this master of "intricate architecture" takes toward this aspect of his craft, his illustration even, in the "he who is delighting me at this moment," of the brief phrases which may look awkward out of the narrative context, but which reveal the skeleton of the work. Without them, the work would appear formless. Form is *natural* to the work of artists, although it manifests itself only after the artist becomes his own critic, discovers the form of his work, sees the few touches needed to bring it out, and provides them.

Proust's notions are related to the better-known esthetic speculations of Joyce which appear in *Portrait of the Artist, Stephen Hero,* the notes which Gorman prints in his biography, and such byblows as the book reviews which he did for the *Daily Express* in 1902–1903.

Joyce's concern is also with the apprehension of that "vital form" which reveals itself to the artist with the sudden power he called epiphanic. Joyce does not write, as James does, of the methods of achieving form; in the early reviews he seems interested not in a novel's craftsmanship but in its revelations of personality. His brother Stanislaus remarks in a note to Joyce's review of A. E. W. Mason's novels that he "was free from bigotry toward the literature of mere entertainment." The reason is that such literature can be as revealing as any other about the mind which conceived it. Joyce cites Leonardo's observation that the mind has a tendency "to impress its own likeness upon that which it creates," and he goes on to find motifs in Mason's novels which were there "without the author's consent." Joyce's favorite word of praise for fiction in the reviews is "epic," and that means, in his famous definition, the "form wherein . . . [the artist] presents his image in mediate relation to himself and others." Like Proust's, then, Joyce's notion of fictional excellence, fictional form, has to do with that which in the Jamesian outlook belongs not to the work but to the author. For Proust and Joyce, fiction is a form of autobiography.

Just about the time that Proust and Joyce were writing the last pages of the works we know as *Jean Santeuil* and *Stephen Hero,* James was writing the preface to *The Ambassadors,* in which he described the perils of the "large ease of 'autobiography' " to which writers had better not yield unless they were prepared *"not* to make certain precious discriminations." James was actually considering the use of the first person, a post of observation he had eschewed in *The Ambassadors* and, as it were, made the almost farcical point of the novel which preceded it, *The Sacred Fount.* His technical warning, however, was directed at "the terrible fluidity" which threatens "self-revelation" of any sort. Since the eighteenth century, when such works as Wieland's *Agathon, The Sorrows of Young Werther, A Sentimental Journey,* and above all Rousseau's *Confessions* came to the fore, and the nineteenth, which saw even more varied mixtures of *Dichtung* and *Wahrheit* (*Adolphe, La Vie de Henri Brulard, The Prelude, Sylvie, David Copperfield, Pendennis, The Way of All Flesh,* and countless others), James' stricture would have served as a corrective; these revelations were usually corrupted by sentimentality or sensationalism, as their forms were by the uncertain postion of the protagonist.

The reliance upon "autobiography" as a source of fiction is related, I think, to the changing conception of character which the novel of analysis helped to bring about. The conception that character is so fluid as to be in fact unknowable determines the construction of such novels as Dostoevsky's *The Devils,* where the planned unpredictability of Stavrogin is a result neither of the author's uncertainty nor of farce (the only genre of which unpredictability is a major component). The fluidity of "characters" as different as Proust's Albertine and Joyce's HCE is also, it seems to me, a product of such a conception.* The notion of the unknowability of character helped to do away with that standard eighteenth- and nineteenth-century novel which depended on the clash of more or less fixed characters around central figures, who become at the end of the novel more or less like one of the fixed figures. When the new conception undermined this form of the novel, many serious writers turned to "autobiographical fiction." Not that writers could know themselves better than they could know others, but at least they knew what they felt, remembered, and believed. This was material for a novel whose chief technical problem would be the position of the narrator-protagonist.

For Joyce, the problem was not as pressing as it was for Proust. His chief stock in trade was not the exploitation of his sensibility: he was not a lyric writer. His first published novel is a clever record of his own experience, experience which he assessed as "young" before he wrote. His later work deals more and more generally with the nature of writing about experience. In his first work he was concerned with guaranteeing the authenticity of Stephen's experience by indicating it had been his own.

---

* Strindberg's famous preface to *Miss Julie,* in which he explains his "characterless" characters, and Pirandello's preface to *Six Characters in Search of an Author* indicate some of the influence the new conception had in drama.

A note by Stanislaus Joyce to the shortest of Joyce's early reviews makes this clear:

> In condemning this novel cursorily, my brother condemns pseudonyms; however, when a year later his own first stories were published, he yielded to the suggestion (not mine) and used a pseudonym, "Stephen Daedalus," but then bitterly regretted the self-concealment. He did not feel that he had perpetrated bad literature of which he ought to be ashamed. He had taken the name from the central figure in the novel "Stephen Hero," which he had already begun to write. Against that name I had protested in vain; but it was, perhaps, his use of the name as a pseudonym that decided him finally on its adoption. He wished to make up for a momentary weakness; in fact, in order further to identify himself with his hero, he announced his intention of appending to the end of the novel the signature "Stephanus Daedalus pinxit." *

For Proust, the fashioning of an "I" took nearly twenty years. It was crucial to his work because his concern was not only the meaning of his experience (the discovery of vocation) but recovery and extension of its extraordinary qualities: his sensibility was both subject and object.

In *Jean Santeuil* he is constantly wrestling the "I." The book begins:

> Should I call this book a novel? It is something less, perhaps, and yet much more, the very essence of my life, with nothing extraneous added, as it developed through a long period of wretchedness. This book of mine has not been manufactured: It has been garnered.

Then follows (according to de Fallois' arrangement) an introduction in which "I" meets the novelist "C" whose novel *Jean Santeuil* is supposed to be. Nothing more is heard of C, but "I" makes frequent appearances alongside C's hero, Jean Santeuil, and occasionally displaces him:

* The French translation of *Portrait—Dedalus: Portrait de l'artiste jeune par lui-même*—brings out the import of the definite article in the English title.

It is a pleasure too—and a very great pleasure—to find ourselves confronted by a certain air of intellectual freedom, in such men who by a word can justify opinions which we ourselves should have liked to express, but have rejected because, in our constant effort to be sincere (I am talking now of natures like Jean's) we feel . . . (p. 352)

and

We do not know whether we still love Madame S_____ [Mme. S. is Jean Santeuil's mistress], but we . . . (p. 582)

There are many other such intrusions.

When Proust told Gide that the writer could tell all as long as he didn't attribute it to "I," he was talking about the necessity of keeping the observer's hands clean, or rather his eyes clear, so that the observations would not be suspect. If a novel's observer is suspect, this becomes one of the objects of the book; this is the case in *The Sacred Fount* and many other novels. The narrator of the *Recherche* is the one who discovers and who acts upon his discoveries; the writer behind the book's "I," Proust, is the object of discovery as well as the discoverer.

For the *Recherche* Proust fashioned a narrator who shared much of his experience and sensibility but who lacked his genius, perversion, and tenacity. It is likely that Proust was helped to work out such a narrator by the critical examinations of writers which he was making at this time for *Contre Sainte-Beuve*. What he says there of Dostoevsky's procedure is remarkably similar to what was to be his own.

Mais il est probable qu'il divise en deux personnes ce qui a été en réalité d'une seule. Il y a certainement un crime dans sa vie et un châtiment (qui n'a peut-être pas de rapport avec ce crime) mais il a préféré distribuer en deux, mettre les impressions du châtiment sur lui-même . . . (*Maison des Morts*) et le crime sur d'autres.

The fact that Proust's discoveries about his own work came (according to de Fallois' chronology) just after the revival of his critical powers in the writing of *Contre Sainte-Beuve* leads to another important difference between the work of Proust and Joyce and that of James and the earlier writers of the autobiographical tradition; that is, the importance of criticism to *and* in their work. James reserved his criticism for his prefaces, and he called these "the story of the story." For Proust and Joyce, whose works are in a sense about themselves, the story of the story, the esthetics and criticism, come into the books. This exhibition of the writer criticizing his work as he forms it provides a logical conclusion to the tradition of "autobiography.*

---

* James himself was to discover the pleasures of "I" when he came to write his autobiographic volumes. Indeed, on the first page of *A Small Boy and Others* he sounds very much like Proust: ". . . to recover anything like the full treasure of scattered, wasted circumstances was at the same time to live over the spent experience itself . . . to see the world within begin to 'compose' with a grace of its own round the primary figure . . . ," and so on, as if he were foreseeing the Proust volume which he was to praise as worthy of Cervantes and Balzac (as Proust records in an article which he had Leon Daudet send to the editor of *L'Eclair* in 1919).

DOCTOR ZHIVAGO AS A NOVEL

For seventeen pages *Doctor Zhivago* * looks like an outline for a Tolstoy novel: three boys, different in character and circumstance, unknowingly interconnected, are treated with the sort of care that makes one anticipate a well-paced unfolding of their careers. End of Chapter One. Chapter Two takes place about two years later, and its first seventeen pages treat Lara Guishar, the book's heroine; her mother; her mother's lover, who seduces her; the cellist Tyshkevich; Olga Demina, an apprentice in Madame Guishar's dressmaking establishment; Faina Silantievna Fetisova, "Madame Guishar's assistant and senior cutter"; the lover's dog Jack; a strike on the Moscow-Kazan railroad; the railroad's divisional manager Fulflygin; the track overseer Antipov; Tiverzin, Khudoleiev, Yusupka, Gimazetdin; a demonstration march from the Tver Gate to the Kaluga Gate; the uncle of the hero, who "saw the fleeing demonstrators from his window"; the—but this will serve. These are but *some* of the characters and events on those seventeen pages. The "summary" is not less confusing than what it summarizes. Nor is the confusion ever dispersed, for the characters and scenes are scarcely developed and almost never exploited unless they are regarded as parts of a confused panorama. Even this explanation will not do, for many of these characters reappear in the novel, not so that one can distinguish them, but because even Pasternak knows that there is a limit to the number of ingredients which can be crammed into one dish. The effects of the first two hundred pages of *Doctor Zhivago* might be compared to a thousandfold

* Boris Pasternak, *Doctor Zhivago*. Translated from the Russian by Max Hayward and Manya Harari with "The Poems of Yurii Zhivago," translated by Bernard Guilbert Guerney (Pantheon, 1959). This review was published in 1959 while the Pasternak cheering section supplied the only literary noise one heard. Dwight MacDonald's blast at the book was published shortly after this one.

expansion of the Hakagawa–Madame de Tornquist–Fräulein von Kulp section of "Gerontion."

Edmund Wilson has called *Doctor Zhivago* a poem (among many other things, including an allegory and a folk tale). But although even narrative poems can slight narrative and get away with it, since they have other charms on which to rely, novels can't. Accretion is not narrative. Pasternak seems to learn this about a third of the way through the book and begins concentrating on his hero, the doctor-poet Yurii Zhivago.

Concentration, however, is a comparative term. Twenty-five pages of Tolstoy or Stendhal would give us the Zhivago of Pasternak's five hundred.

The weakness of Pasternak's work derives from serious errors in presentation, and these in turn depend in large part on the book's form, or rather the impulses to form, at which, since they are not fulfilled, one may only guess.

Pasternak seems to have had two major formal notions for the novel: the first was to write a large, Tolstoyan work, full of characters and scenes which would render the flavor of society; the second was to write a sort of *Red and Black,** an historical chronicle focused on a hero's life. This twofold scheme proved impossible for him to execute. In the first place, a Tolstoy novel works not with characters and scenes † but with situations which "pick up" characters and scenes as they are needed. Second, the Tolstoy situations exist in terms of each other as parallels, contrasts, or continuations. In *Zhivago* there are no real situations, no intrigues which are followed closely, developed suspensefully and in depth. The closest approach to a situation is the love of Zhivago and Lara, but this is so interspersed with other material and so larded with capricious coincidence that one never has the sense of effort a serious love story must have.

---

* Two of the five books Zhivago mentions in the Varykino chapter are *War and Peace* and the Stendhal novel.

† Despite Tolstoy's midnight cry of despair that he had forgotten to put a yacht race into *Anna Karenina.*

No wonder Wilson and other critics have tended to think of *Zhivago* as an allegory; its narrative is too sparse to nourish a reader.

If this thin diet starves the Tolstoy impulse—unfortunately not to death, for we keep meeting characters till the very end— it is fatal to the Stendhalian one. The novel of careers lasts until the death or retirement of the hero; if you begin with the hero as a young boy, and at the same time do a kind of Tolstoy and have three boys, you set up an immensely long novel, even if all the careers end as early as Julien Sorel's. Even with one hero, Stendhal—unlike, say, the author of *Jean Christophe*—centered the career about two parallel situations, one provincial, one Parisian, and thus brought off his chronicle as well as his career novel. Stendhal's controlling idea—something like "What would become of a Napoleon in the antiheroic Restoration?"—looks like the ideal model for Pasternak, whose root idea would seem to be "What happens to a good man in the bad times of revolution and collectivism?" Ambition overlaid and ruined this central notion. Although I do not believe that Pasternak went so far as to attempt what Edmund Wilson suggests—"a phase-by-phase chronicle of Soviet policy, and a discussion of the development of Russian literature which touches on almost all its great figures from Pushkin to the school of modern poetry" or "a historical-political fable—see Larisa's relations with Zhivago, Komarovsky, and Pasha" *—I do believe that the ambition to present the

---

* I think it just as likely, indeed far more likely, that there are *roman-à-clef* elements in *Zhivago*. For Larisa Guishar I suggest the Soviet writer Larisa Reisner, at whose death in 1926 Pasternak wrote the poem "Pamyata Reisner" (*Stikhot voreniya v odnom tome*, Leningrad, 1933, pp. 289–90). In Reisner's book of sketches, *The Front* (1924), appear such Zhivagesque passages as

> The revolution wears out its professional workers unconscionably. It is a harsh master with whom there is no use talking about a six-hour day, maternity benefits or higher pay. It takes everything—men's brains, wills, nerves and lives—and, having sucked them dry, having wounded and exhausted them, deposits them on the nearest scrap heap . . .

career of a good man in bad times was fatally jostled by the attempt to simultaneously present the careers of a good many people drawn from many levels of society.

The scheme Pasternak employs to solve the problems of such a work consists in presenting the fictional matter in short, rapidly shifting scenes, or in Irving Howe's excellent description in "clipped vignettes . . . apparently meant to suggest a Tolstoyan breadth and luxuriousness of treatment." These scenes, or fragments, are "clipped" by a variety of narrative sins which succeed in blighting almost every breath of life in the book. Here are some of them.

1. Unwarranted, unsignaled transitions:

> Nikolai Nikolaievich refused to believe him and dashed out but was back in a minute. He said bullets whistled down the street knocking chips of brick and plaster off the corners. There was not a soul outside. All communications had stopped.
> That week Sashenka caught a cold. (p. 190)

2. Displacement of dramatic narrative by curtailed observations:

> For some time they sang the "Marseillaise," the "Varshavianka," and "Victims You Fell." Then a man who had been walking backwards at the head of the procession, singing and conducting with his cap, which he used as a baton, turned around, put his cap on his head, and listened to what the other leaders around him were saying. The singing broke off in disorder. Now you could hear the crunch of innumerable footsteps on the frozen pavement. (p. 35)

We see no more of the man walking backward; we don't know what "the other leaders were saying." This is the longest of the eight paragraphs which "present" the march from the Tver Gate to the Kaluga Gate.

3. Coincidence: There is more coincidence in this novel than would be justified in a farce. The whole of Russia is like the lobby of a small-town hotel. People simply cannot get away from

each other no matter how far they travel (nor is this the point). Coincidence is Pasternak's way of appearing to continue the Tolstoyan novel when he has really abandoned it for the novel of Zhivago's career.

4. Inability to relate an anecdote:

> While they were waiting for Dudorov he told the story of Dudorov's marriage . . . The improbable gist of this story consisted in the following:
>
> Dudorov had been drafted into the army by mistake. While he was serving and his case was being investigated, he was constantly punished for absent-mindedly forgetting to salute officers in the street. For a long time after his discharge he would raise his arm impulsively whenever an officer came in sight, and often he imagined epaulettes where there were none.
>
> In this latter period his behavior was erratic in other ways as well. At one point—so the rumor went—while waiting for a steamer at a Volga port, he made the acquaintance of two young women, sisters, who were waiting for the same steamer. Confused by the presence of a large number of army men and the memories of his misadventures as a soldier, he fell in love with the younger sister and proposed to her on the spot. "Amusing, isn't it?" Gordon said. But he had to interrupt his story when its hero was heard at the door. Dudorov entered the room. (p. 176)

Stories are frequently interrupted or broken off entirely (p. 71, 262). Or, as in this case, the stories are deprecated: the clause which follows "Dudorov's marriage" is "which he thought was comical." Such deprecation is allied to the next zhivagary.

5. Deprecation of the philosophical speeches: After Zhivago has made a profound speech about life and death:

> "What's come over me?" he thought. "I'm becoming a regular quack—muttering incantations, laying on the hands . . ." (p. 69)

Or a comic Tolstoy disciple after making one of the famous ideological speeches in the book:

"I haven't understood a word. You should write a book
about it." (p. 42)

Or the speaker is said to be drunk (p. 182). The author's lack
of self-confidence is contagious.*

6. Inadequate preparation (or proper sequence):

"And now since you've been so frank with me, I'll be
frank with you. The Strelnikov you met is my husband,
Pasha, Pavel Pavlovich Antipov, whom I went to look for
at the front and in whose death I so rightly refused to
believe." (pp. 298–99)

This revelation is sidestepped not only into but around. Zhivago
responds to it in this way:

"What you say does not come as a surprise. I was prepared for something of the sort." (p. 299)

Or

Mademoiselle called up Kolia and told him to find Dr.
Zhivago a good seat on the train, threatening him with
exposure if he did not. (p. 155)

We never learn what it is that can be exposed.

I shall end the list with a passage which displays one of the
novel's stylistic faults which cannot, I think, be blamed on the
translators.† This is the book's overinvestment in simile and
metaphor.

Narrow dead-end streets ran off the square, as deep in
mud as country lanes and lined with crooked little houses.

* After reading Mrs. Mandelstam's account of artistic hell (*Hope
Against Hope*), I'm inclined to think the deprecations were Pasternak's
way of coping with the censor. In the case of *Dr. Zhivago,* they did not
help.

† Wilson is the only critic I've read [1959] who seems to have read the
original Russian text as well as the Italian and English versions. His
demonstration of the inadequacy of the last is fairly convincing, although he praises, indeed overpraises, its naturalness ("it does not sound
translated"), finds that it cuts through some stylistic defects of the original and is a good deal better than the English versions through which
Tolstoy and Turgenev first made their reputations here.

Fences of plaited willows stuck out of the mud like bow
nets in a pond, or lobster pots. You could see the weak
glint of open windows. In the small front gardens, sweaty
red heads of corn with oily whiskers reached out toward
the rooms, and single, pale thin hollyhocks looked out
over the fences, like women in night clothes whom the
heat had driven out of their stuffy houses for a breath of
air.

The moonlit night was extraordinary, like merciful love
or the gift of clairvoyance . . . (p. 142)

Wilson complains that the translators sometimes lop off fine
figures of speech. Though this is translator treason, *Zhivago*
could use more of it. I have gone through a partial list of the
narrative flaws † in order to hint at the page-by-page difficulty
of reading *Zhivago,* if you're reading it as a novel and not as an
"historic utterance" (Howe) or as "one of the great events in
man's literary and moral history" (Wilson).

What we have in *Doctor Zhivago* is a jumbled accretion
nervously strewn over a great many pages. Its occasional lovely
descriptions and speeches float to the surface like the splintered
witnesses of a shipwreck. For paragraphs here and there, the
novel sounds like Tolstoy (p. 84) or Dostoevsky (p. 155); in
fact, one might assemble an anthology of passages modeled on
the great Russian fiction writers from Gogol through Chekhov.
Here and there too are suggestions that apparently capricious
events or isolated descriptions are truly related to each other,
not in the artificial fashion of "The Rowan Tree" chapter, but in
the subtle one which Stuart Hampshire claims exists between the
natural scene and the narrative events. The trouble is that the
formal collapse and botched rendering obscure desired connections and indicate undesired ones. The errors of conception and
presentation corrode the novelistic ambition almost beyond
guessing.

A melancholy event for a reader of fiction, a melancholy

† The original piece dealt with others. (*See Kenyon Review,* Winter
1959.)

event for the citizen. For two years, readers have been waiting for this novel, their appetites sharpened by the early reports and bizarre publication history. That a great poet was treating one of the great themes of modern history, and from the lip of the grave itself, might well be a great event in "literary and moral history." It is understandable that when the novel did appear, many fine critics saw in this version of their own intellectual history a heroic and beautiful utterance.* For those less close to the ideological fire, this misshapen bequest from Soviet Russian literature testifies to what the book itself explicitly mourns, the dissolution of that sense of individual life which the great Western novel celebrates.

---

* Writing in *Dissent,* Lionel Abel confessed as much: "My liking for this book is a personal fact without significance for literary judgment; it is an accident of my own intellectual history; there is no reason why it should influence anybody else."

HENDERSON'S BELLOW

1

The first forty pages of *Henderson, the Rain King* * are packed
with enough material for two or three novels, odd, passionate
relationships between husbands and wives, fathers and children,
landlords and tenants, intricate, suspenseful, and disposed of
with quick brilliance that is the first of this book's surprises. The
next three hundred pages leap from this material into territory
few novelists in the world are energetic enough to enter. Or
rather to construct. Scanting his marvelous gift of reupholstering
the world's furniture, Bellow sends his hero into a country where
almost nothing is familiar.

> The way grew more and more stony and this made me
> suspicious. If we were approaching a town we ought by
> now to have found a path. Instead there were these jum-
> bled white stones that looked as if they had been combed
> out by an ignorant hand from the elements that make least
> sense. There must be stupid portions of heaven, too, and
> these had rolled straight down from it. I am no geologist
> but the word calcareous seemed to fit them. They were
> composed of lime and my guess was that they must have
> originated in a body of water. Now they were ultra-dry
> but filled with little caves from which cooler air was ex-
> haled—ideal places for a siesta in the heat of noon, pro-
> vided no snakes came. But the sun was in decline, trum-
> peting downward. The cave mouths were open and there
> was this coarse and clumsy gnarled white stone.

This country is neither conscientiously symbolic nor artificial;
but seen through the eyes of Henderson, the regal, knowledgeable, keening slob who narrates the book, its topography has
personality, one which seems to both objectify and spur the
novel's bizarre notions.

Are there precedents for this sort of construction? In a way,

* Saul Bellow, *Henderson, the Rain King* (New York: Viking, 1958).

there aren't. Utopians, satirists, dream visionaries have been contriving countries for millenia, but to greater or lesser degree their contrivances are unlikely. Either the landscape is unearthly and the brute creation articulate, or the hero arrives by time machine or dream. In Bellow's Africa custom and belief are strange, but all—including a semidomesticated lion—*seems,* real. Fantasy is reserved for speculation, where it can be accommodated as an early stage of knowledge.

There is a much more important difference in *Henderson,* and that is its hero. The Gullivers, Candides, and Connecticut Yankees may be scalpels, sensitometers, blank slates, mechanical pens, victims, physicians, PA systems, or even types, eccentric and amusing, but they are never characters whose fates mean more than their discoveries and situations. Eugene Henderson outlasts both what he learns and what happens to him, and constantly he pulls the book out of the perilous abstract. His American memories corkscrew through the African present tense with an ease which makes Ford and Conrad look elephantine; his grab-bag miseries and splendors—battered hulk, largesse, sweet ambitions, ever aching conscience—domesticate the unfamiliar. The book stays grounded in the real.

Henderson proceeds from the narrator's want. He's had the world and it isn't enough. It's what Bellow supplies for his want that makes the book a different sort of reading experience for faithful Bellovians.

2

An account of the difference might begin with a paragraph from *Augie March:*

> In his office Simon wore his hat like a Member of Parliament, and while he phoned his alligator-skin shoes knocked things off the desk. He was in on a deal to buy some macaroni in Brazil and sell it in Helsinki. Then he was interested in some mining machinery from Sudbury, Ontario, that was wanted by an Indo-Chinese company. The nephew of a cabinet minister came in with a proposi-

tion about waterproof material. And after him some sharp character interested Simon in distressed yard-goods from Muncie, Indiana. He bought it. Then he sold it as lining to a manufacturer of leather jackets. All this while he carried on over the phone and cursed and bullied, but that was just style, not anger, for he laughed often.

There in a single paragraph out of *Augie*'s thousand or so, the great know-how is at work, the skipping facts, the bunched variety more lively than life ever is, four or five different sorts of sentence, all held in and charged with Augie's tone. Places, things, people, pointed description, key movements—the alligator-skin shoes knocking things off the desk—and the characterizing summary, this is the way it goes, more brilliantly packed with the commodity and stuff of the world than anything in American literature since *Moby Dick*. "It was like giving birth to Gargantua," Bellow said of it, and that comparison may indicate why it stopped, for to the reader it looks as if it might go on as long as the world supplied Augie with objects to handle and people to watch.

. *Henderson* starts where *Augie* leaves off. Augie was a knocker at doors, a Columbus of the "near at hand." Henderson is a Columbus of the absolute, fifty-five, not twenty, a man for whom doors have opened but who dislikes what's inside.

The problem for *Henderson*'s writer is that the absolute is barely furnished, and what furniture it has consists of those Biedermeier hulks of fiction, ideas.

The strategy of idea novels amounts to working out a form of concealment: the action is tied into idea as illustration or contradiction. The organizing idea of a novel close to *Henderson,* Mann's *Felix Krull,* is something like the reality of fakery, and the book is cluttered with crooks, magicians, illusionists of all sorts, glorious-looking champagne bottles containing miserable champagne, actors seen first under lights and then backstage, a spectrum of fakery drawn from department store windows to interstellar space. The picaresque adventures are sunk into this detail, which is assembled to illustrate, or rather to compose, the themes. On the other hand, in such a book as *The Magic Mountain* the characters do things which contradict the notions they expound. (A humanitarian pacifist challenges a Jesuit convert to a duel, and the latter kills himself.) *Henderson* takes neither one of these routes; its actions are discrete from the notions which make up much of the book—Henderson's, those of the two beautiful obesities, the women of Bittahness, and those of the William James-reading, almost-MD totem king, Dahfu. *Henderson*'s notions glow like actions, its actions signify. (It is a truer expression of the Eliot-Pound thesis of sensuous ideas than most of what they wrote.) So toward the end of the novel King Dahfu is in the midst of a Reichian analysis of Henderson's posture:

> You appear cast in one piece. The midriff dominates. Can you move the different portions? Minus yourself of some of your heavy reluctance of attitude. Why so sad and so earthen? Now you are a lion. Mentally, conceive of the environment. The sky, the sun, and creatures of the bush. You are related to all. The very gnats are your cousins. The sky is your thoughts. The leaves are your insurance, and you need no other. There is no interruption all night to the speech of the stars. Are you with me? I say, Mr. Henderson, have you consumed much amounts of alcohol in your life? The face suggests you have, the nose especially. It is nothing personal. Much can be changed. By no means all, but very much. You can have a new poise, which will be your own poise. It will resemble the voice of Caruso, which I have heard on records, never tired because the function is as natural as to the birds.

Dahfu tells Henderson to get down on his hands and knees and bellow. "Be the beast!"

> And so I was the beast. I gave myself to it, and all my sorrow came out in the roaring. My lungs supplied the air but the note came from my soul. The roaring scalded my throat and hurt the corners of my mouth and presently I filled the den like a bass organ pipe. This is where my

heart had sent me, with its clamor. Oh, Nebuchadnezzar!
How well I understood that prophecy of Daniel. For I had
claws, and hair, and some teeth, and I was bursting with
hot noise . . .

Dahfu's speech is so wily a mixture of the lyric and admonitory,
the descriptive and conceptual, that even if it were not couched
in gorgeous Bellafrikanisch it would advance the narrative at
least as well as more obvious action. Dahfu's assessment leads to
Henderson's roar, the roar leads into further assessment. "I was
the beast . . . [I roared] . . . the note came from my soul . . .
This is where my heart had sent me . . ." The scenic extrava-
gance, a large man on hands and knees bellowing like a maniac,
is put into an intellectual context which makes it not only right
but moving. Behind it is the sort of momentum Swift gave the
scene in which Gulliver kisses his master's hoof farewell, one of
the most beautiful in eighteenth-century fiction.

As for the ideas themselves, they exist in terms of Henderson's
need and have as much relation to belief as Bellow's Africa to
Tom Mboyo's. The major one—a version of the notion that we
are in large part the product of the images we absorb—can be
found in such different places as the beginning of Plutarch's Life
of Timoleon, *Felix Krull,* and the somatic psychology of Wilhelm
Reich. What counts in the novel is that Henderson's reaction to
them reveals and deepens his character; and for Bellow, as for
Malamud and some of the other fine novelists of the time, character is back in the middle of the novel, not where their great
predecessors—Mann, Joyce, and to a somewhat lesser extent the
greater novelist Proust—put it, into a thematic scheme which
trimmed every fictional element to size.

Henderson is a bridge between *Augie March, Seize the Day,*
and those thematic novels. The difficulty is that the bridge must
bear the weight of constant invention, invention which can
hardly draw at all on the home detail in which the other novels
luxuriate. An original like Bellow can't lean too much on the
secondhand views of travelers and movies; he must be on alert

for those special clichés which menace writing about the exotic. Consequently, much of *Henderson*'s detail is landscape, physiognomy, and a few clothing props, and the investment there is great. Bellow readers, used to commodity markets, Mexican resorts, Evanston haberdasheries, Machiavellians, and con men, must go into another gear. They will be helped by the fact that *Henderson* is a stylistic masterpiece.*

The *Henderson* prose had a wonderful tryout in a long story, "Leaving the Yellow House," which appeared a year or so ago in *Esquire.†* The story's about a sort of female Henderson—but on her last legs—who drips out like hourglass sand in the Utah desert. Its clean sentences are now galvanized by the popping energy of *Augie,* and the result is such paragraphs as this:

> Itelo protruded his lips to show that I was expected to kiss her on the belly. To dry my mouth first, I swallowed. The fall I had taken while wrestling had split my underlip. Then I kissed, giving a shiver at the heat I encountered. The knot of the lion's skin was pushed aside by my face, which sank inward. I was aware of the old lady's navel and her internal organs as they made sounds of submergence. I felt as though I were riding in a balloon above the Spice Islands, soaring in hot clouds while exotic odors rose from below. My own whiskers pierced me inward, in the lip. When I drew back from this significant experience (having made contact with a certain power—unmistakable!—which emanated from the woman's middle), Mtalba also reached for my head, wishing to do the same, as indicated by her gentle gestures, but I pretended I didn't understand and said to Itelo, "How come when everybody else is in mourning, your aunts are both so gay?"

3

There are, I think, three very different sorts of literary experience: the writer's, the reader's, and the critic's, the last two being

* After *Mr. Sammler's Planet* I'm tempted to reserve this description for it; but a dozen years ago there was nothing prettier than *Henderson*'s prose.

† Reprinted in *Mosby's Memoirs and Other Stories.* (New York: Viking, 1969).

as distinct as the first from them. If we analogize the writer to an assassin, the reader is the corpse, the critic the coroner-detective. The feelings of the assassin and his victim are notably different, but at least for our purposes they can be called powerful ones. In the former's case, they are organized by purposiveness, in the latter's by force (scarcely conceived and rapidly terminated). The coroner-critic is the rationalist, the reconstructionist; he cannot alter the responses of the reader-victim, but he can, in a sense, alter those of future readers in such fashion that their reactions will be affected by his notions. An early Monet critic could instruct viewers to stand a certain distance from the canvas. (Indeed, the feelings of someone who knows he has been murdered—knows, because "murder" is defined—are surely different from those he'd have if he were run down by a truck.) I bring this up because my reactions first as reader and then as critic of *Henderson* are distinct.* As reader I respond more easily to the Bellow I am used to, the parts of *Henderson* which deal with his American experience—his pig farm, bad teeth, Sevčik violin exercises, his fights on Highway Seven, his high rides with the bear Smolak, his wives and children. As critic, however, that part of me which reading has not yet slain, I admire the boldness and brilliance of the whole, the "originality" and the style, and the other tributaries of great narrative. And I believe my feelings will in future readings catch up with my admiration.†

---

* As a matter of fact, I feel in small part with the assassin, perhaps as accessory after the fact. I read an earlier version of *Henderson* and some of my initial reactions to it turned out to be similar to Bellow's as he went over the book, so that changes were made which make me feel—proudly—implicated. (I reminded him that a scene in which Henderson killed some monkeys who turned out to be the lovers of some of the women was out of *Candide*. The scene of the dynamited frogs was substituted.) The point here is that I feel I know what effects were wanted at certain moments; I also feel "in" on such genetic factors as Bellow's interest in Reich. Such knowledge alters, and alters seriously, my responsiveness to the "magic" of the book.

† I've never reread *Henderson*.

PNIN'S DUST JACKET

It is not often that one has to hurdle the praise of writers one respects to come to an accurate appraisal of a book, but the dust jacket of Mr. Nabokov's *Pnin* * throws a lot of dazzling dust in one's eyes.

The most fantastic claim on the jacket is Edmund Wilson's:

> [Nabokov] turns out to be a master of English prose— the most extraordinary phenomenon of the time since Conrad . . . [He is] something like Proust, something like Franz Kafka, and, probably, something like Gogol . . . [but he] is as completely himself as any of these other writers . . .

Even with the bracketed additions and the dots, even knowing that Mr. Wilson doesn't think much of Kafka, even with the strangely timid "probably," the ambiguous phrases "completely himself" and "the most extraordinary phenomenon of the time since Conrad," there remains "turns out to be a master of English prose." Or could it be that the Nabokov supplied in the brackets was originally—who? Grace Zaring Stone? Just as likely. It must be that Mr. Nabokov has a house at Wellfleet † or helped Mr. Wilson learn Russian, because even the ear that discerned the death rattle of Western poetry in its finest poetic hour in a hundred years ‡ could not, without some extraliterary prompting, acclaim such gimcrackery as

> Some people—and I am one of them—hate happy ends. We feel cheated. Harm is the norm. Doom should not jam.
> (p. 25)

* Vladimir Nabokov, *Pnin* (Garden City, N.Y.: Doubleday, 1957). The Nabokov tide will, I think, subside, leaving the delightful *Lolita* and a few stories.

† A pretty fair guess. Since then, the two old grumblers squabbled on literary pages.

‡ Edmund Wilson, "Is Verse a Dying Technique?" *The Triple Thinkers.*

Or, if that is considered the burlesqued property of *Pnin*'s ghostly narrator, then this example will serve:

> The bells were musical in the silvery sun. Framed in the picture window, the little town of Waindell—white paint, black pattern of twigs—was projected, as if by a child, in primitive perspective devoid of aerial depth, into the slate-gray hills; everything was prettily frosted with rime; the shiny parts of parked cars shone; Miss Dingwall's old Scotch terrier, a cylindrical boar of sorts, had started upon his rounds up Warren Street and down Spelman Avenue and back again; but no amount of neighborliness, landscaping, and change ringing could soften the season; in a fortnight, after a ruminant pause, the academic year would enter its most winterly phase, the Spring Term, and the Clementses felt dejected, apprehensive, and lonely in their nice old drafty house that now seemed to hang about them like the flabby skin and flapping clothes of some fool who had gone and lost a third of his weight. (pp. 29–30)

This pile of clauses is neither comic nor rhythmically pleasing, the imagery is either trite or wrong, there is useless filler ("of sorts"), and the overall effect has a complex pointlessness ("projected . . . hills") which would suggest some private joke if it were consistent. Nabokov's style exhibits almost every stylistic vice from the baroque vocabulary ("canthus," "calvity," "zygomatic,") which strays into neologistic ugliness ("reminiscential," "hostelic") to mistakes in idiom ("arrived at last to," "twice bigger," "up the country") which are pardonable, but not on the grounds that the narrator is a Russian émigré, because the mistakes are not frequent enough to be explicable, achieve no effects but awkwardness, and should have been taken care of along with a number of annoying mechanical blemishes ("Are they only mechanical?"). The alliteration ("proceeded to impress upon Pnin the following points") is so annoying that again one wonders "Is it planned? Is it funny?" There is a similar mania for parentheses *—"so as to have the one he wanted among the

---

* The reader of the book may notice that Nabokov isn't the only devotee of the parenthesis.

rest (thus thwarting mischance by mathematical necessity)"—
funny names (Dr. Rosetta Stone), and a Conradian excess of
qualifiers. There is, occasionally, a good paragraph (see last
half of page 120).

Style, however, is a question of manner. What are we to say
to Mark Schorer, whose rapture centers about more basic issues?

> How to describe it or its effects? I'll settle for profoundly
> delightful, because under the wonderful and hilarious com-
> edy, which any academic person at least will recognize at
> once and delight in, there is a deep pathos that takes us
> out of all academies into the befuddled sufferings of hu-
> manity at large . . . I honestly haven't enjoyed a novel so
> much in a long time.

Mr. Schorer is a novelist and a critic of the novel, and though
he considers imagery patterns of novels more important than I
do,* he knows the shapes of fiction, long and short. *Pnin* is no
novel, and mere publisher's thirst for the commodity should not
conceal the fact. *Pnin* contains material for a novel, notes for a
novel, but even the strange final chapter in which the narrator at
last appears more conspicuously than in an aside—"the kind
Russian lady (a relative of mine)"—and tries to organize some
of the events of the book cannot conceal the indirection, the
waste of character and incident, the false soliciting of expectation which come from jamming these casual sketches into the
"novel" category. Notes for *a novel,* because there is a moving
situation, a clumsy, comic, sentimental, good-hearted Russian
émigré isolated in a country whose ease and mechanism he
adores but who is victimized by them and almost all the people
who surround him. Such summary does too much honor to these
one hundred and ninety pages. The book's only continuous lines
are Pnin and the setting. They sit around waiting for anecdotal
movement. The end of the book uncovers the narrator—the

* Mark Schorer, "Technique as Discovery," *Hudson Review,* 1 (Spring
1948), 67–87.

popular lecturer who is to take Pnin's job—listening to the anecdotes.

The reader who says about this device, "Look, you've just pointed to the clever, original form of the book," will be guilty of Nabokov's own makeshift notion of form. As *New Yorker* sketches the *Pnin* stuff had some charm. Not as a novel. The academic wisecracks trip over each other; the notation of American detail ("a copy of Gertrude Käsebier's photographic masterpiece 'Mother and Child' "), Pnin's crying spells, the pedagogical parentheses—"He picked up his *portfel'* (briefcase)"—the Pninisms—" 'Unwrap,' said Pnin"—get heavier and heavier, until the last hope that they are going to function in a moving work is lost and one waits out the end.

OUT OF LITERARY PHASE

One of the great twentieth-century novels is Christina Stead's *House of All Nations,* which Simon and Schuster published in 1938 and few have read since. Its world is international finance; its characters are dominated by markets, manipulations, making money from gesture, rumor, or even occasionally real goods. The place is usually Paris, the time just before the great gold crisis of 1933, the knowledge of the world such that no work known to me better reveals the relationship of money to personality and politics. It is, perhaps, the leading Stendhalian novel in English.

Like all novels of experience its problem is narrative structure; but like almost all fine novels of experience it works out ways of saying what it has to say. The book is constructed around characters arranged in a hierarchy of finance as the *Inferno*'s are in a hierarchy of sin. The characters are more vivid than exemplary, and there is no sense that they are not controlling the novelistic process; a reader who misses that process —the ruination of character and society by money men—can still be charmed by the book.

House of All Nations appeared in a bad time. The reviews were, as they say, mixed.* The main thing here, though, is that the book has not yet become a part of literary culture; and that culture, and the social-political-esthetic standards which spring from it, is the weaker for it. It appeared, then, out of literary phase, against the time's grain, as that is expressed in commerce. An irony for a book about this phenomenon.†

* Louise Bogan said it was neo-Ouida, Alfred Kazin that the author's great gifts would show up better in other novels; John Chamberlain and Elliot Paul thought it terrific.

† The book is even more out of phase than Miss Stead's later, weaker, and less ambitious but still excellent novel *The Man Who Loved Children,* which was revived after years of touting by Randall Jarrell and his friends. *House of All Nations* has just (1972) been reissued by Holt, Rinehart and Winston.

Very powerful books often spring up out of phase, and God knows how many rot away unknown. The fact is a romantic cliché but the sort that's useful to keep recalling. The recall keeps some control over the narrowing of literary culture.

In these days, that culture is dominated by two sorts of work. The first is the splendid literature of comic self-revelation, the idiomatic poetry of great cities, the discovery of the comedy and beauty of more and more new, offstage (ob-scene) material. The American Jewish writers perform these urban excavations as American Southern writers performed them in the country.

The other tradition of great but in my view lesser richness is the experimental one, an international tradition whose esprit is close to that of modern painting (the art world as laboratory), but which is even more handicapped (sheltered?) than that world by the ubiquitous accomplishment of its greatest practitioner, James Joyce. The French public is the most alert to this tradition partly because of the excellent national training in language and the concomitant fatigue with its classic postures (which take more than a Céline to somersault). The French experimenters are, in my view, a most refined and intelligent group, but the closest they come to work of independent power (work which doesn't gasp out of critical water) is in the fiction of the émigré Irishman Beckett.*

I've just [1969] read—and write now to signal the appearance of—a new novel in the French vein by an American, Austin Wright.† The experimental novel of Wright is less conspicuously a machine for making philosophical comments about narrative than the French works, or even those of Borges (although his are independent and beautiful in no small part because of his

---

* Where Joyce kept all the naturalistic stuff in the novel and then worked his wonders organizing it, his young friend Beckett worked the other end of the street, and got rid of more and more. His job is maintaining narrative interest. He does wonderfully for thirty or forty pages at a crack.

† Austin Wright, *Camden's Eyes* (Garden City, N.Y.: Doubleday, 1969).

short forms). Wright's book should be noted, not for the general reader who can read almost any good "novel of experience" with pleasure, but for those who treasure narrative form and feel its complex relationship to the forms of awareness. Wright's plot, like that of most experimental work, depends on the familiarity of its story (middle-class adultery), but its power comes from the shifting ratios between incremental knowledge and ever reforming narrative versions of it. The texture is Jamesian— slow (incremental and interdependent), limited almost entirely to the world of the fable, witty, wise, and usually beautiful, sentence by sentence. Its modernity is in the shift of narrative person ("I" can become "he" in the same sentence) and syntactic shock (sentences dangle, usually to avoid spelling out what the narrator—and the reader—can guess). Once you pay the high price of admission, the stylistic excitement is high. The excitement of texture is close to that of the narrative excitement, which is largely sexual. In a way the book is a kind of anti-*Portnoy*, not as immediately pleasing or lyric and not as brave (or *je m'en foutiste*), but it deals with harder matters and requires subtler organization.

I mention *Portnoy* and began with *House of All Nations* in the small hope of averting the quick demise of Wright's book. For both deep and commercial reasons, this is *Portnoy*'s time.* The depths are those of the comic dispersal of psychic shadows; the commerce has to do with the packaging of this new morsel of liberty. *Camden's Eyes* is the butt end of a tradition. It speaks to self-denial rather than self-expression, to the intensification of character rather than its liberation from unhappiness. Its comedy is quiet and its beauty is economic rather than caricaturistic (a visitor's list tells a saga in a few lines, the first such innovation since the party names in *Gatsby*). It is also heavy with the stigma of the difficult book, very long paragraphs, with conversation seldom set out from the margin. In short, a loser.

The hope here is that this little work, published out of literary

* 1969.

phase and against the grain, will be read by twenty or thirty thousand Americans and become to some extent a part of literary culture now. Although its disappearance would not be as grave as that of Miss Stead's marvelous book, it would be graver than that of much that is daily celebrated.

CATCH-22

The human interior is full of violent gripes against life; books which don't draw on them seldom get beyond decorous amusement. But between gripe and *The Brothers Karamazov* come craft, intelligence, and imaginative power. *Catch-22* * has the comedy and fervor of gripes, but its lack of craft and measure cripple it. A portrait gallery, a collection of anecdotes (some of them wonderful), a parade of scenes (some of them finely assembled), a series of descriptions, yes, but the book is supposed to be a novel. It's supposed to add up, to build, to sow and harvest. You can say it's much too long, because its material—the cavortings and miseries of an American bomber squadron stationed in World War II Italy—is repetitive and one-note; or you can say it's too short, because none of its many interesting characters and actions is given enough play to organize your sympathy. Heller's like a brilliant painter who decides to throw all the ideas in his sketchbook onto one large canvas, relying on their charm and shock to compensate for the lack of design. A Rembrandt talent could not survive such procedure.

If *Catch-22* were intended as a commentary novel such as *USA* or *The Idiot,* then such sideswiping of character and action might be taken care of by the thematic commentary, but every other page heads it into farce or fantasy. No mood is sustained long enough to register for more than a chapter; the result is emotional chaos.

All right, what about *Tristram Shandy*? Isn't it an open invitation to say anything? Yes, but its energy and pathos constantly

* Joseph Heller, *Catch-22* (New York: Simon and Schuster, 1961). I stick with this review, though rocks have been heaved at it for years. It appeared in the Sunday book section of the New York *Times* on about page 70. Happily for Heller and his millions of fans, the review didn't do much harm. Indeed, on the book's tenth anniversary, the *Times* used the front page to rebuke its old reviewer.

retrieve its "waste matter." And, furthermore, it doesn't keep making concessions to the standard novels of its day. *Catch-22* does. It's as if it suddenly sees its nuttiness in the mirror and then decides to be a good novel and play it straight for a while. So it has its little mode of progress: the decent get killed off, the self-seekers prosper, and there is a last-minute turnabout.

If Heller had let himself go all out, or shortened the book till there was nothing ordinary in it, if he'd burlesqued not only the insanity of war's detail but the literature which recorded it, *Catch-22* might have been a first-rate book.

MALAMUD'S *TENANTS*

Harry Lesser, "a serious man," is the last inhabitant of a New York tenement. Levenspiel, the owner, pleads with him to get out so wreckers can make way for an income-producing building. Lesser, a hard man but not a stone one, understands Levenspiel's plight but sticks to his legal guns.

Thirty-six, author of one good and one bad novel, he is finishing up his third. Ten years he's been at it, the end is in sight, he cannot tear himself from his routine now. But the end won't come, it won't quite come.

"For Christ' sake," Levenspiel asks him, "what are you writing, the Holy Bible?"

Who can say till it's finished? Not Lesser. Stench, prowlers' filth, cold, decay, and the implorations of Levenspiel mount the six flights and maroon Lesser with his manuscript.

One day he hears the plokkity-plok of a typewriter. Had he "left himself hard at work somewhere around while he was out getting his groceries"? No. In the abandoned apartment down the hall, bent over a huge old typewriter which resembles "a miniature fortress," is "a goateed man, darkly black-skinned," another serious man, another writer, Willie Spearmint (nom de plume, Bill Spear).

Had Levenspiel booked "this act" to spook him? No. Willie is there because he can't work at home while his "bitch" fiddles around. So the two writers, black and white, work side by side in the dying tenement.

This beautiful, bare, intense situation is the center of Bernard Malamud's new novel.* In the classic fashion of the short novel or story Malamud worked out in *The Assistant, The Magic Barrel,* and *Idiots First,* the protagonists grind each other either

* Bernard Malamud, *The Tenants* (New York: Farrar, Straus and Giroux, 1971).

until they are interchangeable or until one or both are trans-figured or dead.

The Tenants, though, has something more. Like so many post-Renaissance makers, Malamud comes up against himself. "What am I? What is a writer?" The book is self-reflexive (not autobiographical).

To work out new versions of this theme is no joke. *The Tempest* is a marvel, Fellini's *8½* a clutter of mirrors. The Malamud version is remarkable, but my early feeling about it is that it has been wounded by the strongest of artistic sirens, the desire to include too much and be too much.

The excess, first, is in story. The marvelous relationship between black and white writers becomes one between black and white and black and Jew. To the degree that our ideas of ourselves and others are verbal creations, this is a fine, novelistic swelling of the basic theme of creation-conclusion, and within it Malamud invents brilliantly: Willie's work is described, its flaws and powers are there on the page. (This tour de force gives the lie to the manacling notion that imagination stops at skin or nation.)

Outside this relationship is Spearmint's "bitch," the white actress Irene, who passes to Lesser, her bleached hair growing back to its natural black. Irene means the end of servitude to writing, and though there is no happy resolution in the sheets she is Lesser's *dea ex machina.* The excess is here. A large portion of the book bends around a love triangle, which, no matter how meaningful, deforms and simplifies it.

There is other excess. Lesser's book is called *The Promised End;* it does not end, it ends Lesser, and in another way it ends *The Tenants.*

We wait for a superb end to this book, we are forced to it; but the investment is so great that it would be hard to imagine an end that would satisfy it. Malamud's doesn't. He wriggles in and out of endings, using clever devices, even meaningful ones, but the book coasts in. On fantasy.

At its best, Malamud's realism is so pure that it becomes parabolic without effort. When his spare little situations work themselves out to their realistic extremities, the craziness, violence, and comedy soar toward mystery without wind machines.

The world is too mysterious for magic, too rapid in turnover for imported ambiguity. (God is subtle, not malevolent, said one of his greatest interpreters.) The world employs, maybe needs, fable and true myth. In literature there is a cozy place for fable; and Malamud has written fine ones which are never in doubt. But when fantasy is confused with metaphor, watch out.

The fantasy of *The Tenants* slides in on a somewhat greased style. Most of it is classic Malamudian, street-fresh, bare, slightly Yiddished American, full of odd turns which double back in the sentence for picturesque force: "Things could be worse and had been."

But there are also dark sentences, with sticky syntax and poetic noise: "What useless dreams intervene? Though he remembers none although his sleep is stuffed with dreams, Lesser reveries one touched with fear: Here's the stranger I meet on the stairs."

All writers like to extend the language. Malamud has and does, but here and there the strain hobbles the narrative.

The final word here is praise. The purity of a book like this exposes impurities more easily than a plain, good storybook. Malamud is a fine craftsman, a fine writer; his intensity is Kafkaesque, his low comedy unexcelled, his literary economy so admirable that it leads him to play with it. *The Tenants* is a much, much better book than his last three; it should be read with joy for a very long time.

LEAKS IN THE UPDIKE

When stories float out of every television set and newspaper (the New York *Times* is called the leading black humorist), the writer of a four- or five-hundred-page novel should perhaps be more wondered at than despaired of. Shouldn't that quixotic industry which assembles places, characters, scenes, and events into some sort of compelling order be allowed to pass without hindrance?

Oddly enough, no. It's the luxury products we examine most closely. Our lunch may be lethal, our air unbreathable, our houses flimsy lumps, but there they are. As for the twenty or thirty novelists who mean something to us, we look them over closely.

So here is John Updike's fifth novel,* four hundred and fifty-eight pages long, and it took a lot of work to put together, and its author is a witty, crafty, intelligent man who's written eight or nine beautiful short stories, one firm, modest novel (*The Poorhouse Fair*), and a few scenes in other novels which bring much pleasure. A relatively precious commodity, and in the nature of things one has been hoping for a marvelous book from his hand. There's all that wonderful Olinger material waiting for Proustian assemblage—the sensitive son with bad skin, the oppressively innocent, virtuous father, the Pennsylvania Dutch land with the snowed-in farms, the high school basketball games, the creaky Pontiacs, the optometrists, drugstores, sweethearts, and the return to them all with the beautiful, resistant wife, the art school diploma, the oblique poetic brushes with the Absolute. All that waits for real treatment, and what do we have?

Sentences: "Her cool thin tone, assumed at the moment when he had believed their intimacy, in this well-lit safe room encircled by the April dark, to be gathering poignant force enough to

* John Updike, *Couples* (New York: Alfred Knopf, 1968).

263

vault them over their inhibitions, angered him" (p. 4). Misprint?
An error in transmission (out of Aramaic via Hungarian). The
book is stuffed with them.

What else?

Dialogues, on this level of wit and insight:

> "We've become slaves to auctions," Roger Guerin was
> continuing. From the square shape of his head Foxy
> guessed he was Swiss and not Parisian French in ancestry.
> Her side was nudged and Freddy Thorne told her,
> "Roger thinks auctions are like Monopoly games. All over
> New Hampshire and Rhode Island they know him as the
> Mad Bidder from Tarbox. Highboys, lowboys, bus boys.
> He's crazy for commodes."
> "Freddy exaggerates," Roger said.
> "He's very discriminating," Ann called from her end of
> the table.
> "That's not what I'm told they call it," Harold little-
> Smith was saying to Janet.
> "What are you told, dear?" Janet responded.
> Harold dipped his fingers into his water goblet and
> flicked them at her face . . . (p. 28)

Etcetera.

A museum of narrative monsters, not grand enough for parody
or even spite.

Then there is the book's chief commodity, love stuff. *Couples*
is the supermarket of Smarmy Enchantment: "Her slick firm
body was shameless yet did not reveal, as her more virginal
intercourse once had done, the inner petals drenched in helpless
nectar" (p. 130). The hope may be that the library board of
Salina, Kansas, or Kirksville, Missouri, might make a fuss about
such shuddering beauty or, perhaps, that the adolescent underground will find here a new *Guide to Doing It.** For *It* is the
book's story, at least coupling (largely heterosexual and gusta-
tory: "To eat another is sacred" [p. 435]). The rest is the fall
of the chief Tarbox coupler, Piet Hanema. The fall, though, is

---

* This was out of date even then.

clumsy, perhaps an afterthought to give a bit of shape to the mass. The whole strikes one as a distended, strophulous version of *Appointment in Samarra*, whose prolific, self-indulgent and -abusing author Updike resembles more and more.

A concluding moral. After a few years of more or less innocent and driven story writing, the fiction writer begins to know that what counts requires a kind of moral tenacity which vanity, indolence, ignorance, and timidity work to sap. No accumulation of craft or knowledge can disguise the loss of this higher fidelity, and on the other hand no failure will erase all its marks.

Except for eighty fine pages about a marital swap, the marks are absent from *Couples*. If the old Olinger conscience will take Updike out to the woodshed, perhaps he can come back a sound writer.* Unlikely. The rot of this fancy, sweating, deformed, profoundly trivial book is a public lesson for a number of us.

---

* *Beck: A Book* (New York: Knopf, 1970) is a clever fake. I haven't read *Rabbit Redux* (New York: Knopf, 1971). Every now and then Updike publishes a lovely story.

SOME THAT GLITTERS IS

The most experimental times have their set pieces, their Annunciations and Madonnas. Ivan Gold's novel * can be hung on lots of the day's topical pegs: the Novel About Writing a Novel, the Belle Bitch Sans Merçi, the Dirge of the New York Jew. But wrapping paper isn't gift, and Gold, Ivan, is as distinct from Gold, Herbert, as he is from Powers, J. F., Paley, Grace, and Johnson, Uwe.† His book is made out of what they sell down at the corner, but he's a good cook and doesn't pass beans off as caviar.

Sick Friends has a very good narrator, a funny idler-writer trying to write another book. Jason Sams is smart and, better, seems exceptionally honest.

In art, honesty is often what sells rotten meat as Rotten Meat; but *Sick Friends* is a book whose form and aroma are confessional—from its dedication to "H.S. who was there" to a biographical note whose dates and places conform to the fictional hero's. Mostly Gold uses internal, Gulliverian devices for "making honesty," footnotes which supply complete texts of documents, the hero's habit of copying other people's diaries and letters and telling readers when he has failed to copy and has to reconstruct something from memory. Most of all, there's the prodding sense that this book is barely able to contain all that happened to him and his friends, and that there is lots more waiting for Guggenheims to be told.

What is told is mostly Jason's difficult time with Christa Sarkissian. Not *the* artist in his huffing thirties, not Russia in war and peace, just Jason. That, if not life, can be fiction, and one needn't deny oneself the involute pleasures of Mlle. Sarraute or the hippo-pirouettes of Gospodin Nabokov to assert that it's

* Ivan Gold, *Sick Friends* (New York: E. P. Dutton, 1969).
† Johnson's *Two Faces* is the best postwar German novel I've read.

the line of pure fiction, Homer through Tolstoy, James, Hemingway, Bellow, and thirty or forty contemporaries such as Gold.
The line is as persistent as grass or flesh and can't be outmoded
by movable type or film. (Of course, *Sick Friends* will be harder
"to teach" than *Jealousy* or *Ada* because it's mostly just there.)

It may be there a little too long. Now and then, counting the
pages left in the chapter, one thinks Gold could use some of the
intensifying devices of the trade, Herzogian letters, or a Spiel-
vogel to encourage the ellipses and poetic condensations of
hysteria. But maybe not. It may be that the depth of Jason's
involvement with Christa needs all the trips to the grocery, the
letters from friends, the sharp business of the street. It surely
needs the sexual detail.

Jason knows Christa sexually; her power is the source of the
instability which is his enthrallment and Gold's book. The description of their sexual life is crucial. Gold's hard-nosed, un-
transfiguring, never-let-anything-by style makes such difficult
pages a good deal more than a how-to manual or his own sexual
calling card; there's none of *Couples'* poetic slime or *Portnoy's*
lyric farce. Just love's labors won and lost. No small trick.

Gold's first book, *Nickel Miseries,* was not bad but nowhere
as good as this one; cleverness blotted most of its good stories.
Gold—as he lets readers know through Jason—went a long way
on it. His novel will probably be rapidly classified and forgotten.
The loss won't be as serious as, say, the loss of Miss Stead's
House of All Nations (1938),* but it would be another oversimplification of a literary scene which is too often divided between the sons of *Ulysses* and a few grandsons of the Russians.
Gold augments the scene; he is one of the few who've almost
mastered the art of seeming artless; he's seldom boring and he
seldom fakes. If you feel an occasional spurt of claustrophobia
reading his book ("There's got to be more in the world than
this"), at least you never say "This is baloney."

* I don't mind pounding the drum for this wonderful book.

For me, the only unworkable Gold stuff is the title and the splendid epigraphs from Mann, Wilhelm Reich, and Dostoevsky. Or does such finickiness earn the Dostoevskian description of the reviewer as "a creature who walks on two legs and is ungrateful"?

9. *Poems*

The authorities
Hand him the forms.

> Donald Justice
> "The Missing Person,"
> from *Night Light*.

Most of my own few poems are controlled by the formal patterns of the 1940s and 1950s; I neither elaborated nor broke with them. I observe poetry a bit better than I write it.

Sculpture and painting are said to pendulum between the "realistic" and the "Byzantine"; so does poetry. Metrical formality is the usual Western sign of "Byzantinism." When poetry moves toward some form of "prosaic realism," it departs from it in other, "poetic" ways—diction, syntax, sound schemes—or in quicker and longer jumps from notion to notion than any but surreal or farcical prose tolerates. So the Eliot-Pound Waste Land–Cantos *departure from Edwardian formalism has as much to do with elusive, rapid intelligence as with broken meters and syntax. The Wordsworth-Coleridge departure from Collins-Gray formality was, via meter loosening, "prose" subject matter and "prosaic" diction; its poetic emphasis is in such innovation as the speeded, elusive narrative (see the* Lucy *poems).*

Of the two books discussed here, Lowell's marked a break with the formal poetry which dominated the 1950s. A student of the formalist Ransom, Lowell had been writing fairly "strict" poems, often in blank verse. In Life Studies *he loosened up. As with much real innovation, his impulse was not formal exhibitionism (not that that can't lead to fine results); Lowell's analyst, the irregular sonneteer Merrill Moore, had suggested he write a therapeutic autobiography. Lowell began with prose, then shifted into "prosaic" verse. The result inaugurated or signaled the confessional poetry of the 1960s.*

The Bowers book is the cream of the most Byzantine of all recent American schools, the one led by Yvor Winters at Stanford. At Chapel Hill in the 1940s Bowers, Donald Justice, and I ate Winters for breakfast and spent time catching each other's meters off his bases. Bowers and Justice went west to become his students, I stayed east, and went further east to Europe, leaving poetry to them that could do it. A few years later, back in Iowa among the trilling birds (Lowell, Shapiro, Berryman, Snodgrass,

271

Justice, and many others), I caught the bug again. I began writing poems, edited an anthology, and did such reviews as the two printed here.

SLOWILL

A book is so often an assemblage of pieces written over years and under varieties of pressure and allegiance that the writer himself marvels that its parts sometimes overrun their occasions to adhere to each other with a kind of "inevitable" fixity. That proper form is "natural" to great matter is a nineteenth-century notion that the twentieth century has largely discarded, but a good case can be made for it when the matter at hand is auto-biographical. A writer's life may not offer him a form, but it does hand him ready-made boundaries of experience and point of view which make his transformation of the matter from flux to object a quicker, easier job.

Robert Lowell's *Life Studies* * does not pose as a full-fledged autobiography. Unlike Wordsworth's, his experience is not selected to show "the growth of a poet's mind" or of anything else; his mixture of prose and verse isn't a Dantesque commentary in the manner of the *Vita Nuova,* nor is it a conscientiously symbolic or transfigured account in the manner of any number of poeticized lives which seem to have been lived for the poetry which would come from them. Lowell's "I" is not his lyric buggy; it's simply the narrator of his memories and his experience. As burgher lives go, it's some experience. Lowell seems to have been and suffered in his own person much of what is said to characterize the first half of the century: religious conversion

* Robert Lowell, *Life Studies* (New York: Farrar, Straus and Giroux, 1959).

and abandonment, the rebellion and domestication of liberalism, contempt for the state, violent pacifism, gentle rationality, and madness. Lapsed Catholic convert scion of great American (and almost, I understand, great Boston) families, "fire-breathing CO," semisocialist stalwart of Beacon Hill, victim of manic-depressive breakdowns, scholar, idler, genteel brawler, family rebel, and chronicler, self-effacing, egoistic, inaccessible, confessional. All this and much more in the ninety pages, so much of fact and emotional revelation that one can hardly believe one owes it to thirty-five pages of prose and twenty-three short poems.

Nor is this experience veiled or dominated by the poetry; if anything, the poetry which Lowell has contrived for this book takes the gloves off the experience, brings it in close-ups to the reader. I think it the most intimate exposure in recent literature; * and it is almost without the shriveling, rhetorical fakery of advertised intimacy.

> After a hearty New England breakfast,
> I weigh two hundred pounds
> this morning. Cock of the walk,
> I strut in my turtle-necked French sailor's jersey
> before the metal shaving mirrors,
> and see the shaky future grow familiar
> in the pinched, indigenous faces
> of these thorough-bred mental cases,
> twice my age and half my weight.
> We are all old-timers,
> each of us holds a locked razor.

Experience here does not yield to the overt signs of verse—regular meter, rhyme, juggled syntax; when convenient, these show up, but the idea seems to be to use verse chiefly as a way of making more rapid transitions than any but surrealist prose

---

* Since Lowell and Snodgrass opened the box, the supply of intimacy has exceeded all rational demand. I'm surprised the movies haven't caught up yet. (The indiscretions of Fellini, Bergman, and Godard are Georgian in their modesty.)

allows. In addition, the verse convention allows the poet to slough off the obligation to full accountability which prose at least promises. The burial of that formal poetry which Lowell wrote for years seems to go with his attempt to bury a raging ego. In the book's opening poem—three regular sonnets—these burials are associated with his leaving the Catholic Church: over the Alps, from Rome to Paris, his

> mountain-climbing train had come to earth.
> Tired of the querulous hush-hush of the wheels,
> the blear-eyed ego kicking in my berth
> lay still, and saw Apollo plant his heels
> on terra firma . . .

The "terra firma" of *Life Studies* is the poet's family. It comes through in these pages with a clarity, detail, and affection which look like his attempt to hold on to it through the ego benders. The sections about his grandfather are close to idylls, except that unlike most idylls they don't float away from detail:

> Nowhere was anywhere after a summer
> at my Grandfather's farm.
> Diamond-pointed, athirst and Norman,
> its alley of poplars
> paraded from Grandmother's rose garden
> to a scarey stand of virgin pine
> scrub, and paths forever pioneering.

Against the solidity, self-confidence, and richness of that time and place, the other lives in this book are broken and eccentric; the idyllic view is shaded by that:

> Mother, you smile
> as if you saw your Father
> inches away yet hidden, as when he groused behind a screen
> over a National Geographic Magazine,
> whenever young men came to court you
> back in those settled years of World War One.
> Terrible that old life of decency
> without unseemly intimacy

or quarrels, when the unemancipated woman
still had her Freudian papá and maids!

I suppose that the general intellectual viewpoint behind this
book is that most frequently associated with the *Partisan Review,*
the view that bourgeois life has persistently cheapened standards
so that the division between the powers and the intellectuals has
isolated and maddened the latter, and brutalized the former. In
Lowell's pages this viewpoint is earned when it is not asserted.
When it is asserted—as in a poem about Eisenhower's first
inauguration—the rhetoric seems inherited, the attitude easier
than the words.

Whether private, like Commander Billy Harkness, the "human
ash-heap," or public, like Santayana, "unbelieving, unconfessed
and unreceived," whether rendered in pruned Flaubertian prose
or the new verse, whether parts of large motifs—Commander
Lowell's leaving the Navy for Lever Brothers—or just framed in
Lowell's interior, the characters are the heart of this fine little
book. These and the moving poems about madness which come
at the end. The very last picture in the book has the poet, his
"mind not well," watching a brave mother skunk swilling garbage in the moonlight. Context implies that the garbage is what's
left for the poet, that this book is the swilling. Such swill nourishes. (For packaging, I'll offer the portmanteau "Slowill.")

THE POETRY OF EDGAR BOWERS

Edgar Bowers' poems * are those of someone who doesn't resort to meter at every robin's appearance. The poems sound like ones the poet seems obliged to write. They are controlled in a way which transforms personal feeling into commentary, rage into a kind of civic anger, tenderness into analysis of tenderness. The poems deal with important, common topics—love, death, reflections on great men, landscapes, dedications. They are rarely idiosyncratic; the aroused feelings are manifestly controlled; reference is explicitly made to them and to their magnitude.

Bowers is master of a complex syntax and a small, fairly common vocabulary composed to an unusual degree of abstract nouns and such words as "bone," "flesh," "light," "shade," and "dark." There are few bizarre qualifiers, no interchanged parts of speech, no *"Erhebungs,"* "concupiscent curds," or "dithering in the drift of cordial seas." Standard meters are employed in a way which seems the inflexible expressions of the feelings' small flexibility. In a century whose favorite poetry has so often been violent, allusive, antisyntactical, and theatrically idiosyncratic in subject and style, Bowers' work looks more conspicuous than it would in an eighteenth-century collection.

Bowers' distinguished teacher, Yvor Winters, wrote that a poem

> is good in so far as it makes a defensible rational statement about a given human experience (the experience need not be real but must in some sense be possible) and at the same time communicates the emotion which ought to be motivated by that rational understanding of that experience.†

* Edgar Bowers, *The Form of Loss* (Denver: Alan Swallow, 1956).
† *In Defense of Reason* (New York: William Morrow, 1947), p. 568.

This clumsy statement * will serve to distinguish the temper of Bowers and the more usual modern poet who, like Miss Compton-Burnett's Lesbia Firebrace, announces on the steps of the house she's come to visit that she has come to offer herself "because I have nothing else to offer. When people say that, they are content with their offering, and expect other people to be."

Bowers' poems are reasoned meditations usually centered about a single experience, a city view, a conversation with his grandmother, an elegy, reflections on a maxim. The poetic pressure comes from an insistent, complicating analysis. There is almost no narrative movement, even in poems whose events seem to beg for narrative treatment,† none of the emotional progress characteristic of Keats' odes, seldom movement which leads to emotional climaxes or turnabouts. The poems revolve about and close in on the experience until its import is transformed. They expose not so much breadth of perception as the serious, complex mind which is stirred into poetry by the original perception. This holds true for the few dramatic poems in the book as well; Bowers' William Tyndale and Joseph Haydn seem like each other and like the person who declares in the prefatory "To the Reader"

> These poems are too much tangled with the error
> And waste they would complete. My soul repays me,
> Who fix it by a rhythm, with reason's terror
> Of hearing the swift motion that betrays me.

"These poems" brood over loss, over the malice of both reason and unreason, and they are nostalgic for the old religion which softened loss and malice by placing them in a larger scheme. (See "The Virgin Considered as a Picture" and "Epigram on the Passing of Christmas.") Other poems deal with the aftermath of World War II seen from the side of the defeated

---

* Consider the uselessness of "defensible" next to "rational," of "given," and of the parenthetical expression, the lack of antecedent for "that rational experience" (stemming from a confusion of the two occurrences of "rational" in the sentence), and the bizarre "motivated."

† Though Bowers is one of the best storytellers I know.

(Bowers was an intelligence noncom in occupied Bavaria), the stones of Venice "in which great works decay," the loss of love, friends, relatives, surety, and innocence. Loss is the book's temper, but its richness comes from the analytic tenacity whose chief instrument is the most elaborate syntax in recent American poetry. The syntax is built not with phrase clusters, parallel constructions, or novel clauses but on such things as brief prepositional phrases which suddenly extend and modify the direction of the poetic sentence:

> Now at the last he lies back, still unspent,
> In passion and in time, relinquishing
> All that he gathered from them to their use,
> Clasps in the dark will he could not refuse
> Ingenuous patience eager with assent.
> > "Oedipus at Colonus"

The stanza consists of rapid modifications of the original view of the ripened, "unspent" king, and its strength is in the syntactic economy of "from them to their use" and the qualifier "Ingenuous."

I should like to look at one of Bowers' poems in order to exhibit some of its virtues and then point to a defect which is related to them. The poem is called "Dark Earth and Summer."

> Earth is dark where you rest
> Though a little winter grass
> Glistens in icy furrows.
> There, cautious, as I pass,
>
> Squirrels run, leaving stains
> Of their nervous, minute feet
> Over the tombs; and near them
> Birds gray and gravely sweet.
>
> I have come, warm of breath,
> To sustain unbodied cold,
> Removed from life and seeking
> Darkness where flesh is old,
>
> Flesh old and summer waxing,
> Quick eye in the sunny lime,

> Sweet apricots in silence
> Falling—precious in time,
>
> All radiant as a voice, deep
> As their oblivion. Only as I may,
> I come, remember, wait,
> Ignorant in grief, yet stay.
>
> What you are will outlast
> The warm variety of risk,
> Caught in the wide, implacable,
> Clear gaze of the basilisk.

The elegiac meditation is an address by the mourner to the one mourned. The tone is quiet but varied; the variations are embodied in a subtle metric which mostly departs from an anapestic dimeter base. A moving, quietly complicated statement leads to resolution in the last stanza.

Bowers balances great weights on tiny pivots, which is fine when the pivots are steady: so the use of "may" for the more likely "can" in the fifth stanza at first seemed a mistake, as did the "yet" in the same stanza; when the connection between the two is understood, an ordinary statement about mourning becomes a refined account of helplessness. If such pivots wobble, however, the poem is damaged more seriously than a poem built from more conspicuous blocks. Thus the confusion which rises from the questionable antecedents of "Removed from life," "All radiant as a voice," and "Caught in the wide . . . basilisk." The punctuation after "time" and the use of "old" to describe the flesh of the dead (if it described the speaker's, it would be an intolerable diversion) leave debate which can't be resolved with the surety which resolved the uncertainty about "may" and "yet." Consider

> All radiant as a voice, deep
> As their oblivion.

Does "All" refer to the apricots? So it would seem, but then why so heavy an investment in this detail, and why further complicate the dubious simile of the "voice" to which they are similar in radiance? Or is it "time" which is radiant? The punctuation would indicate that, but "their" makes this impossible, unless "their" refers to the apricots. Or "All" could refer to all the scene's components; but the difficulties attendant here are insurmountable. The point is that the "clear statement" is sometimes unclear, and the cause isn't intellectual difficulty but mechanical complications of expression derived from the poet's practice of never letting a simple statement stand. The practice accounts for much of Bowers' success, but out of the firm control it constantly requires, it mars lovely poems.

There are also, I think, two "mistakes" in diction which twist the poem away from the straightforward, if complex, situation toward false complication of the speaker's character (he becomes "literary"): "basilisk" and "precious in time," miscalculations of the strain that traditional diction exerts on poems. Such mistakes seem to me the sort which Bowers' difficult procedure invites and makes conspicuous, but the procedure is responsible for some of the most beautiful poems in recent American poetry.

10. Joyce, Eliot, Pound

Leaving the trail, we struck directly across the country, and took the shortest cut to reach the main stream of the Platte.

Francis Parkman
The Oregon Trail

These three "non-English" writers did more than any other English-language artists to make literature once again the form of mentality which made sense and beauty of more thought, behavior, scene, and feeling than any other. Their prime subject was the relationship of what people did, felt, and said they did and felt to what the dominant traditions of—largely—Western culture said people have felt, and done and should do. They treated the discrepancies on the realistic scale from rage through farce. Joyce's Bloom, a wastebasket of the culture, is en route to something else; he is a rendition of the extraordinary-ordinary man whose emotional life takes over the center of contemporary English and American literature. In Joyce the character is a pretty strictly controlled part of a large, formal scheme. The artistic "schemes" of the post-midcentury writers have been —on the whole—more closely related to the incidents which will best describe the emotional curve of the central characters. This has meant broader excavations of the inner life and views of the world clearly distorted by the ionized sensibilities of the characters. (Both Bellow and Robbe-Grillet can fit under this rubric.) I would guess that those of us writing now, whether conscious of it at the core of our work or not (and it will be mostly not), pour the stuff of such interior life over one traditional assumption after another. Whether we begin with a lust for novelty or just a desire to write about a person or situation as strongly as possible, the best results will deepen and re-order consciousness along the now hidden lines of the world's new strength. New energies, new scarcities, new gains, and new sorts of misery will be registered and worked out in the new constructions of literary art. The results, not the job, will be new. (Some results already match the work of the three old masters of the century.)*

Eliot, Pound, Joyce, and Proust took up a lot of my apprentice time. Eliot's poems, notes, and essays gave me my reading lists; Proust and Joyce were graphs of literary possibility; Pound, through an accidental meeting in Venice,* made me feel the life

*Cf. page 209

behind the textbooks. (My one meeting with Eliot was a small-joke scene. He "misheard" my name, and said, "Ah, Stearns. You're from Watertown, Mass." I said, "I'm afraid you're a hundred miles, two letters, and a few other things wide of the mark, Mr. Eliot." "Ah well," he said, "families wander in a generation.") Since then the old masters sometimes seem much closer at hand, sometimes impossibly remote. (Friends are too close for useful perspective.) These few small pieces were done for little magazines or Chicago newspapers. The one on Pound as a translator was my second critical piece (the first was a Rilke review in Poetry). *Perhaps they're more devotional than practical, but that may be the right way to close out the miscellany.*

JOYCE'S VANISHING ACT

For half a century Joyce scrutinized his own life. The results were remarkable books and a remarkable personality. Richard Ellmann has written an account of this autobiographical career * that not only extricates it from Joyce's versions of himself but explains the reasons for his versions. Explains, that is, what is explainable, for after eight hundred pages stoked with discoveries and insights Ellmann wisely permits Joyce to remain mysterious.

The mystery begins about halfway through Joyce's adult life, as he leaves Trieste for Zurich and begins the large-scale excavation of *Ulysses.* Up until this point Ellmann dominates his subject, judging with intimate severity the sponging egoism of the early years. In this ugly cocoon one of the subtlest imaginations in the world has been forming, one that resists the classifications of

* Richard Ellmann, *James Joyce* (New York: Oxford University Press, 1959).

biographer, wife, brother, or itself. Ellmann keeps describing
Joyce, but he makes clear that we are seeing less and less of what
counts. (Even photographs of Joyce in these years capture little
more than blank features.) The most nomadic of European
writers inhabits himself. Almost everyone who meets him—
Busoni, the composer, Jung, the psychologist, intellectuals from
all over the world—senses the rare interior power. One of them,
Archibald MacLeish, after decades spent with men famous in
politics and art, described his reaction to Ellmann in 1954:

> I don't know what "greatness" in a man is though I think
> I know what it is in a man's work. But a great *man!* I've
> been close to some accounted so but it was always the
> deeds or the work I felt—not a greatness in the man him-
> self. But in Joyce you felt a hard, strong actuality that, if
> not greatness, was at least something you were always
> conscious of.

Eliot said that a work of art "is not the expression of personality" but an escape from it. This famous claim will not hold
up in Joyce's case. Ellmann's book shows that Joyce's work
involved so thorough an exploitation of his personality that it
may fairly be said that there was nothing "accidental" in his life.
Joyce seems never to have had a useless experience. His ability
to transform detail into signposts lies behind his fantastic super-
stitiousness and behind the ease of seeing in a Dublin advertising
canvasser Ulysses, Christ, Shakespeare.

It is because Joyce's life and work together form a track which
leads to what are still formal, linguistic, moral, and emotional
frontiers that Ellmann's biography is also a work of criticism.
Its strength, as well as its length, derives from this double load.
That it is also a wonderfully amusing and very touching, even
heart-rending book is a tribute Ellmann must share with his subject. The account of Joyce's efforts on behalf of the tenor John
Sullivan would make a comic novel (the climax Joyce's cry in
the Paris Opera House that he has miraculously recovered his
sight). A very different novel would contain the scene in which

Joyce stands quietly at the railroad station while his insane daughter screams bloody hell at him. Ellmann subdues the scenes so that the biography is never anecdotal but cumulative and telling. When, on the last page, Joyce is buried, his wife stretching out her arm to the coffin while a deaf man across the way shouts "Who is it? Who is it?", this reader for one felt like answering "The greatest man around."

POUND VS. JOYCE

In 1912 Ezra Pound, thrashing hints of modernity out of the London bush, turned out a quatrain of invocation:

> Sweet Christ from hell spew up some Rabelais,
> To belch and . . . and to define today
> In fitting fashion, and her monument
> Heap up to her in fadeless excrement.

A year later the spew arrived in the manuscripts of a thirty-two-year-old Berlitz teacher living in Trieste. By the time Pound's enthusiasm and impresario energies had run their course, the new monument maker had himself become a monument. As for the heaped-up matter, the supply turned out to be greater than the invoker could manage.

"I am perhaps a little more phallic and less interested in the excrement and feces of men and beasts," he wrote the Rabelaisian supplier, and his editorial shears tried clipping a few Joyce bits from Bloom's relaxed session in the garden privy. No great harm done, but it was a sign of growing distance between discoverer and discovery.

This finely edited book * tells a great deal about the relationship. From it, and from the wonderfully edited letters of Joyce (the work of Stuart Gilbert and Richard Ellmann), one can see much and guess more. One of the guesses is that neither Pound nor Eliot would have bitten off half as much without the discoveries of Joyce; another is that the atmospheric receptivity Pound created enabled Joyce to attempt far more than he otherwise would have. Thus we have documentation for a major change in human expression. Short of finding a transcript of Jonson's talks with Shakespeare, we're not likely to do better.

* Forrest Read, ed., *Pound/Joyce*. The letters of Ezra Pound to James Joyce, with Pound's critical essays and articles about Joyce (New Directions, 1967).

The Read book contains the notes for at least one extraordinary story. Within the bawdy jockeying, complaints, and sensitometer reports, one sees the brilliant American revolutionary coming up against the first man whose genius and tenacity are clearly greater than his own. He yields pride of place, assists him, advances him, and then discovers that the demands of his own work and ego force him to reconstruct both; the reconstruction makes him devalue the other man and ignore his development. "Nothing so far as I make out," he wrote Joyce after trying the early pages of *Finnegans Wake,* "nothing short of divine wisdom or a new cure for the clapp can possibly be worth all the circumambient peripherization."

Receiving this, Joyce "despaired," then resisted his own never forgotten sense of deep obligation to contend with Pound in the later sections of *Finnegans Wake.* "If I can't upset this pound of pressed ollaves [bards olives] I can sit up zounds of sounds upon him." (The sound man, Joyce, assailing the imagist, Pound.)

The contention was serious, but the contenders remembered each other's splendor. Joyce's last letter advised his brother to call on Pound for help, and four years later, thirty-three years after his quatrain, Pound invoked the liveliness of his dead companion:

> and Jim the comedian singin'
> 'Blarney Castle me darlin'
> You're nothing now but a StOWne'

POUND STERLING

Ezra Pound, A Close Up by Michael Reck

If Benedict Arnold had written *War and Peace,* his name wouldn't be a curse; the derelictions of Dante and Sir Francis Bacon are shadow depths in our perspective of them. Ezra Pound is neither Arnold nor Dante; but in a black period of his life his not wholly misdirected rage at the war-linked cultures of industrial society became a frenzy of imprecision, and it was not difficult to lump him with far more evil men and events. Indicted for treason, he agreed to accept the verdict of four psychiatrists that he "suffered from a paranoid state which renders him mentally unfit to advise properly with counsel or to participate intelligently and reasonably in his defense." He was remanded to the criminally insane ward of St. Elizabeth's Hospital in Washington, D.C., where he spent the next dozen years seeing his wife and other visitors two hours a day and turning out a tremendous amount of brilliant work. Released as an "incurable" in 1958, he returned to Italy, where not long ago he said: "Everything I touch, I spoil. I've always blundered."

> I knew at fifteen pretty much what I wanted to do. I resolved that at thirty I would know more about poetry than any man living, that I would know the dynamic content from the shell, that I would know what was accounted poetry everywhere, what part of poetry was "indestructible," what part could *not be lost* by translation, and— scarcely less important—what effects were obtainable in *one* language only.

His quest and practice altered the language and literature of this century. "There are very few living poets, even if they are not conscious of having been influenced by Pound, who could say 'My work would be exactly the same if Mr. Pound had never lived.' " This from Auden, not his great admirer. He was a

* New York: McGraw-Hill, 1967.

kind of Nils Bohr of the arts, not only a great practitioner but the creator of climates in which other men did their best work. "Ezra was the most generous writer I have ever known," wrote Hemingway. "He helped poets, painters, sculptors, and prose writers that he believed in and he would help anyone whether he believed in them or not if they were in trouble."

Joyce, Eliot, Yeats, Frost, Cummings, Ransom, and Marianne Moore received crucial help from him. He edited the fat out of *The Waste Land,* brought Yeats' greatest poems to boil, sharpened Binyon's translation of Dante's *Comedy* (the finest in English), directed Rouse's brilliant Homeric translations; one could add fifty or sixty instances of the same order.

> And the days are not full enough
> And the nights are not full enough
> And life slips by like a field mouse
>   Not shaking the grass.

He wrote volumes of poetry and criticism and worked on the *Cantos,* the only modern American poem that can approach the *Comedy, Faust,* and the classic epics. Still unfinished after fifty years of work, this poem breathes, and sometimes gasps on, the historic and economic studies Pound began making after World War I, when he first felt what he had long thought, that the arts were intimately connected with the creation and distribution of other social goods and services. The occasional slaver on Pound's expression of his notions has led them to be dismissed as those of a crank or a genius strayed from his proper playground. In the mouths and on the pens of men whose salaries derive from the reiteration of hand-me-down falsehoods, such dismissal smells.

As for the poems, they will mostly take care of themselves; there is some good critical assistance here, and it won't be long before the thorniest canto can be grasped as easily—well, almost as easily—as *The Waste Land* or Part Two of *Faust.* For those in search of blemishes, there are plenty of these as well.

Reck was one of the people who went to see Pound in St. Elizabeth's. Unlike such visiting cranks as Horton and Kaspar, or some of the gushers and hand lickers, he stood up to diatribes against Roosevelt and Morgenthau. Pound appreciated his independence, enjoyed his presence, and this little biographical memoir is the result. It's a kind of amiable calling card, and it can bring people who know little of Pound to know his outlines. One recommends any vehicle which will get readers within reach of what counts.

What counts for a handful of people is the frail, laconic man in the odd hats who celebrates his eighty-seventh birthday on October 30 [1972]. What counts for the cultural historian is the man's life and contacts. What counts for people with an ear for verse is

> Evening is like a curtain of cloud,
> a blur above ripples; and through it
> sharp long spikes of the cinnamon,
> a cold tune amid reeds

and

> "Respect a child's faculties
> "From the moment it inhales the clear air
> "But a man of fifty who knows nothing
>   Is worthy of no respect."

and

> Died some, pro patria
>   non "dulce" non "et decor" . . .
> walked eye-deep in hell
> believing in old men's lies, then unbelieving
> came home, home to a lie,
> home to many deceits,
> home to old lies and new infamy . . .

I myself used to see Pound about once a week from November to March in 1962–1963. It was a cold winter in Venice; Pound was in bad shape, recovering from surgery, teeth not fixed, feeling the cold. He talked little, but now and then opened up and made jokes. Often, though, these tea times were efforts to pump social life into the room. I felt that his old friend Miss Rudge wanted the occasional visitors to do that. One day Pound picked up something I said about Peggy Guggenheim, who lived down the street five light years away. He accused me of making things up. It relieved him, he said, because now he didn't have to blame his memory. I was angry and sat there brooding while Miss Rudge and another friend tried to make conversation. They left and I started to follow without more than a nod, but I went over to the bed, held out my hand for what I believed would be my last good-by there, and said: "I'm sorry, Mr. Pound. You're right in a way. Most of this social talk is just baloney." He held my hand tight, drew me down to the bed and looked in my eyes. "No," he said. "Wrong, wrong, wrong. I've always been wrong. Eighty-seven percent wrong."

The huge, grooved, leonine old head was broken with sadness. It was hard for me to talk, but I said something to the effect that, yes, you may have been wrong, but the people who accuse you aren't even in the same world of right and wrong as you. He said: "You don't know what it's like. To stray off the path, and not be able to get back." I said something about his having hit the bull's-eye plenty in his life. But he was not ready for encouragement. My hand was still gripped hard and he went on, quoting Dante, saying what the loss of memory meant and more that I have lost now in the years. I put this here in the midst of these little pieces on Pound to make "the historical record." (The emotional aftermath led me to write the novel *Stitch*.)

POUND AS TRANSLATOR

The Spirit of Romance * is Pound's "shortish account" of some major works of the Romance literatures between the troubadours and Camoëns. It was first issued in 1910 and has been neither superseded nor matched in the interim. Considering the work done on nearly everyone discussed in the book since that time (including articles by Pound), this is quite a tribute. No other short book of the kind has covered so much territory and yet convinced the reader that the whole was, if not a continuum, at least a kind of Common Market † presided over by an extremely efficient and knowledgeable official. This is to say that the book hangs together—and hangs together less because of the "definite plan" which Pound claims for it than because he was already, at twenty-five, able to examine a large body of complex material and to judge it with authority.

Pound is not an original critic in the sense that he provides a radically new way of reading a text or of looking at a period. Yet he is important in critical history as a bridge between the textual reading of nineteenth-century scholarship and the textual interpreting of twentieth-century critics. For other than textual work Pound relies pretty generally on accepted scholarship; for instance, his view of the "softening up" of the classical Latin tradition by influxes of personalism, mysticism, and antiauthoritarianism was the standard view of Mackail and others. If he rates a poet more highly than most scholars do, he usually has a substantial backer; thus he follows Dante's estimate of Arnaut Daniel.

Where Pound devotes himself to "criticism pure," however, he opens up worlds. For instance, he analyzes the troubadour

* Ezra Pound, *The Spirit of Romance* (New Directions, 1955). This was my second published piece of criticism. It appeared in 1953.
† The original had *Zollverein*.

sensibility in a fashion which anticipates Eliot's analysis of the metaphysical one:

> Did this "chivalric love," this exotic, take on medium-istic properties? Stimulated by the color or quality of emo-tion, did that "color" take on forms interpretive of the divine order? Did it lead to an "exteriorization of the sen-sibility," an interpretation of the cosmos by feeling? (p. 94)

Pound writes either a sort of shorthand Roman-historian prose or a jerky, idiomatic one stuffed with metaphors from Physics 2 and music. The whole gives the impression that the writer's been around and is anxious to get you around. The jerkiness helps one see that the coherence of a book like this is one of an ever available sympathy, a negative way of defining a very good book.

Pound's originality is something quite different from either his prose or his critical insight; he is the Sir Francis Drake of foreign literatures. For all their fine translating, Rossetti and Swinburne never really brought home anything but squinty-eyed Rossettis and Swinburnes; for all his "historicism," Browning never left Wimpole Street. As everyone knows, Pound brought Arnaut and Cavalcanti and even Dante to English and American poets and into English and American poetry on a grand scale. (Landor and Shelley had done it before in smaller and, I think, more eccentric ways.) Not only did he usually translate as if nothing but gauze lay between the centuries and tongues, but his own verse began to ring with the imported voices. He thus extended the sensibility of English and the modes of poetic expression.

Both *The Spirit of Romance* and *The Translations of Ezra Pound* * show him in the act of translating—the *act* because it is the printed show of energy that makes for much of the marvel and also much of the peculiarity of Pound's work.

---

* *The Translations of Ezra Pound.* Containing text and translation of fifty or so poems by Guido Cavalcanti, ten poems by Arnaut Daniel, commentary on and translations of some of the Noh plays, *Cathay* (mostly poems by Li-Po), *The Seafarer,* six miscellaneous poems, and some maxims of Rémy de Gourmont.

The marvel comes mostly when Pound, in the line of Golding, North, and other great Elizabethan translators, is releasing the force of a text by spotting the origins of the force and duplicating them. Often this involves using English cognates of foreign words in such a way that they will assume the slightly different meaning of the original and even some of the original phonetic value. This can be so slight an extension as the rendering of *Tan m'abelais vostre cortes deman* as "So pleasureth me your courteous demand" (where "request" is the more precise rendering of the last word); or it can become unnecessarily violent as in the translation of *Adsonat Terei puella subter umbram populi* into "There, in the poplar shade the Tyrrean girl" (where "Tyrrean" is the poem's only reference to Tereus).

The last example, taken from *The Spirit of Romance,* can be glossed over there. Within "pure translation," however, Pound often runs into the difficulty of operating without a didactic framework yet wanting to say something about the total *oeuvre* of a poet which doesn't seem to be adequately said in the text. The section on the Noh plays is in a sense, therefore, the most satisfying in *The Translations,* despite the fact that the plays themselves are dull as dirt away from the highly stylized dances for which the texts are settings or causative agents. The Noh section is in the style of *The Spirit of Romance,* and Pound has been able to "set" the translations with commentary and thus produce the atmosphere of discovery and initiation which is so special a part of his work. Another reason for the success of this section is that Fenollosa had apparently worked so close to the texts that they lost the difficult, archaic quality they are said to have for modern Japanese and appear in Pound's English simple and classical.

What is peculiar in Pound's translating shows up mostly in the famous versions of Cavalcanti and Arnaut Daniel. Away from the didactic context, Pound burdens some of the translations with an antique weight (perhaps in order to carry what has since become staple or cliché or what has vanished altogether from the tradition):

> 'Tis he hath hurled the dart, wherefrom my pain,
> First shot's resultant! and in flanked amaze . . .

is the version of

> Lanciato m'ha d'un dardo entro lo fianco;
> Si giunse il colpo dritto al primo tratto . . .

It would be difficult to imagine a great translator slipping further away from a text, or from poetry itself: "pain" and "amaze" are not in the Italian, "flanked" is a mangled echo of *fianco,* and "First shot's resultant" is blown up with Pound's desire to say something about the mechanical-spiritual correspondence which is often the key to Cavalcanti's strategy—or at least about something else which, in *The Spirit of Romance,* went properly into prose. So in the latter work Pound has told us that Arnaut is often jazzy; and, sure enough,

> Tan pareis genta
> Cella quem te joios
> Las gensors trenta
> Vens de belas faisos!

has a jazzy or, let's say, Castillian lyric quality to it. Pound's version sounds like John Gower in Shubert's Alley:

> She's so the rarest
>   who holdeth me thus gay,
> The thirty fairest
>   can not contest her sway.

Unfortunately, there's a great deal of this.

Yet this is dust on a bright halo. Generally Pound's energy and tact are unmatched. When there is a textual alteration, you bend with the remover to remove; the alteration is the gambit which snares the prey. It may be slight ("When dry words rattle in my throat" for *Quand' io ti rispondea fiochetto e piano*) or wholesale, like the consistently less lyric version of Laforgue that Pound gives in order to emphasize the sad glitter and wit of the original:

Your eyes! Since I lost their incandescence
Flat calm engulphs my jibs,
The shudder of *Vae soli* gurgles beneath my ribs . . .

for

Il me faut, vos yeux! Dès que je perds leur étoile,
Le mal des calmes plats s'engouffre dans ma voile,
Le frisson du *Vae soli!* gargouille en mes moelles . . .

The finest English verse in *The Translations* comes in *The Seafarer* and *Cathay*. There whatever is sporty, cagey, antique, or labyrinthine in other sections of the book drops away and we have the pure, emotionally subtle, moving verse which most English readers have Pound alone to thank for knowing.

The sort of "faults" cited above are like those Pound is often accused of committing. Students are told "not to stop at Pound." I think one wouldn't do too badly "stopping with Pound" except that it would mean having missed the swing of his criticism-translation—which is hortatory. Pound mostly says, "Look! There's marvelous stuff here and there; here is a chunk of it and here's what it's about and what it has to do with this or that," and so on, until his voice seems to go up with defiant expectation and you've taken off around the corner to buy the Provençal *Chrestomathy* and Portuguese, Spanish, and Chinese dictionaries. It's like getting a wonderful postcard from the Fiji Islands —you'd always thought there were only stumps and crayfish there, but now you sell your train ticket to California and take steamship passage.

STUMBLING INTO MODERNITY *

In October 1921, Thomas Eliot, a thirty-three-year-old American living in London, realized that he was on the verge of a nervous breakdown. A few years before he'd given up an academic career, although he'd finished a doctoral dissertation (on the philosopher F. H. Bradley). Against his family's wishes he left the United States and settled in England. He got a job in Lloyd's Bank, specializing in their foreign department; after hours he wrote reviews and articles for technical magazines and literary pages and gave evening lectures to working people on a great variety of subjects. In 1915 he had married an English girl whose neurotic instability reinforced what he later discovered to be his own lifelong "aboulie and emotional derangement." Abulia, "loss of will power," was an undercurrent of a few remarkable poems he'd written and published in literary magazines. The poems brought him to the attention of an ebullient and energetic American a few years older than himself, Ezra Pound, already a well-known figure in London literary life. Pound, a discoverer, had found his America. He got Eliot's poems published (borrowing money for the printing costs); he got an American lawyer named Quinn to help Eliot negotiate with reluctant American publishers; and he observed, with growing anxiety, that Eliot would soon be lost to poetry under the burdens of his wife's invalidism and the fierce schedule required to pay her doctors. In October 1921, under the additional strain of a visit from his mother, brother, and sister, Eliot was told by a specialist that he would have to get off by himself for three months. The bank—where he was now a valued employee specializing in debts and claims complicated by the various peace

* T. S. Eliot, *The Waste Land*. A facsimile and transcript of the original drafts, including the annotations of Ezra Pound; edited by Valerie Eliot (New York: Harcourt Brace Jovanovich, 1971).

treaties—gave him paid leave, and he went off, first to Margate, then to Lausanne. For two years he had thought about writing a long poem; his convalescence gave him the opportunity to write it, indeed consisted in his being free to write it. In January 1922 he came back to London with the poem. But not quite the poem with which he had left Lausanne. That poem was a much longer, clumsier affair. En route to London, he had stopped off in Paris, where Pound then lived. Together they went over the batch of manuscript-typescript and eliminated whole sections and great parts of other sections of the poem. The end result was one of the triumphs of literature, a poem generally regarded as the chief poetic expression of twentieth-century modernity.

This story has been known for a long time, but the details of the Parisian operation on the clumsy creature which became the *The Waste Land* have been hidden, because the batch of manuscript was lost. In gratitude for John Quinn's help, Eliot gave him the manuscript drafts and revisions. At Quinn's death, the uninventoried treasure was put in a storage box, where it wasn't discovered until the 1950s. Quinn's niece sold it for eighteen thousand dollars to the Berg Collection of the New York Public Library, whose curator finally informed the second Mrs. Eliot of the acquisition in 1968. Mrs. Eliot has now edited this facsimile edition with a transcript, an introduction, and notes. In this important labor of love she had the assistance of Pound, whose short preface calls this " 'mystery of the missing manuscript' pure Henry James."

One mark of modernity is its passion for the inside story. Given a choice between a New Testament and the inside story of the Old, it would opt for the latter. Process fascinates the modern, products only briefly enchant him. When process involves so important a transformation as the one this book exhibits, the modernist reader feels like a participant in creation.

A good account of the making of *The Waste Land* will be a long endeavor, but here are some rough speculations.

A man of enormous energy, intellectual experience, and ambition has been driven into an emotional corner. While this has been happening to him, the stupidest war in centuries is going on. His and everyone else's "individual lives are so swallowed up" "that one almost ceases to have personal experiences or emotions . . ." With the war's end, there is an enormous release of energy and the creation of enormous problems of adjusting to it. This affects him personally to the point of breakdown. A poet, he is not a first-person celebrator or complainer. He adopts a strategy he has used in early poems, dramatic monologues, and dialogues, and he writes a series of poetic scenes and lyrics in other voices. He has an organizational principle picked out of a scholar's book on the degeneration of a religious ritual—that of an impotent king and his sterile land—into poetic romance. The theme of sterility undoubtedly touches the poet in many ways; and the book supplies much of the imagery and symbolism of his poem as well as its eventual title. The original title, "He Do the Police in Different Voices," is taken from a bit of *Our Mutual Friend,* which deals with a half-witted foundling named Sloppy who is said to be "a beautiful reader of a newspaper. He do the Police in different voices." The poet, with that familiar aristocratic mix of inverse snobbery and true affection for working-class life, will write a good deal of this poem in (his idea of) working-class speech. (Too straight to sentimentalize its virtues —or anyone else's—he still gives it the poem's only note of earthly warmth.) The ugliness which has driven him to the corner is everywhere—palaces, pubs, past, present, inside Western culture and inside his life. The poems exhibit as many social and cultural scenes as he can manage, each written in a metric which comments on it (one of the many tricks picked up from Joyce).

This procession of long, varied poems was what Eliot brought to Pound. What he took away a few days later was a poem which, though still made up of discrete parts, was also of a piece. A footnote proclaiming Tiresias the poem's center was as yet unwritten and probably unconceived, but this new poem had a center: the judgment of a sensibility made clear in every allusion and meter. From the lush, "Shakespeherian" blank verse describing the society boudoir to the fresh, irregular lyrics of the fourth and fifth sections, not only is that sensibility felt but its convalescence is charted. The end of the poem is a collection of fragments, a microcosm of the Pounded poem, that rapid, jagged, elliptic juxtaposition of brilliant scenes and cultural shards which became the flag of modernity. Under Pound's guidance, Eliot had stumbled into it.

Years later a confident, prosperous, public-minded Eliot said of *The Waste Land:*

> Various critics have done me the honour to interpret the poem in terms of criticism of the contemporary world, have considered it, indeed, as an important bit of social criticism. To me it was only the relief of a personal and wholly insignificant grouse against life; it is just a piece of rhythmical grumbling.

If every artist who felt or said such things about his early work could cause their oblivion, there would be very few beautiful poems or pictures left in the world. Eliot wrote nothing finer than his "grouse."

BIBLIOGRAPHICAL AFTERWORD

The pieces that appeared originally in the following periodicals have been combed, trimmed, beheaded (and headed with new titles), footnoted, updated, and/or arranged: *Accent:* "Pound as Translator." Chicago *Daily News: "In Cold Blood";* "Coach Lombardi"; "Malamud's *Tenants.*" Chicago *Sun-Times:* "Out of Literary Phase"; "Leaks in the Updike"; "Joyce's Vanishing Act"; "Pound vs. Joyce"; "Pound Sterling." Chicago *Sun-Times Book World:* "The Post-lapsarian Marilyn"; "The Playboy Revolutionary." *Chicago Review:* "The Poetry of Edgar Bowers." *Commentary:* "Slowill"; "In Response to a Questionnaire." *Encounter:* "On the Johnson Library." *Harper's:* "Chicago." *Kenyon Review: "Doctor Zhivago* as a Novel"; "Henderson's Bellow"; "Proust and Joyce Under Way." *The Nation:* "Yarmolinsky, Eisenhower, and the Cannibal"; "On Camera"; "The Revolutionary Test"; "The Books in Fred Hampton's Apartment"; "Farming the Tundra"; "A Memory of Forster"; "The Politics of a Mason." *New York Review of Books:* "Indians and Settlers." *The New York Times: "Catch-22";* "Some That Glitters Is." *Paris Review:* "Aurelia Frequenza Reveals." *Prairie Schooner: "Pnin's* Dust Jacket." *Shenandoah:* "Flannery O'Connor." *Teeth, Dying, and Other Matters:* "The Pursuit of Washington." *University of Chicago Magazine:* "Two Scenes from *Dossier: Earth.*" *Western Review: "Picaresque Extra Cuvée."* *Yale Review:* "Events, Happenings, Credibility, Fictions" (also in *American Literary Anthology* III).